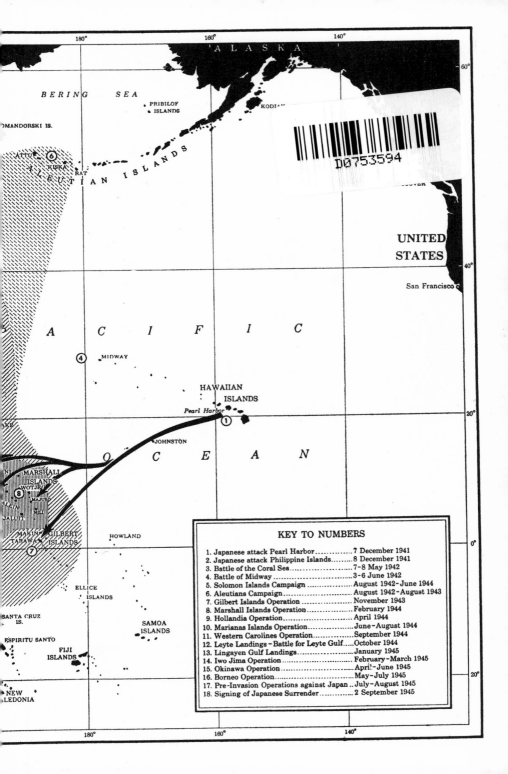

180°   160°   140°

'A L A S K A

60°

B E R I N G   S E A

PRIBILOF
ISLANDS

KODI

OMANDORSKI IS.

ATTU 6   KISKA   RAT
A L E U T I A N   I S L A N D S

UNITED
STATES

40°

San Francisco

A   C   I   F   I   C

4   MIDWAY

HAWAIIAN
ISLANDS

Pearl Harbor
1

JOHNSTON

O   C   E   A   N

20°

MARSHALL
ISLANDS
WOTJE
8   MAJURO

JALUIT

MAKIN GILBERT   HOWLAND
TARAWA ISLANDS
7

ELLICE
ISLANDS

SANTA CRUZ
IS.   SAMOA
ISLANDS

ESPIRITU SANTO

FIJI
ISLANDS

NEW
LEDONIA

0°

20°

KEY TO NUMBERS

1. Japanese attack Pearl Harbor.............7 December 1941
2. Japanese attack Philippine Islands........8 December 1941
3. Battle of the Coral Sea.....................7-8 May 1942
4. Battle of Midway.............................3-6 June 1942
5. Solomon Islands Campaign .... August 1942-June 1944
6. Aleutians Campaign........................... August 1942-August 1943
7. Gilbert Islands Operation ....November 1943
8. Marshall Islands Operation.................February 1944
9. Hollandia Operation...........................April 1944
10. Marianas Islands Operation.................June-August 1944
11. Western Carolines Operation...............September 1944
12. Leyte Landings–Battle for Leyte Gulf.....October 1944
13. Lingayen Gulf Landings......................January 1945
14. Iwo Jima Operation .... February–March 1945
15. Okinawa Operation............................April?–June 1945
16. Borneo Operation.............................May–July 1945
17. Pre-Invasion Operations against Japan ..July–August 1945
18. Signing of Japanese Surrender..............2 September 1945

180°   160°   140°

THE
MAGNIFICENT MITSCHER

THE
MAGNIFICENT
MITSCHER

THEODORE TAYLOR

With a Foreword by Admiral Arthur W. Radford and
an Introduction by Jeffrey G. Barlow

NAVAL INSTITUTE PRESS
ANNAPOLIS, MARYLAND

Copyright © 1954, 1991
by the United States Naval Institute
Annapolis, Maryland

Originally published 1954 by W. W. Norton & Company, Inc., New York

Library of Congress Cataloging-in-Publication Data
Taylor, Theodore, 1922–
    The magnificent Mitscher / Theodore Taylor ; with a foreword by
Arthur W. Radford ; and an introduction by Jeffrey G. Barlow.
        p.   cm.
    Reprint, with new introd. Originally published: 1st ed. New York :
Norton, 1954.
    Includes bibliographic references.
    ISBN 1-55750-800-3
    1. Mitscher, Marc Andrew, 1887—1947.   2. Admirals—United States—
Biography.   3. United States.   Navy—Biography.   4. United States—
History, Naval—20th century.   5. World War, 1939–1945—Naval
operations, American.   I. Title.
E746.M5T3   1991
940.54'5973'092--dc20
[B]
                                                                91-14412
                                                                CIP

Printed in the United States of America on acid-free paper ∞

9 8 7 6 5 4 3 2

First printing

Contents

Illustrations

ix

The *Essex* at the moment of impact with a *kamikaze*

The *Bunker Hill* fighting a flight-deck fire after being hit by a suicide plane

Mitscher decorated on his way home late in 1944

Mitscher in San Diego with his wife, Frances

Peacetime—Mitscher with Secretary of the Navy James Forrestal

Mitscher—oil portrait by Commander Albert K. Murray, USNR

Acknowledgments

The Commandant of midshipmen at the United States Naval Academy in 1950, Captain Robert B. Pirie, now a rear admiral, knew that leadership could not be learned from books, but he thought a biography of a recent war leader might serve an inspirational purpose at Annapolis and chose Admiral Marc A. Mitscher as the subject. Pirie convinced writer Stacy V. Jones that Mitscher's life was one of the great untold naval stories, that Mitscher exemplified true leadership. Jones began preliminary research, but soon found himself hemmed in by other commitments. At that point, I began work. I am therefore pleased to express my appreciation to Admiral Pirie for the idea, and to Stacy Jones for the rich inheritance.

Most military leaders have kept diaries and papers in quantities sufficient to fill at least a small file cabinet and in some instances several rooms in a warehouse. There was no reason to believe that Admiral Mitscher had not gathered at least a file cabinet of papers. But after ferreting exhaustively through Washington files and interviewing many of Mitscher's fellow officers, I concluded that Admiral Mitscher had no formal papers. A few letters, several charred by an aircraft-carrier suicide bombing, and some impersonal official correspondence were all that could be located. In later stages of research, I discovered a letter in which Admiral Mitscher declared he stored thoughts in his mind, not in ribboned bundles.

This biography is an "all hands" product, with contributors

ranging from Fleet Admirals Nimitz and Halsey down to mess stewards with hash marks trellised up their forearms. It draws upon memories, which must be hopefully trusted, photographs, flight records, battle-action reports, unpublished manuscripts on Admiral Mitscher by J. R. Eyerman and Rear Admiral George R. Henderson, and an assortment of personal logs, written by shipmates, on various phases of the Pacific war. I have extracted liberally from books and periodicals.

I wish to thank the United States Naval Academy for permission to examine Admiral Mitscher's Academy records; the Bureau of Naval Personnel for permission to extract from his personnel jackets, including fitness reports and official correspondence; the Office of the Chief of Naval Operations for permission to examine action reports, war diaries, ships' logs and war summaries; the Naval Aviation History Unit for access to many papers and records.

Mrs. Marc A. Mitscher not only provided much material but, more important, gave me the trust and warmth of her friendship. Mrs. Zoe Mitscher Hoevel, the Admiral's sister, devoted time and energy to the reconstruction of Mitscher's boyhood, and even located a spry, ninety-year-old lady who taught the Admiral in grade school in Oklahoma. Captain Herbert Underwood, USN (Retired), was my main source for the Academy days.

Perhaps two hundred Navy and Marine officers, active and retired, could be listed as cohelpers. Rear Admiral Arleigh Albert Burke contributed much material, lent counsel, and steered the author into many unexplored channels. His role in the life of Admiral Mitscher was important; his role in assisting preparation of this book was commensurately important. Rear Admiral William A. Read, USNR, likewise counseled and encouraged, giving me free access to his vivid recollection of the days on Guadalcanal, and later in the fast-carrier forces; and permitting me to make use of a detailed narrative memorandum on his experiences with the staff or Task Force 58/38.

My sincere appreciation also goes to Mr. Adrian Van Wyen, head of the Naval Aviation History Unit, Office of the Deputy Chief of Naval Operations for Air, who painstakingly checked the manuscript, and gave expert guidance from the beginning of the first paragraph.

I am grateful to Lieut. Barrett Gallagher, USNR, for his help in gathering many of the pictures used here, and for his own magnificent photographs of the carrier navy in action.

For their valuable assistance and many major contributions, I am grateful to Vice Admiral Patrick N. L. Bellinger, Vice Admiral Alfred Melville Pride, Vice Admiral A. W. Johnson, Lieutenant General Field Harris, USMC, Rear Admiral George R. Henderson, Rear Admiral Stanhope C. Ring, Rear Admiral Truman Joseph Hedding, Rear Admiral Claude S. Gillette, Captain James Flatley, Captain Ernest Snowden, Captain John T. Hayward, and Commander Everett Eynon—all of whom served with Admiral Mitscher; Captain Elliott W. Parish, Jr., and Captain Louis J. Kirn, for their technical assistance; Miss Loretta I. MacCrindle, of the Navy Historical Records section, for the location of many records; Miss Mary Baer, of the still library, Naval Photo Center, for assistance in research on photographs; Captain Walter Karig, and Commander J. Burke Wilkinson, for their literary advice, and former Navy pilot Edwin P. Weigle for supervising the department of air terminology. However, the author accepts full responsibility for all material.

Finally, I humbly wish to thank my wife, Gweneth Goodwin Taylor, not only for her labors on the manuscript, but for her patience and devotion.

If some of what Admiral Mitscher said and thought and did is recorded in this book, and if it shows something of the genius he had for leading other men to do great deeds, then it will have served its purpose.

Foreword

The Magnificent Mitscher is the story of a man. It is a well documented story, complete with names and places and great events in American history. But it is more than that. In the larger sense, it is a history of a technological revolution in warfare, and specifically, in the United States Navy.

Theodore Taylor, himself a Navy man, traces the life of Marc Andrew Mitscher from the cradle to the grave. In considerable detail, he outlines this aviator's early interests in air power, from the days when the age of flight was little more than a dream, to the fierce Battle of Okinawa. The progress of the air arm of the U. S. Navy, from converted coaling ships to armadas of fast carriers, is recorded with the life and accomplishments of Admiral Mitscher.

The book is good reading. In addition, it lives again those stirring times when the United States of America turned back so dynamically the tides of aggression. Each American can feel proud of his tradition. He can face the future with the certain confidence of previous experience.

ADMIRAL ARTHUR W. RADFORD, USN
Chairman, Joint Chiefs of Staff

2 June 1954

Introduction

TODAY, several decades after the death of Admiral Marc Mitscher and, for many members of the generations born since 1945, seeming light years away from the events of World War II in the Pacific that brought Mitscher public acclaim, it is hard to conjure up the memory of this reticent naval aviator. Those who trained him or flew with him in the early years of naval aviation, fellow pioneers such as Jack Towers, Pat Bellinger, Ken Whiting, and Mel Pride, have gone on to join him in that special corner of Heaven reserved for aviators—those most ebullient, self-assured, independent, stubborn members of the naval profession. We are fortunate, indeed, then that Theodore Taylor wrote his biography of Mitscher in the early 1950s, when most of these individuals were still alive and their memories of Pete Mitscher were fresh. But for his dutiful work, the details of Mitscher's fascinating life would be lost to us.

Marc Andrew Mitscher entered the United States Naval Academy in July 1904, not because he had any great wish for a naval career but because his father wanted a son to go there. During his plebe year, he acquired his nickname "Pete" (originally "Oklahoma Pete") after a fellow Oklahoman who had bilged (flunked) out of the Academy the previous year. During his time at Annapolis, Mitscher was anything but a model midshipman. He was an indifferent student with a lackluster sense of military deportment. The resulting combination of a low academic performance and a high number of demerits forced his resignation from the Academy in his youngster year. Through the efforts of his father, though, he secured another appointment and reentered the Naval Academy with the class of 1906. When he finally graduated in June 1910, his class standing was anything but impressive. Graduating 107th out of a class of 130, Pete Mitscher stood but a few bare points above the anchor man, Herbert Hein.[1] No one then could have imagined that this unlikely Annapolis graduate would one day wear an admiral's stars.

During Mitscher's first years as a passed midshipman and ensign, he served in a variety of surface ships. In 1911, however, he acquired an interest in aviation and thereafter began barraging the Bureau of Navigation with requests for a transfer to aeronautical duty. Finally, in September 1915 he was ordered to the armored cruiser *North Carolina,* Pensacola's station ship, for instruction in aeronautics.[2] Marc Mitscher reported to Pensacola in the fall of 1915 as one of thirteen students in the first formal class at the flying school. Among the officers who were there when he arrived were instructors John Towers and Patrick Bellinger. Also there were Robert Saufley, Henry Mustin, John Rodgers, and Kenneth Whiting. Whiting, the commander of the flying school, soon became a close friend to the new student aviator.

In 1915 a formal training organization was still lacking at Pensacola, which had opened as a naval aeronautics station only in January of the previous year. Ground school dealt only with the technical aspects of flying. It was assumed that the students, being Naval Academy graduates, were already thoroughly conversant with subjects such as navigation. The training was largely a hands-on experience, as the students were taught to tear down and rebuild aircraft engines, how to repair tears in the biplanes' fabric wings, and how to tighten or replace the bracing wires holding together the framework of the pusher seaplanes they flew.[3] This practical training had a great appeal for Mitscher, and he excelled in his studies at Pensacola in a way that he never had been able to do at Annapolis.

The flying itself was fairly straightforward. The seaplanes would be pushed down a plank incline into the water. Once up to takeoff speed, they would lift off the water and stagger into the air. Given the nature of the aircraft, aerobatics were pretty basic—side slips and wing turns, not the Immelman turns and barrel rolls common to their wartime, land-plane cousins. Nonetheless, Mitscher found in flying an exhilaration that he had never experienced during his tours in surface ships.

He graduated from the flying school in June 1916, designated as Naval Aviator #33. That same month he was assigned to the staff of the air station at Pensacola, commanded by Henry Mustin. In addition to receiving additional aviation training during this duty assignment, Pete Mitscher served as the station's engineering officer, responsible for keeping Pensacola's aircraft in flying condition. In April 1917, with the United States now in the war against Germany and her allies, he was detached from Pensacola and assigned to the first of several wartime duty stations.

Two years later, this balding, thirty-two-year-old lieutenant, whose wizened visage made him look much older than his contemporaries, was assigned as the pilot for NC-1—one of three huge flying boats scheduled to make the first transatlantic crossing by airplane. The three aircraft took off from Trepassey, Newfoundland, on 16 May 1919, headed for England, with intermediate stops at the Azores and Portugal. The folllowing day, after becoming lost in heavy fog, NC-1's plane commander, Pat Bellinger, made the decision to land the seaplane in the ocean to see if they could figure out just where they were in relation to their initial stopover point in the Azores. During the landing, the plane was disabled by choppy seas. Mitscher and the others in NC-1's crew were out of the race. They radioed their estimated position but were quickly picked up by a Greek freighter that chanced upon them that afternoon. The second of the three flying boats, NC-3, under the command of Jack Towers, suffered a similar fate but managed to reach Ponta Delgada in the Azores, as a surface craft, after some fifty hours of battling the winds and waves.

The last of the planes was luckier. On 27 May 1919, NC-4 left the Azores headed for Lisbon, Portugal. Arriving there safely that evening, the aircraft became the first one to complete a transoceanic flight. Four days later, plane commander A. C. "Putty" Read and his crew landed safely at their final destination—Plymouth, England.

Once back in the United States, the daring aviators were awarded medals by the Navy Department. Marc Mitscher was awarded the Navy Cross for "distinguished service in the line of his profession as a member of the crew of the Seaplane NC-1, which made a long overseas flight from Newfoundland to the vicinity of the Azores in May, 1919."[4] The department's official recognition, however, did nothing to erase Mitscher's feeling of failure—NC-1 had not successfully completed the transatlantic flight upon which he had embarked with so much anticipation. Indeed, even later in life, when he looked back upon those events, the admiral was unable to rid himself of a sense of bitter dissatisfaction that fate had intervened to rob NC-1 of success.[5]

In 1926, Mitscher received orders that would mark him as a carrier aviator—for most naval aviators, the pinnacle of a flying career—from that time forward. He reported to the USS *Langley,* the navy's first aircraft carrier, as head of its Air Department. Six months later, with the navy's third carrier, *Saratoga,* nearing completion, he was assigned to the American Brown Boveri Electric Corporation in Camden, New Jersey, in connection with her fitting out.[6] Ken Whiting was her new executive officer and Pete Mitscher her air officer. Lieutenant Commander Mitscher stayed with *Saratoga* in that vital but usually unheralded job as air boss for some thirty-one happy months.[7] In June 1929, he returned to the *Langley* as her executive officer. Following a year on board "the Covered Wagon," Mitscher was ordered to several noncarrier assignments before returning to the *Sara* as Ken Whiting's exec in June 1934. Thereafter, he waited seven long years for a coveted carrier command. In August 1941, Pete Mitscher left his job as the assistant chief of the Bureau of Aeronautics for an assignment as prospective commanding officer of the aircraft carrier *Hornet,* which was fitting out at Newport News Shipbuilding and Dry Dock Company. Once the *Hornet* was commissioned in October 1941, it didn't take old friends long to find out about it. One classmate, Lieutenant Commander T. A. Nicholson, USNR, wrote to the proud CO:

Congratulations!!—Although we did stand more or less at the bottom of our class, thank God we are still living, enjoying ourselves, and our feet are still on the ground!

The picture of you [in the newspapers] looks like—well, it reminds me very much of when you were a little bit unsat in navigation or mechanics. You always did look worried and serious when you were studying. How about sending this office a picture of yourself with a grin on?[8]

The command of a new carrier was something that Pete Mitscher had been looking forward to for a very long time. In answer to his friend Captain George Murray's letter of congratulations, he noted, "You are entirely right in your letter of some time ago, stating that I would be very much pleased to get out of Washington and get back to sea. Since leaving Washington I have not been back, and with the possible exception of one visit before we sail, I do not expect to go back."[9]

The new skipper picked a top-notch group of men to be his senior department heads. Mitscher's executive officer was George Henderson, his old exec from his first ship command—the seaplane tender *Wright*. Henderson, like Mel Pride, had come into the regular navy from the reserves during World War I. The air boss in *Hornet* was Apollo Soucek, an experienced carrier aviator who had garnered some measure of fame from setting world altitude records in 1929 and 1930. Mitscher and the others orchestrated a flurry of activity in November and December 1941, getting the new ship ready for sea. Some three weeks after the Japanese bombed Pearl Harbor, the *Hornet* sailed from Norfolk on her shakedown cruise. It was to mark about the last quiet time the ship was to see.

In February 1942, Mitscher was selected for flag rank. Among his letters of congratulations was one from Admiral Royal Ingersoll, Commander in Chief, Atlantic Fleet. In his letter of thanks, Pete Mitscher took the occasion to praise Ingersoll's son, who was an officer in the *Hornet's* gunnery department. He told the admiral, "I feel that I should mention that in my career in the Navy it is seldom ever that I have encountered a 'chip off the old block', but I can assure you that your son is one of the most progressive and efficient officers that it has ever been my pleasure to serve with."[10]

In April 1942, the *Hornet* served as the launching platform for Lieutenant Colonel Jimmy Doolittle's B-25 raid on Tokyo, and in June, Mitscher's ship was one of the three U.S. aircraft carriers that turned the tide at the Battle of Midway. It was in the aftermath of this battle that Pete Mitscher's concern for his men began taking a toll on his health. From his early days in naval aviation, Mitscher was known as an officer who looked after his people, but few realized how deeply he felt the loss of the men who flew with him or for him. The heavy casualties in the *Hornet's* air group during Midway proved a difficult burden. Yet, one of the first losses in the *Hornet* was in the ship's company. A *Yorktown* fighter had crash-landed on the *Hornet* when its pilot had ignored the signals from her landing signal officer. In the crash, the aircraft's .50-caliber machine guns began firing directly into the ship's after control station. One of the victims was Royal Ingersoll. A sorrowful Mitscher was forced to write the admiral of the tragic accident. In his letter he commented:

It is my regrettable duty to inform you personally of the death of your son, Royal, on board this ship on June 4th, while we were in action in the so-called Battle of Midway.

As I have said before, Royal was one of the most efficient officers it has been my pleasure to serve with and his death is mourned by the whole ship's company, officers and men, who considered him the Rock of Gibraltar in the Gunnery Department of the ship.[11]

Another loss that was keenly felt by Pete Mitscher was that of Lieutenant Commander John C. Waldron, the commanding officer of the air group's torpedo squadron, VT-8. Waldron was one of those officers for whom Mitscher had the greatest respect—one who was hard-working (even "driven" in his need to excel), thorough, and demanding of the best that his men could give. Thus, when Waldron and his squadron were lost while pressing home their attacks on the Japanese carriers in the face of withering fire, Mitscher was deeply affected. In July 1942, Mitscher wrote to Mrs. Waldon of the high regard in which he had held her husband. He told her, "I am convinced that your husband, together with his whole squadron, will prove to be one of the greatest heroes of the war. His gallant conduct, and that of the squadron under him, leaves him outstandingly the inspiration for all America."[12]

On 30 May 1942, just a few days before the battle, Mitscher had received an appointment as a temporary rear admiral, and so, barely a month later, he left the *Hornet* for his first duty as a flag officer.[13] After nine months of rear-area assignments, on 31

March 1943 he arrived on the island of Guadalcanal, reporting in as Commander, Air, Solomon Islands (ComAirSols)—a combat command. Guadalcanal had only been secured some two months before, and strong Japanese ground, air, and naval forces were still established throughout the northern Solomons at bases such as Rabaul, Buka, Kahili, and Munda. The American air and ground forces on Guadalcanal were woefully short of facilities—airfields, camps, hospitals—but were gradually building up fighting strength.

Mitscher's four months as ComAirSols were hectic ones. His most important job in the first weeks was instilling a new offensive spirit in his troops. As Captain W. A. "Gus" Read, Mitscher's assistant chief of staff for administration on Guadalcanal, later expressed it, " . . . most of all, down there at that time we needed a new point of view. We had been on the defensive so long, hanging on by the skin of our teeth at times, short of planes, short of fuel, short of ammunition and bombs, that the whole atmosphere of the place was one of dogged defense."[14] Mitscher proceeded to instill a fighting spirit in his Allied forces in record time. It was during his first month there that army P-38 fighters under his command successfully intercepted over Bougainville and shot down the Betty bomber carrying Admiral Isoroku Yamamoto, Japan's greatest naval leader and the man who had planned and commanded the Japanese fleet's attack on the American battleline at Pearl Harbor.

As ComAirSols, Mitscher was continually directing bombing missions against Japanese airfields on New Georgia and Kolombangara. As the result of the air operations of both sides, however, dogfights between Japanese and American fighters were taking place in the air over the Solomons almost daily—sometimes directly over Guadalcanal. The admiral's nighttime hours on the island were often occupied sitting in a dugout waiting out Japanese bombing raids by small numbers of hecklers. Given his mission of keeping superior Japanese air forces on the defensive with inadequate combat resources, the constant stress he was under, and the long stretches of time on the island when he got little sleep, it is no wonder that in later years Pete Mitscher looked back on his days at Guadalcanal as some of the toughest of the war.

In July 1943, Mitscher was ordered to San Diego as Commander, Fleet Air, West Coast—largely a rest and recuperation billet for the exhausted officer. A few months with a light workload and plenty of time for fishing worked wonders on Pete's health. In early January 1944, a rested Mitscher was detached from his duty at San Diego and ordered to report as Commander, Carrier Division Three.

Mitscher's assignment to the carriers at this time was fortuitous. Admiral Chester Nimitz, CINCPAC, was looking for a commander for the Fifth Fleet's fast carrier force, and Pete Mitscher was both qualified and available for the job. Pete Mitscher was the first of the pioneer naval aviators to be given a major wartime carrier aviation command, and as the news became known, his old aviator friends were delighted to hear that one of their own had finally made it to the top. One man who was not happy with this new situation, though, was Rear Admiral Frederick Sherman, a late-comer aviator who had commanded carrier task groups since early in the war.[15] On 11 February 1944, he expressed his dissatisfaction with Mitscher's appointment in his diary:

The air operations are under Mitschen [sic] and subdivided into three task groups. . . . Mitscher and [Charles A.] Pownall [whom Mitscher relieved] are both inexperienced in handling large task forces and Spruance [Commander, Fifth Fleet] is unqualified to handle air and I think his staff work is very poor. I seem to be engineered into a position where I know more about the game than my bosses and they know it and are jealous of the fact. . . . I feel that the present set-up is no place for me.[16]

Whatever Sherman's misgivings, Pete Mitscher settled into the job as though he had been doing it all his professional life. His first assignment as Commander, Task Force 58 was the attack on the Marshall Islands (Operation FLINTLOCK). From 29 January through 15 February 1944, Task Force 58's four carrier task groups attacked targets on Roi, Kwajalein, Wotje-Taroa, Eniwetok, and Majuro, dropping 1,300 tons of bombs and destroying some 145 Japanese aircraft on the ground and in the air.[17] Further carrier strikes against Truk in the Carolines and Saipan and Tinian in the Marianas from 16 through 24 February (Operations CATCHPOLE and GATEWAY) netted some 339 additional Japanese aircraft.[18]

It was on the way back to Majuro for refueling and rearming after the attacks against Saipan and Tinian that Admiral Mitscher received word that he was getting a new, non-aviator, chief of staff. Mitscher's then chief of staff, Captain Truman Hedding, selected the name of his replacement from a list of possible choices after the admiral refused to have anything to do with it.[19] The man Hedding selected was Captain Arleigh Burke, who had gained fame as the leader of Destroyer Squadron 23 (the "Little Beavers") in some of the most successful night naval engagements of the Pacific war. Though neither Mitscher nor Burke would have believed it during the first few months of their association, Burke's arrival on board the flagship began a partnership and eventual close friendship that was to last until Admiral Mitscher's death almost three years later.[20]

Over the following several months, Task Force 58 was occupied with supporting General Douglas MacArthur's Hollandia invasion and hitting Truk for a second time. It was during these weeks that Pete Mitscher's long years of practical aviation experience began paying off in the skillful way he handled his force. One aspect of this skill was his great compassion for his people, particularly his pilots.[21] Arleigh Burke recalled:

One of the most important things that I learned from Admiral Mitscher was that he looked out for his personnel. . . .
There are many ways that men can be affected. One of the principal ones is if they feel that their top command[er] is paying complete attention to his people. Admiral Mitscher had this quality to an extreme condition. Consequently, his pilots worshipped him.[22]

Mitscher went out of his way to see that if shot down, his pilots would be picked up, and he never willingly expended them.[23] As a result, his people gave all of their attention to getting the job done, knowing that Pete Mitscher would be there doing everything to bring them back safely. Similarly, Pete's feel for the tactical situation—his appreciation of Japanese intentions, his ability to use weather fronts to the task force's advantage, and his flexibility in adapting his plans to changing enemy conditions—was phenomenal. One of the ways he kept up with the tactical situation was by debriefing personally the strike leaders and other selected pilots after their missions. As Burke commented, "He got the pilot's idea of what was over the target, what the targets looked like, what they thought about the situation, what they would recommend doing the next time. . . ."[24] The result of this personal involvement was a much better appreciation of emerging enemy conditions—one that ultimately benefited the Fast Carrier Task Force in increased fighting effectiveness and decreased combat losses.

In May 1944, Marc Mitscher received a temporary appointment to vice admiral. That same month, while he and his staff were planning Task Force 58's part in the Marianas operation, Mitscher learned that he might be relieved of his carrier assignment and ordered back to duty in Washington. Rear Admiral John McCain, a late-comer aviator who had just finished a tour as the first deputy chief of naval operations for air, supposedly was slated to relieve him.[25] Rear Admiral J. J. "Jocko" Clark, one of Mitscher's task group commanders, wrote to Rear Admiral Arthur Radford of this impending change. He commented, "Admiral Mitscher has told me that he may be leaving. I suppose it is not for me to express any opinion, but I am sure you agree with me that it is not a good idea to take Miller Huggins away from the New York Yankees in the middle of the World's Series."[26]

Before Pete Mitscher received formal notification of his relief as commander, Task Force 58, however, Admiral Nimitz went to bat with Admiral King to retain him in his present duty. Nimitz wrote the chief of naval operations:

As you know, McCain took passage with Spruance and is undoubtedly enjoying his grandstand seat for the operations now in progress. From the comment appearing in the press, it appears possible that the agitation for consolidation of the services has subsided, and that Mitscher's services may not be so urgently needed in Washington. If this proves to be the case, I hope that he may remain in the billet which he is filling to my complete satisfaction, and in which he has the confidence of all concerned.[27]

Nimitz's plea proved successful with Admiral King, and a few weeks later he was able to write to Pete Mitscher, "For your personal information only, Admiral King has accepted my recommendation that you remain in the Fleet. McCain will come to sea, also, for duty similar to yours. In this manner it will be possible for you both to have a blow [rest] from time to time."[28] Under the concept worked out during the following weeks, Mitscher and McCain were to alternate in command of the Fast Carrier Task Force. While one was directing carrier strikes during a particular operation, the other would be drawing up plans and preparing to take over the carriers during the next operation.

With Nimitz's strong backing, Admiral Mitscher remained

with the Fast Carrier Task Force, as Task Force 58 had
become known, through the pivotal First Battle of the Philippine Sea, when, in what came to be known as the Marianas
Turkey Shoot, Mitscher's fighters downed some 395 Japanese
carrier planes for a cost of only 130 American aircraft. At the
beginning of August 1944, he was looking ahead to fleet
operations in the Philippines. He wrote his wife, Frances, "I
may go back to Pearl for a conference if I am to go on the next
one. . . . If I go on the next one it should be over by mid October
then I am sure to be relieved, as I believe . . . [McCain] and
myself are to alternate expeditions."[29] In early October 1944,
Mitscher's carriers (as Task Force 38) were part of Bill
Halsey's Third Fleet, which was readying itself for supporting
operations during the upcoming invasion of the island of Leyte
in the Philippines. Because of Pete Mitscher's confident
handling of the carrier force, Admiral Halsey was reluctant to
have McCain relieve him until after the Third Fleet's portion of
the operation had been completed. He wrote Nimitz, "Mitscher,
under my directive, has planned the forthcoming operations. . . . Because of this, and the importance of the next
move, I had decided to hold Mitscher until its termination
around 25 October. Mitscher's handling of the Task Force has
been so uniformly superb, that I have been loathe to let him
go."[30] As a result of this decision, Mitscher's steady presence
was with the carriers during the Battle of Leyte Gulf (23 to 26
October 1944) when the Japanese Navy attempted to crush the
Leyte beachhead. During the battle, Pete's sure hand had the
intended effect, particularly against Admiral Kurita's central
force the first day, when U.S. carrier aircraft sank the Japanese
superbattleship *Musashi*.

Upon the battle's completion, Mitscher and his staff were
relieved by Admiral McCain and his people. Pete headed back
to the States for a well-deserved leave with his wife. Thereafter, once back at Pearl, Admiral Mitscher, Commodore Burke,

and the others prepared plans for strikes against Tokyo and the Japanese mainland and support for operations to seize Iwo Jima and Okinawa.

At the end of January 1945, Mitscher relieved McCain as commander of the fast carriers. After supporting the Iwo Jima operation (10 February–5 March) and attacking Tokyo in late February 1945, Task Force 58 headed for Okinawa, where landings were scheduled for 1 April. Mitscher wrote his wife, "The Japs are still going after us and we may have a fight before this undertaking is over, if we do it will be the last one because after this undertaking the Pacific will be quiet for a time, anyway."[31] From mid-March until late May 1945—some eighty-two consecutive days at sea—the task force was required to operate in a fairly restricted area off Okinawa, in order to furnish direct support to the invading forces struggling to conquer the island in the face of fanatical Japanese resistance. It was during this period that the carriers were subjected to a very serious pounding from Japanese kamikaze (suicide) air-craft.[32] For most of that time, Mitscher's flagship, the carrier *Bunker Hill,* led a charmed life, even as ships throughout the fleet were being damaged or sunk in kamikaze attacks. This all ended, however, on 11 May 1945, when the *Bunker Hill* was hit by two suicide aircraft that arrived during a lull in the action, just before ten in the morning. Captain Gus Read, who was the duty officer on the flag bridge at the time, remembered the kamikazes' arrival vividly. He recalled:

Within a few seconds the first plane hit the ship. He dropped a bomb through the flight deck, then dove into the [CAP] fighters warming up on the stern, demolishing three, and going overboard himself. Since these planes were fueled to capacity, this immediately started fires aft.

A second plane flew in on his wing, swung past the port side with a roar, climbed steeply, did a wingover and dove into the ship, crashing it into the flight deck at the side of the island and dropping a bomb through it into the hangar deck, prior to impact. The plane itself tore across the gallery deck and exploded in one of the pilots' ready rooms there, killing all hands. This, of course, started bad fires amidships and, unfortunately, wrecked the damage control station on the hangar deck. . . .[33]

Those members of Admiral Mitscher's staff who were not on duty at the time of the attack were badly hit by the subsequent fires. Three officers—Captain Ray Hege, the newly attached staff flight surgeon who was staying in Arleigh Burke's in-port cabin, Lieutenant Commander Frank Quady, the assistant operations officer, and Lieutenant Commander Charlie Steele, the admiral's flag secretary—and ten enlisted men on the staff were killed. Many others were wounded.

With thick smoke from the fires making working conditions on the flag bridge impossible, the decision eventually was made to transfer the flag. A weakened Pete Mitscher was carefully helped up over the front of the bridge by Arleigh Burke and down a Jacob's ladder to the deck.[34] Mitscher transferred to the *Enterprise* with a skeleton staff that afternoon. Less than three days later, on 14 May, the *Enterprise,* too, was hit by a suicide aircraft. The ensuing fires destroyed the carrier's flight deck, together with all of its parked aircraft. In the attack more of Mitscher's staff were wounded. The *Enterprise* withdrew with the rest of its task group for refueling. Once in the refueling area, Mitscher and his remaining staff members transferred for the second and final time to the *Randolph,* Rear Admiral Jerry Bogan's flagship, since there were no undamaged carriers available without a flag aboard.[35]

A weary and frail Pete Mitscher rode out the last of the Okinawa battle in the *Randolph.* On 27 May 1945, Bill Halsey took command of the fleet from Spruance, and Pete was relieved by "Slew" McCain. His fighting was over for the duration. His physique weakened by the stresses imposed by his many months of combat, Marc Mitscher died of a heart attack less than two years later.

Pete Mitscher was regarded by most naval aviators as the best carrier admiral of the war, and with good reason. An inspiring leader and gifted tactician who was fortunate to be backed up throughout his time with the fast carriers by a top-notch staff, Mitscher was the father of the navy's major air victories in 1944 and 1945.

The idea of a biography of Marc Mitscher had originally been suggested to writer Stacy Jones in 1950 by then Captain Robert Pirie, who first had served with Mitscher in the 1930s, when the latter was the chief of staff to Commander Aircraft, Base Force.[36] Jones had served as a civilian assistant to Assistant Secretary of the Navy for Air Artemus Gates during the last year of the war. He undertook the assignment with the expectation that it would have a topical interest if he emphasized the fact that Mitscher had fathered the idea of the flush-deck aircraft carrier, which had been killed by Secretary of Defense Louis Johnson in 1949 but had been reinstated by Congress in 1951.[37] He set to work on the project, but after doing some preliminary research, decided to give it up, perhaps because of the lack of substantive written material on Mitscher's career.

The project then was taken up by Theodore Taylor, who carried the book through to completion. Taylor was a graduate of the U.S. Merchant Marine Academy who had served during the Second World War as third officer in merchant vessels and, at the end of the war, in the Pacific in the USS *Draco* (AK 79) and the USS *Sumner* (AGS 5). Following the war, he became a newspaper man. During the Korean War, he was recalled to active duty and served in several public information offices in the navy and the Office of the Secretary of Defense.[38]

Theodore Taylor was an excellent choice as Mitscher's

biographer. His background as a merchant marine officer and later as an officer in the U.S. Navy provided him with a familiarity with nautical subjects denied to most civilians. Also, his training as a newsman served him well in interviewing Mitscher's friends and shipmates. He was helped in his task of writing about Pete Mitscher by having access to a great number of people who had served with the admiral over the years. In the early 1950s, most of the key figures of naval aviation were still around to talk with, and talk with them he did. In researching Mitscher's life, Taylor interviewed or corresponded with naval aviators such as John Towers, Patrick Bellinger, Alfred Pride, William Halsey, Apollo Soucek, and J. J. Clark. These and many other people were able to relate stories about Pete Mitscher that otherwise would have been lost to us.

The chief problem that Taylor ran into in his research was the paucity of letters and official documents written by Mitscher during his career. This absence of correspondence was due to the intentional action of Admiral Mitscher in the last months of his life. Before he died, he burned all of his personal and official papers, so that no one could be harmed in the future by the discovery of criticisms he may have written about particular individuals or events in the heat of the moment.[39] The only Mitscher material that Theodore Taylor found to use were a few official documents, an occasional letter to a friend or classmate, some letters of congratulations, and condolences to Mrs. Mitscher on the admiral's death.[40] The author did his best to overcome this by relying on official documents to provide information concerning Admiral Mitscher's wartime assignments. He was helped in this effort by the Navy Department, which allowed him to see certain Action Reports, War Diaries, and Operations Plans that were still classified at the time.[41]

The result of Theodore Taylor's patient effort is an excellent biography of Marc Mitscher. Through Taylor's fluid writing style and his recounting of interesting anecdotes supplied by

Mitscher's friends, we are given access to Mitscher the naval aviator in a way that makes him come alive again. And if we are not similarly treated to as detailed an account of Mitscher the man, it is not through lack of effort on the author's part. Pete Mitscher was a very phlegmatic individual who, in his later years particularly, was not given to speaking much about himself to those who served with him. Thus, Taylor's biography of Mitscher is the best one can hope to obtain. Although, here and there, it does contain an occasional inaccuracy, the book measures up well to the demands of biography under such difficult circumstances.

Since Taylor's book first came out, a vast number of competent histories have appeared on the events of the Second World War in the Pacific and, to a much smaller extent, the emerging role of naval aviation in the U.S. Navy. Any number of these would serve the useful purpose of adding further information about the events that shaped or impinged upon Marc Mitscher's life. One that readily comes to mind is Clark Reynolds's book on the development of carrier aviation in the U.S. Navy.[42] Recently, we have begun to see the publication of biographies of some of the other pioneers of naval aviation. One such is Paolo Coletta's book on Patrick Bellinger.[43] Similarly, Clark Reynolds is now hard at work on his long-awaited biography of Jack Towers, portions of which have appeared as articles in Naval Institute publications during the past several years. Finally, the close working relationship between Mitscher and Arleigh Burke has been explored to a certain extent in a recent biography of the latter by E. B. Potter.[44] It is hoped that other biographies of important naval officers of Mitscher's era are also under way.

Nonetheless, books of this sort can only be complementary to (not substitutes for) Theodore Taylor's account of Mitscher's life. Certainly, now that the vast documentary record of official reports and correspondence on the U.S. Navy's role during the

Second World War has been declassified, we likely will see the appearance of an increasing number of books that can provide exact details of operations that were denied to nongovernmental historians in the days when Taylor wrote his book. But such information can only supply the backdrop against which we view Marc Mitscher, for in the intervening years, most of the men who knew Mitscher have gone to join their shipmates. It is this fact that continues to give Theodore Taylor's biography of this magnificent man its importance.

I am grateful to my grandfather, Francis G. Barlow, an Army Signal Corps pilot on active service in France, 1918–1919, and to my father, Captain John F. Barlow, USN (Retired), a naval aviator of varied experience in the postwar U.S. Navy, for encouraging the interest of a young boy in the multifarious activities of aviation. I would also like to thank Admiral Arleigh A. Burke, USN (Retired), for the many hours of conversation over the years about Marc Mitscher that brought to life this remarkable man in a way nothing else could have done.

JEFFREY G. BARLOW

EDITOR'S NOTE: This book was photographically reproduced from the original text. The following are corrections to that text.

On page 85, line 3, Mitscher actually reported to the *Langley* on 27 June 1929.

On page 92, line 10, the correct designation of the command to which Mitscher was ordered was Aircraft, Base Force.

On pages 98 and 99, Admiral King was Commander Aircraft, Base Force, flying his flag on the *Wright,* when Mitscher joined the ship as CO in May 1937. He did not become Commander Aircraft, Battle Force until January 1938.

On page 347 of the bibliography, line 1, this memorandum—*to* the Judge Advocate General—was prepared by Captain Arleigh Burke, then the head of Op-23.

NOTES

1. *Annual Register of the United States Naval Academy [,] Annapolis, MD. [:] Sixty-Sixth Academic Year 1910–1911* (Washington, D.C.: Government Printing Office, 1910), 44.

2. Unless otherwise noted, specific references to dates and duty assignments during Admiral Mitscher's early career are taken from Bureau of Navigation document 7591- Nav-327-MK, "CAPTAIN MARC ANDREW MITSCHER, UNITED STATES NAVY Re: Service of," 31 July 1941; "MITSCHER, MARC A. ADM" Folder, Box 453, Officer Bios Collection, Operational Archives, Naval Historical Center (hereafter cited as OA).

3. A pusher aircraft had the propeller in the rear of the wings. Becoming familiar with the framework wiring on these pre–World War I biplanes took a great deal of effort in itself. The different kinds of wires on airplanes of the time included such esoteric types as aileron balance wires, anti-drag wires, and bottom-bracing wires. Ernest Larue Jones and Lester D. Seymour, "Glossary Of Aeronautical Terms," typewritten manuscript, n.d. [early 1920s], 81–82; author's collection.

4. Navy Cross citation, quoted in officer biography—"Admiral Marc Andrew Mitscher, U.S. Navy," 1 May 1946, 1; "MITSCHER, MARC A. ADM" Folder, Box 453, Officer Bios Collection, OA.

5. Interviews with Admiral Arleigh A. Burke, USN (Retired).

6. *Saratoga* was commissioned a year after he joined her, in November 1927.

7. The author possesses a 1928 photograph of a smiling Marc Mitscher posing at San Diego in front of a parked F3B with the pilots of Fighting Three.

8. Letter from Nicholson to Mitscher, 21 October 1941; "MARC A. MITSCHER PERSONAL CORRESPONDENCE" Folder (first of three in box), Box 1, Papers of Marc A. Mitscher, Manuscript Division, Library of Congress (hereafter cited as MD-LC).

9. Letter from Mitscher to G.D. Murray, 3 November 1941, same folder.

10. Letter from Mitscher to R.E. Ingersoll, 5 February 1942; "MARC A. MITSCHER PERSONAL CORRESPONDENCE" Folder (third of three in box), same folder.

11. Letter from Mitscher to Ingersoll, 9 June 1942; "MARC A. MITSCHER PERSONAL CORRESPONDENCE" Folder (second of three in box), same folder.

12. Letter from Mitscher to Mrs. Adelaide Waldron, 4 July 1942; same folder.

13. Unless otherwise noted, specific references to dates and duty assignments for Admiral Mitscher during the war are taken from Bureau of Naval Personnel document Pers-3270-ghb 7591, "VICE ADMIRAL MARC ANDREW MITSCHER, U.S. NAVY Re: Service of," 5 September 1944; or

[Bureau of Naval Personnel] document Pers-5321-lmc 7591, "ADMIRAL MARC ANDREW MITSCHER, UNITED STATES NAVY, ACTIVE, DECEASED Re: Service of," n.d. [1947]; both in "MITSCHER, MARC A. ADM" Folder, Box 453, Officer Bios Collection, OA.

14. Untitled manuscript speech by Captain W. A. Read, USNR, n.d. [probably 1946], 1; "FILE NUMBER 101" Folder, Unnumbered box, Papers of Arleigh A. Burke, OA.

15. Sherman had been designated an aviator in March 1936, after serving some twenty-five years in surface ships and submarines. Bureau of Naval Personnel document Pers-3270-ghb 7562, "REAR ADMIRAL FREDERICK CARL SHERMAN, U.S. NAVY Re: Service of," 5 September 1944, 1–2; "SHERMAN, FREDERICK CARL ADMIRAL USN" Folder, Box 573, Officer Bios Collection, OA.

16. Carbon copy of typed, largely uncorrected, manuscript labeled "Wartime [WW II] diary of Adm Frederick C. SHERMAN" (brackets in original), May 1942–March 1946, 63; "SHERMAN FOREST C. ADM. [sic]" Folder, Box 292, Indiv. Pers. Records, World War II Command File, OA.

17. "TASK FORCE FIFTY-EIGHT [Statistical Summary]," attached to "TASK FORCE FIFTY-EIGHT CALENDAR," n.d. [late February or early March 1944]; "MARC A. MITSCHER MISCELLANY" Folder, Box 3, Mitscher Papers, MD-LC.

18. Ibid.

19. Vice Admiral Truman J. Hedding, USN (Retired), Interviews by Dr. John T. Mason, Jr., February–May 1971, transcript, U.S. Naval Institute Oral History Program, Annapolis, Md., #1—61–62.

20. For an engaging account of Admiral Mitscher's later career as viewed by Admiral Burke, see Arleigh Burke, "Admiral Marc Mitscher: A Naval Aviator," U.S. Naval Institute Proceedings, 101 (April 1975): 53–63.

21. Interviews with Admiral Burke.

22. "Narrative by: Commodore Arleigh A. Burke, USN [—] Experiences as Chief of Staff to Admiral Mitscher," recorded 21 August 1945, 1; "BURKE, A. A., ADM #417-3" Folder, Box 5, World War II Interview Collection, OA.

23. Ibid., 1–2.

24. Ibid., 2.

25. McCain, like Frederick Sherman, had been awarded his wings in 1936, after spending a lengthy career in surface ships. [Bureau of Naval Personnel] document Pers 5324a-bh 5368, "VICE ADMIRAL JOHN SIDNEY MC CAIN, UNITED STATES NAVY, ACTIVE, DECEASED Re: Service of," 15 September 1945, 1–2; "McCAIN, JOHN S.—ADM" Folder, Box 407, Officer Bios Collection, OA.

26. Letter from Clark to Radford, 26 May 1944; "Admiral Radford #1 Personal Corres. April–July 1944" Folder, Box 27, Papers of Arthur W. Radford, OA. See also entry for 24 June 1944, Sherman Diary, 69.

27. Letter from Nimitz to King, 13 June 1944; "ADMIRAL'S LETTERS—1944 Folder #1 Personal File," Series XIII, Papers of Chester W. Nimitz, OA.

28. Letter from Nimitz to Mitscher, 8 July 1944; "MARC A. MITSCHER PERSONAL CORRESPONDENCE" Folder (second of three in box), Box 1, Mitscher Papers, MD-LC.

29. Letter from Mitscher to Frances Mitscher, 1 August [1944]; "Mitscher, Marc A (VADM) Personal Papers (1917–1951)" Folder, Box 3, Fragmentary Personal Papers, OA.

30. Letter from Halsey to Nimitz, 6 October 1944; "#15 CORRESPONDENCE with COMMANDER THIRD FLEET, 1944 (HALSEY)" Folder, Series XIII, Nimitz Papers, OA.

31. Letter from Mitscher to Frances Mitscher, n.d. [postmarked 27 March 1945]; "Mitscher, Marc A. (VADM) Personal Papers (1917–1951)" Folder, Box 3, Fragmentary Personal Papers, OA.

32. For a contemporary recounting, see "Narrative by: Commodore Arleigh A. Burke, USN [—] Carrier Force Pacific—Tokyo Strike, etc."; "BURKE, A. A., ADM #417-2" Folder, Box 5, World War II Interview Collection, OA.

33. W. A. Read speech, 16–17.

34. A few days before, he apparently had suffered a slight heart attack, and on the day that the *Bunker Hill* was hit he was in poor shape to climb over obstacles by himself. Interviews with Admiral Burke.

35. "Narrative by Commodore Burke—Tokyo Strike," 20.

36. Theodore Taylor, *The Magnificent Mitscher* (New York: W. W. Norton & Company, Inc., 1954), xi.

37. Letter from Stacy V. Jones to Admiral Arthur Radford, 16 August 1951; "J" Correspondence Folder, Box 33, Radford Papers, OA.

38. Information on Theodore Taylor's background comes from biographical sketches attached to several articles he wrote for *U.S. Naval Institute Proceedings* in the 1950s.

39. Interviews with Admiral Burke.

40. These, which later were donated to the Manuscript Division of the Library of Congress by Frances Mitscher, consist of three document boxes of miscellaneous material—some 900 items; most of little value to a biographer.

41. See Taylor, *The Magnificent Mitscher*, 347–48.

42. Clark G. Reynolds, *The Fast Carriers: The Forging of an Air Navy* (New York: McGraw-Hill Book Company, 1968).

43. Paolo E. Coletta, *Patrick N. L. Bellinger and U.S. Naval Aviation* (Lanham, Md.: University Press of America, 1987).

44. E. B. Potter, *Admiral Arleigh Burke: A Biography* (New York: Random House, 1990).

THE
MAGNIFICENT MITSCHER

Culmination

⚓ ⚓

WASHINGTON week ends, by November, 1945, were beginning
to return to normality. Government workers and soldiers and
sailors, previously occupied six or seven days a week by the
Pentagon or the offices in its war pipelines, could be seen ex-
amining the Lincoln Memorial as if it were newly discovered,
and the traffic along Constitution Avenue was thick with automobiles no longer restricted by gasoline rationing.

Some government officials, however, continued to work at a
wartime pace. On the third Sunday in that month, Secretary
of the Navy James V. Forrestal was in his office in the sprawling, ramshackle Navy Department building awaiting the arrival
of Vice Admiral Marc A. Mitscher. It was not unusual for the
Secretary to work on Sunday. The Navy was unraveling during this period, and Forrestal spent seven days a week trying
to organize an orderly demobilization and at the same time plan
for the future. Ships had to be laid up or scrapped, bases inactivated, and several million men processed home.

Mitscher, on the other hand, had been making every effort
to keep away from the frustrating headquarters by the Poto-
mac. Six days out of seven at the desk of Deputy Chief of
Naval Operations (Air) was quite enough for him. However,
he reported gladly to Forrestal. He admired the dynamic
financier who was later to become the nation's first Secretary of

3

Defense. Also, he knew his trip would not be wasted in idle chatter, for Forrestal used words sparingly, which was to Mitscher's liking. In addition, Mitscher thought he knew most of what the Secretary wanted to discuss.

Earlier, during September, Forrestal had requested Mitscher's comments on the composition of the "Post-War Navy," and the preface to the resulting memorandum by Mitscher sets the tenor:

In accordance with your request I am outlining to you views on my conception of a Post-War Navy, as briefly as it is possible to do so. I invite to your attention the fact that my ideas are based solely on my own observations through the years during Fleet maneuvers in peacetime and actual combat operations in war, and the lessons learned therefrom. I am not a graduate of the Naval War College, but have operated under their precepts for many years and find I cannot agree with many of their past conclusions. A paper of this nature will be subjected to many adverse arguments, but I can assure you I was the first aviator to operate with the so-called modern battleship after this war started, and at the time I was as enthusiastic as any Naval officer should have been, but in my operations in the Pacific I have definitely come to conclusions, which are stated below, and I am convinced I am right.

Point by point, in the five-page, single-spaced document, Mitscher covered what he thought to be the ideal composition for the future Navy, fingered the Soviet Union as the threat to peace, and spoke rather sharply of naval officers who still viewed naval aviation as an unruly and prodigious stepchild. Certainly Forrestal had expected Mitscher to place aircraft and aircraft carriers in the lead position in the postwar Navy, and to relegate battleships to the bottom of the list. And Forrestal, a World War I Navy pilot, agreed completely, it was later established. They talked for about an hour on various aspects of the memorandum and on problems facing the nation. In his diary for November 20, 1945, Forrestal wrote:

There is strong pressure to bring the Americans out of China, particularly the Marines. If we do so, we invite a vacuum of anarchy in Manchuria, and it is obvious that into that vacuum ultimately either the Japanese or Russians will flow. In this connection I referred to a conversation with Admiral Mitscher on Sunday, in which he pointed out that in any future war between a combination of Russian and Asiatic powers, the manpower available to such a combination would be so tremendous and the indifference to loss of life so striking that it would present a very serious problem to this country.[1]

When the conference ended and the Admiral prepared to return to his Shoreham hotel apartment, Forrestal abruptly offered Mitscher the position of Chief of Naval Operations, to succeed Fleet Admiral Ernest J. King. Mitscher was stunned. Never had a professional aviator held the Navy's supreme command. The offer was tantamount to recognizing the successful end of a naval revolution in which planes and aircraft carriers had replaced the hallowed battleship, a crusade in which he had fought for thirty years. Furthermore, there were five or six admirals very much senior to Mitscher and entirely eligible. Normally, they would be given the first consideration and the first opportunity.

The position Forrestal offered Mitscher is the goal every Naval Academy graduate is supposed to dream about, work for, and fight for. Only forty-one men in the history of the country had held it. No naval officer could ask for more honor and prestige to culminate his career. But Mitscher declined.

His reply, he told his aide, Commander Everett Eynon, was,

[1] "Here, in very nearly its full form, was the dilemma that was to bewilder the Truman administration from that day forward. Mitscher's, and Forrestal's prevision was to be tragically confirmed just five years later, in 1950, when that huge and expendable Communist manpower, conscripted in the service of Communism, rolled down upon our armies in northern Korea."— Comment by Walter Millis in *Forrestal Diaries*, edited by Walter Millis with the collaboration of E. S. Duffield (New York, Viking Press, 1951).

"No, thank you, Mr. Secretary, I'd want to make too many changes around here."

It is probable that Mr. Forrestal understood the polite excuse. He knew that the wrinkled little man seated in front of him loathed long mahogany desks, baskets of papers, and the veneer of official Washington. Although Mitscher might have made a superior CNO, he would undoubtedly have been the unhappiest admiral ever to occupy that throne.

Mitscher was a fighter and a pilot and an expert in operating massive groups of flattops. Office work didn't become him. It was quite obvious that, as he told Vice Admiral Patrick Bellinger later, Forrestal's offer had filled him with overwhelming pride. But he was out of breath from four years of sprinting, and Constitution Avenue was hardly the place to rest. Also, he had just finished the one job, perhaps the only job, that was precisely tailored for him. If Admiral Marc Mitscher hadn't been around during World War II, then the Navy would have found it necessary to manufacture a reasonable facsimile of him.

Less than two years after the Sunday session in Forrestal's office, Mitscher, then Commander in Chief, Atlantic, died in the Naval Hospital, Norfolk, Virginia. The four years of war had overtaken him. He was a combat casualty.

For days afterward, tributes and letters of condolence were received at his headquarters in Norfolk. There were letters and wires from enlisted men and admirals, from the President of the United States and from foreign governments. Frances Smalley Mitscher, his wife, was profoundly moved by messages from persons she presumed to be complete strangers. There were letters from three enlisted men who had named their first sons after Mitscher. Gordon A. Reeves, who had served in the U.S.S. *Hornet*, wrote: "I feel that history has not given your late husband full credit for his part in the Japanese war.

CULMINATION

The average American does not know him, but every man who
served under him knew his greatest quality—human understanding. His sensible qualities kept us alive and willing to go
anyplace, providing he led us."

A couple in Tampa, Florida, wrote: "Knowing nothing of
Admiral Marc's life beyond what we read about his nobility in
the line of duty, we would like to have his officer's biography,
for Marc Stanley when he is older."

Who did know Marc Mitscher?

As the days passed and the shock of his sudden death began
to subside around Atlantic Fleet headquarters, many of his
shipmates found themselves asking that question, in one way or
another. The feeling was not confined to the fleet. On February
4, Henry Suydam, of the Newark *Evening News* had written
an editorial about Mitscher. His first paragraph read as follows:

Admiral Marc Andrew Mitscher was one of the greatest admirals whom the American naval service has produced. Yet of
him it could be said that he died unknown, except as a war hero.
He shunned self advertising in all its forms. He never made a
speech, even at the height of his fame, that he could avoid. He
was a silent man in an age of self expression. Hence, to some he
seemed remote and baffling.

Other editorial pages around the country echoed Henry
Suydam: Here was a man who had passed swiftly and glori-
ously through moments of American history and had "died
unknown, except as a war hero."

Of course, Mitscher the fighter—not the man—was generally known to the Navy, especially to the officers and men of
naval aviation. To them, he was Admiral Pete, or Little Pete,
or Uncle Pete, an enigmatic sailor-pilot who ran fast-carrier
task forces with rocking-chair ease. He was admirably
equipped to do it, and had spent an entire lifetime preparing

to fight air battles over the sea. He understood the sea, and the air masses above it.

But even within the family of the Navy the story of the leader of Task Force 58 had little more than the substance of a legend, for his rise to fame had been sudden and Mitscher seldom talked about the past. Without consciously doing so, he had provided fertile ground for the legends which always flourish during battle.

His appearance alone made him legendary. He was a small man with a wizened face and a thin, soft voice, and remarkable composure. The skin on his face was of parchment quality, aged beyond its years. His forehead was pleated and chevroned. Piercing, light-blue eyes, which could look through a man without hurting him, were set beneath bushy, reddish-brown eyebrows, and shaded by the inevitable long-billed cloth cap, a fixture over his bald, sunburned pate. He was variously described as dwarflike and gnomelike. Actually, he was neither.

The legend pictured him as incapable of excitement even when flaming Japanese bombers plummeted toward his bridge. It was said that he was a Jap-hater with a hate so passionate that it was sometimes distasteful to those around him; that he rescued pilots from under the snouts of enemy guns; that he'd flood the fleet with light to bring home his pilots on black nights in enemy waters. This was the naval airman's legend of "Pete" Mitscher. It was almost immune to attack, and it ignored the possibility of the man's inadequacies.

But if the slight, impeccable figure, so indelibly placed on the wing of a fast carrier's bridge, mysteriously riding backward in his swivel chair, and barely whispering his orders, were to be brought alive again today it is improbable that the legend would tarnish. Much of it is gospel.

Now he is recognized *within the Navy* as one of the greatest combat officers in the history of air or sea warfare—a nautical Jeb Stuart who hid beneath weather fronts to make his attacks, and was engaged in every major naval battle in the Pacific during World War II except Coral Sea. He fought more naval engagements than Farragut and John Paul Jones combined. He introduced or sponsored most of the intricate tactics used by fast-carrier task forces. He was the father of the U.S.S. *Forrestal*, the first of today's so-called "supercarriers."

Yet Mitscher's full contributions toward the building of the mightiest naval air arm in the world, perfecting carrier tactics, and developing American military aviation are relatively unknown. Already his name is fading into the silence that was always typical of him.

This story of his life is addressed to the thousands of men—the pilots, aircrewmen, and sailors—who fought at Midway, in the Solomons, the Marshalls, the Carolines, the Marianas, the Philippines, and Okinawa. It is addressed to the aviation pioneers who flew with him in orange-crate planes. It is addressed to the strangers who wrote Frances Mitscher after his death. It is addressed to Henry Suydam, and to all the other people who expressed regret at not having known Admiral Marc Mitscher.

Their regret is understandable; he was a magnificent man.

PART ONE

⚓ ⚓
⚓

The Air above the Sea

CHAPTER

⚓ 1 ⚓

Early Days

FORTUNATELY for the United States Navy, Marc Andrew Mitscher's grandfather, Andreus Mitscher, woodworker of Traben, Germany, had what appears to have been an intense wanderlust. His kit of fine German tools had supported him in a half dozen countries before he finally took passage aboard an immigrant packet bound for America. He landed in New York in the early eighteen-fifties and there met Constantina Moln, a German girl who had immigrated as a child. They were married in 1854 and Andreus's days of wandering ended.

How the Mitschers hit upon Hillsborough, Wisconsin, is unknown; perhaps they were drawn to this wilderness area because many of its settlers were of Austrian and Bavarian origin. Andreus built a home and a small shop, and became Hillsborough's cabinetmaker, furniture dealer, and funeral director. He made fine coffins to order, and Constantina, between bearing her own children, became the village midwife.

Marc Mitscher's father, Oscar, was their second son. He was a child who caused much consternation in the otherwise placid dwelling on Water Street. High-strung, unpredictable, and a thorough extrovert, he refused to enter the cabinetmaking trade and became a clerk in the mercantile firm of T. J. Shear, the village tycoon.

Shear's daughter, Myrta, was a school teacher. Of pure English stock, Myrta was the complete opposite of Oscar Mitscher. She seldom spoke unless something important needed to be said. Never hurried, never excited, she balanced Oscar's impetuosity. She wanted nothing more than a comfortable home in Hillsborough, a small family, and a span of peaceful years in the rich Vernon County farmlands. They were married in 1883, and it turned out to be a profitable as well as companionable arrangement. Soon the sign in front of the store said "Shear & Mitscher." Oscar was an enterprising young man. But in a few years, suffering from rheumatism and touched with Andreus's wanderlust, he pulled up the family roots and moved them into the Oklahoma Territory of the roaring land-rush days.

On January 26, 1887, before they left Hillsborough, their second child, Marc Andrew, was born. A sister, Zoe, had been born two years earlier, and a brother, Tom, was born in Oklahoma City in 1894.

Oklahoma City, in the period between 1890 and 1900, the peak of its boom-town, plank-walk days, had the proper blend of adventure and opportunity for Oscar. On arrival, after having had a land claim jumped at nearby Guthrie, he opened a haberdashery at the corner of Grand and Robinson streets, and it quickly prospered and grew to be a general store, with several partners. Marc often played between the bins of goods.

Myrta disliked the dry, windy pioneer town and returned to cool Hillsborough each summer with the children. For young Marc, however, there was always plenty of excitement in Oklahoma. There was an Indian-raid false alarm one night, and once he was present when a deputy marshal drove up in a buggy and shoved out the body of a slain outlaw. The crowd rushed forward and Marc's nose was pressed into the desperado's chest, an experience he did not forget for a long time. Storms were frequent. A tornado, one of many, demolished their home on West Fourth Street; Oscar promptly built a new one on Choctaw Street.

Early in this period Oscar became involved in politics, and he was Oklahoma City's second mayor, serving from 1892 to 1894. He was also an unsuccessful candidate for governor several years later. None of this interest, however, filtered down to his eldest son, who was always a sideline observer of political affairs, and even as an adult generally refused to discuss them.

Oscar and Myrta were happy despite the temperamental differences between them. The home atmosphere was congenial. Strife was rare. The Mitschers were never wealthy and never poverty-stricken.

It seems apparent that his happy childhood and his mother's nature were the sources of Marc Mitscher's emotional stability. Oscar supplied persistence and affection and other less well-defined legacies. He was an attentive father, certainly, and a good companion on hunting trips and occasional rambles over the plains. He taught young Marc to count by playing cards with him, and Mitscher later became a good bridge player and a formidable poker opponent. They were chess partners for years, checking and countering by mail.

Most of the things Mitscher liked as a youngster he still liked as a four-star admiral. Myrta made huge pots of noodle soup for him and always had enough when he asked for more. Forty years later, he still favored it. In many ways, he remained throughout his life much as he was during his mid-teens. Obedient, gentle and respectful, it is certain he loved his parents deeply, yet he seldom showed this feeling. His relationship with Zoe was affectionate, but, again, without demonstration. He was never close to Tom, possibly because of the difference in their ages.

Oklahoma days were also days of riding bareback on Ingie, a spirited Indian pony given him by Oscar. Mitscher broke him handily, and was the only one in the family who could cope with the cantankerous beast. They were days of meandering by buffalo wallows and over the dusty prairie. He became expert with a lasso and also with his fists. Myrta frequently saw her son arrive home from school in disorder, a trickle of blood on his lips, and in brooding silence. He didn't pick fights, his sister has said, he simply couldn't avoid them. With Uncle Wesley Shear he went to a baseball game one afternoon. On the way to the park, he was ridiculed because Myrta had dressed him in a frilly suit, but he walked calmly beside his uncle, apparently ignoring the taunts. To Shear's utter disappointment, Marc made no mention of the incident, nor did he voice threats to get even. But the next day he ambled into the kitchen with a bloody nose and torn shirt, and announced that the score was settled. The family story indicates that he took on four or five boys and beat them all.

When it mattered to him, Mitscher usually "settled the score," during his youth and later. There were several incidents in which an almost vindictive urge was revealed. Mitscher had strong likes and dislikes and the dividing line was sharp.

In his school work Mitscher was below average, but he did not seem upset by his low grades, most of them barely passing; nor did he express interest in anything except horses, baseball, and football. In the classroom, according to his former teacher Ada Jarboe, he was shy "and blushed easily and avoided girls of any age."

In 1900, to the family's delight, Oscar was appointed agent for the Osage Indian reservation at Pawhuska, a reward for steadfast adherence to the Republican Party in a Democratic stronghold. The Osage hills brought back memories of Vernon County. Myrta was content at last.

Although Marc, by now fourteen, would have preferred

to stay on the reservation the year around, chasing jackrabbits over the Osages, or watching dances and pony smokes in the village, Oscar decided the Indian school was not a suitable place to educate his children. Therefore, when W. S. Field, formerly of Hillsborough, and one of Oscar's Oklahoma City store partners, offered to school Marc and his sister during the winter months, Oscar promptly accepted.

The Fields lived in Washington, D.C., in a rambling old house on Eleventh Street, S.E., that is now an undertaking parlor. There, away from all the influences of home, Marc remained the same tranquil youngster. There were many parties, and some of the people who attended them remember that he would come into the parlor, gaze soberly at the gay group, and then slip quietly away. He read many books, mostly popular adventure fiction, and could frequently be found in the Fields' large library, munching on sugar toast and engrossed in the latest Dick Merriwell episode.

Apparently timid elsewhere, he was aggressive on the athletic field, but even there he would not take over leadership until it became obvious that no one else would. He played sand-lot football because the Maury School coach, fearing that the slight boy might be injured, refused to give him a uniform. He weighed less than a hundred and ten pounds at the time but was compact and evenly muscled. The sandlot games, held almost every afternoon during the fall, were played behind the old Washington carbarn at 13th and D, Southeast. Marc had a team he defiantly called the Second Maury, and many of the games were played against a squad captained by Penn Carroll, who eventually became a Navy commodore.

Sometimes these autumn afternoons afforded glimpses of his incipient leadership. A fight started during one game and was developing rapidly into a junior riot when young Mitscher moved into the center of it and stood between the fighters. They towered over him. He reminded them that they were playing a football game. If they wanted to fight, he told them, they could wait until the game was over. After the final whistle, Mitscher drew off a ring and asked a bystander to referee; then he stood between the crowd and the fighters and kept perfect order.

"I think I saw the first signs of his ability to cope with a situation," Commodore Carroll said. "He knew when to take command."

But the winter months in Washington were only a seasonal bridge between the periods spent in Pawhuska and the Osages. He was enchanted with those lonely hills. There, in summer, he spent much of the day on horseback and frequently chummed with a lad named Clarence Tinker—the same Major General Tinker who was lost en route to the Battle of Midway. Sometimes Marc played shinny with the Indian boys in the village, his thick, whitish-blond hair, soon to vanish, an easy target for the wildly flung sticks. Often he camped out in the hills. He was a good shot and acquired a wide knowledge of the habits of local wild life.

It appeared at this point that Mitscher might choose some kind of outdoor work, although he was never specific about it. In the summer of 1902, however, Byron Shear, clerk of the court in Oklahoma City, visited Pawhuska for a few weeks. Uncle By Shear was a frustrated cavalryman and saw in Marc an opportunity partially to compensate for his own failure. He began a storytelling campaign designed to route his nephew to West Point and then into Army cavalry.

However, Oscar suddenly made it known that he had always wanted a son to enter the United States Naval Academy, and since young Tom would not be eligible for some years, Marc became the immediate candidate. Oscar sabotaged Shear's plans by entering Marc in a private preparatory school in Washington and driving ahead to secure an appointment at Annapolis for him. Mitscher, it is certain, had little interest in ships, and none in the Navy, but he seems not to have objected.

Oscar experienced no difficulty in placing his son's name on the list through his long-time crony, Congressman Bird S. McGuire. On May 3, 1904, McGuire forwarded a letter to the Navy Department and Mitscher's career was underway.

CHAPTER

⚓ 2 ⚓

The Naval Academy

IN THE summer of 1904, Ernest J. King, later the craggy, flint-coated fleet admiral, was but an ensign in the cruiser *Cincinnati*, plowing around Asiatic waters; another famed fleet admiral, William F. Halsey, Jr., had just graduated. That same summer, on June 22, seventeen-year-old Marc Mitscher took his Annapolis entrance exams and immediately skidded to the foot of the class. The Navy grades on a percentage system, with 4.0 as the highest mark, 2.5 as passing. Perhaps Mitscher's appalling entrance grades were prophetic. He made 2.6 in geography, 2.5 in arithmetic, 2.8 in history, and failed geometry with 2.2. In English, he fared little better.

Judged only on scholarship, Mitscher was one of the most unlikely candidates for flag rank ever to log in at the staid, strict school on the banks of Maryland's Severn. In contrast, among his original classmates were such brilliant students as Jerome Clark Hunsaker, later one of the nation's top aeronautical engineers, and Richmond Kelly Turner, Willis Augustus Lee, Jr., and Thomas Cassin Kinkaid, all notable flag officers by the end of World War II.

Mitscher acquired his nickname that fall semester. The

first midshipman from Oklahoma, Peter Cassius Marcellus Cade, Jr., had "bilged out"—Academy slang for failing—in 1903. When the upperclassmen returned from September leave and found the Pawhuska towhead in the place of Cade, it was decided some tribute must be paid the latter. Mitscher was forced to repeat Cade's full name each time he was approached. In a few weeks, he was being called "Oklahoma Pete" Mitscher. By midwinter, this had become plain "Pete" Mitscher, and it remained that way.

His troubles came from the stacks of books. He was no match for Dandell's *Principles of Physics* or Meras' *Syntaxe Pratique* or Cotterill and Slade's *Lessons in Applied Mechanics* or Genung's *Outlines of Rhetoric*. He even failed the "crip" course in mechanical drawing that year.

He had other troubles too. Martinets ran Annapolis and harsh discipline was both a game and a way of life. "Sundowning," the studied practice of hazing, was a leftover from the sail Navy. Mitscher rebelled, and only inborn stubbornness kept him going. Hazing was cheered on by the sundowners, and Mitscher was hazed with the rest, although there is no evidence he was unduly manhandled. By now, he had acquired a reputation as "touge," "a red mike," and "wooden." The Severn translation: tough, a woman hater, and poor student.

In his second year he joined freely in the hazing of plebes. Then tragedy struck the Academy in November, 1905. A member of Mitscher's group, James R. Branch, was killed in a class "fight." Congress demanded action—the abolition of hazing, class fighting, and other traditional violence aimed at converting boys into men. Some two hundred midshipmen had been involved in hazing, a lengthy investigation proved, and Mitscher was among them. Punishment was ordered.

Academy records indicate he was forced to resign because of scholastic difficulties. However, his classmates blame it on his involvement in the hazing, plus the accumulation of 280 demerits against an allowable 250. They point out that Mitscher would have been permitted a re-examination in the spring of 1906 if academic reasons alone had been involved. Whatever the cause, he was asked to vacate the premises on March 16, 1906. The painful letter of resignation to the Secretary of the Navy, scrawled on cheap tablet paper, is still a part of the Admiral's official record.

Oscar Mitscher fumed and threatened. He told his son to remain at Annapolis and then hurriedly arranged for the same Congressman McGuire to make a reappointment. But the two years of school were wiped off the calendar. Mitscher was allowed to re-enter as a supposedly chastened plebe, and start all over again. He was ordered to report back to Annapolis in June, 1906.

Outwardly tough, Mitscher was also deeply sensitive, although this was seldom revealed to any but his most intimate friends. Now a bilger, he had received a crushing blow. Apparently, it only made him more determined. At nineteen, with a black mark on his file card, looking about as old as he did twenty years later, he took up residence once again. To the fresh, eager plebes of 1906, several years his junior, it often appeared he carried a small man's chip on his shoulder.

One 1906 classmate said: "He was more like a private in the rear rank. He made aside remarks. He was negative and antisocial. He swore. He was dry and uncommunicative. He was inclined to ignore orders and advice."

But another member of the class saw Mitscher differently: "Yes, he was tough, and didn't make friends too easily. But he was the kind of man you'd most want around when you got into trouble. The bilging had hurt him."

Mitscher appeared sober indeed, but never somber. In the limits of his room, or in the company of close friends, the inner warmth came out. But it was a warmth that needed long, careful kindling. One of his closest companions was Harry

"Cash" Cecil, a kindly, chubby Tennessean, who was later killed in the crash of the dirigible *Akron*. Another was hot-headed Frenchy Lamont, a "convict." Frenchy couldn't keep out of trouble. There were also moon-faced Fats Roesch, penny-ante partner T. A. Nicholson, studious and witty Herbert "Judge" Underwood, and Mitscher's "wife," roommate Papa Mike Foster, who shared his toothpaste, shaving cream, and money. With the exception of Judge Underwood, they were all poor students.

Apparently there wasn't a strategist or hero, a Mahan, Dewey, Farragut, or John Paul Jones, in the lot. In fact, Underwood boned them up constantly in the fight to survive.

Mitscher began picking up demerits again for various misdemeanors, and kept a sizable balance of them until he graduated. The violations ranged from "button off reefer" to "smoking" to "card playing" and "room in disorder." Some were more serious, and at times he came close to 250 demerits, the maximum allowable. Once, he accumulated a hundred in less than twenty-four hours and again teetered on the brink of dismissal.

One evening in March, 1907, the room which he shared with Papa Mike, a sterile, bleak cubicle with a pair of green-reflectored hanging lights and twin porcelain wash basins, was the scene of a drinking party. The midshipman grapevine warned that officers were about to raid the party, and Mitscher and Underwood dragged Papa Mike, who was pleasantly tight, off to a safe hiding spot. Then Mitscher, clad in a turtle-neck sweater with 1910 emblazoned across the chest, returned to the monastic cell. The raiders had arrived, and he was scooped up, with four other classmates, and marched to the dispensary. There he was pronounced "under the influence."

Mitscher emphatically denied the charge, claiming he had not touched a bottle since September leave. He was in training for wrestling at the time. Denial was not according to naval custom. It was permissible to explain, but not to contradict or accuse. Mitscher would have none of that. He hadn't been drinking and he planned to say so. He penned a short statement of complete denial, but, Underwood quickly pointed out, in doing so he was contradicting the doctors; more than that, he was calling them liars.

On the morning of March 12, Mitscher was called before Captain W. S. Benson, the Academy Commandant, later Chief of Naval Operations. Benson was outraged at the impudence of the Oklahoma boy and demanded that Mitscher withdraw or rewrite his statement.

But, standing within an arm's length of the feared, gruff Navy professional, he quietly, stubbornly, refused. Benson, angry, fined Midshipman Mitscher fifty demerits on the spot, charging him with gross disrespect.

Underwood pleaded with Mitscher to let him draft an explanatory statement. Calmly, Mitscher answered, "No. Benson knows I'm telling the truth."

Benson had ordered Mitscher to return to his office the next day. He apparently supposed a night's reflection might change the mind of the obstinate youngster who was kicking up the traces of naval custom.

So on March 13, Mitscher reported again to Benson. Certain he had won a victory, the Commandant greeted Mitscher warmly, requested the new statement, and lifted his hand to receive it.

Mitscher said, "I have no new statement."

Benson gave him fifty more demerits for gross disrespect, and Mitscher answered, "My statement is the unvarnished truth and therefore can't be gross disrespect."

Benson ordered him out, but soon removed the alcohol charge from his record. Although Mitscher intensely disliked the stern disciplinarian the rest of his life, it was noticed that

Benson appeared to have considerable respect for the young midshipman after the showdown.

In stubbornness, there was little difference between Midshipman Mitscher and Admiral Mitscher. If you could convince him he was wrong, which was not easily done, he would back down. But otherwise Mitscher would follow his own convictions to the end, regardless of interruptions, distractions, cost, danger, or consequences. His salvation, at Annapolis and later, was an exceptional amount of common sense and a capacity for judgment which seldom erred.

He was tattooed in the summer of 1908. When the U.S.S. *Olympia* reached Norfolk the captain decided to disembark forty-four midshipmen to relieve overcrowded conditions. Mitscher was among the midshipmen sent back to join the lowly plebes for a dull summer of tacking around Chesapeake Bay.

Resentment at having to leave the *Olympia* ran high for several weeks. "We took it out in raising as much hell as possible," Underwood remembers. To cement the common misery, thirteen of them visited a tattoo artist and received identical tattoos on their upper right arms. The design was a bluish-colored buzzard, pierced by a purple dagger dripping blood. It was hideous enough, and they all felt better. But in later life, Mitscher was rather sensitive about this gaudy decoration.

His studies continued to mire him down although he devoted every free moment to his books. His scholastic records from 1906 to 1910 are filled with borderline marks. His last failure was in 1909 (Marine Engineering and Applied Mechanics) but he slithered past the 2.5 mark on a re-examination. However, he displayed aptitude in such subjects as seamanship and gunnery. His highest mark in the final year at Annapolis was registered, appropriately enough, in Naval Warfare.

By and large, when the 130 midshipmen marched up for their diplomas on June 3, 1910, the prospects of Marc Andrew Mitscher were not promising. He had not qualified as a midshipman officer. If he had leadership ability, it was so deeply buried that nothing short of smelting and remolding would bring it out. There was no indication of social polish which would enable him to carry out the quasi-diplomatic duties required of a flag officer, and he was only a few places away from "anchor man," lowest on the list.

Of course, there had been an earlier "wooden" graduate named William "Bull" Halsey. Scholastic records, Mitscher and Halsey proved, are not always reliable indications of military ability.

Mitscher's page in the 1910 Naval Academy yearbook, *The Lucky Bag,* caricatures him in both poetry and prose:

> Pete dislikes all allusions or mirth
> On the hue of his hair or its dearth
> It gives him much pain
> When he has to explain
> That he's not an albino by birth

The stern looking face of this whitened patriarch belies his true nature. Often Pete endeavors to frown upon the light and happy side of life, but he never really succeeds. 'Tis said a grass widow trampled on his heart Youngster [sophomore] leave, whereat he swore that he was forever done with the eternal feminine, and sought solace in his pipe and a book. But time proved she is eternal and not many hops had passed ere Pete again graced the gym with his presence, confiding to the stag line, with a smile, that he was roped in on a fussing game and warning them off the hazardous rocks and shoals of that treacherous sea. The one thing that will make Pete smile and continue to do so for many days is to put "one over" on Papa Mike. The remainder of the time he spends in combing his hair to hide the bald spots. Pete is a man who never says much, and his smiles gain by their very rarity. We know him for a true friend and a man on whom one can depend.

Mitscher had requested duty in the U.S.S. *Colorado*, a Pacific Fleet armored cruiser, and was assigned to it, reporting aboard at Seattle in July, 1910 as a passed midshipman. In those days, all midshipmen were on two years' probation before being commissioned ensigns.

CHAPTER

⚓ 3 ⚓

First Sea Duty

THE *Colorado*, although a spit-and-polish ship, was a welcome relief from the Academy. Mitscher began to grow. In his first fitness report his grades ranged from 3.3 in navigation to 4.0 in efficiency and ability, and he was described in it as "calm and even tempered." [1]

But Mitscher's conduct still was not exemplary, and occasionally he ran afoul of naval law and discipline. At Valparaiso, Chile, in the fall of 1910, an escapade which involved Mitscher threatened the harmonious relations between Chile and the United States for several hours. A barroom fight between American officers and Chilean civilians turned into a riot. Mitscher is remembered standing erect in the middle of the melee, swinging happily at anyone who came within range. *Colorado*'s entire group of passed midshipmen lodged in a

---

[1] Mitscher's fitness reports, thirty-four years of evaluation by every commanding officer he served under, were examined each time he came up for promotion. Mitscher saw them only two or three times in his entire career. It is interesting to note that this same evaluation, "calm and even tempered," appeared in every fitness report through 1946, although no reporting skipper had knowledge of the analyses made by previous skippers.

Valparaiso jail that night. On the same cruise, with Claude S. Gillette, now a retired rear admiral, he also missed the last liberty launch to the *Colorado* at Chimbote, Peru; both of them narrowly escaped being dismissed from the Navy. They caught the *Colorado* by rowing a fisherman's boat over the churning waters of Ferrol Bay.

Nineteen eleven was an eventful year. In May, the *Colorado* inched into Puget Sound Navy Yard at Bremerton, Washington, for repairs. Gillette announced wedding intentions and Mitscher witnessed the nuptials on May 25, but he had trouble concentrating on the principals because of the maid of honor, a beautiful, brown-eyed, buttermilk blonde.

She was Frances Smalley, daughter of a Tacoma lawyer, and at the party afterward he openly campaigned for her attention; he saw her again at a dance and finally coaxed her to the *Colorado* for dinner. Frances did not realize it, of course, but Mitscher had already made up his mind to marry her.

Just as his parents had been poles apart, Mitscher, in choosing Frances Smalley, selected a girl who was clearly his opposite. She was gay; he was silent. She loved to dance, loved parties; he disliked both. She was not inclined to marry, least of all to marry the unromantic Midshipman Mitscher. He dated her again that summer as the *Colorado* paraded up and down the coast. Then the armored cruiser sailed for the Far East, and Frances wondered whether she would ever hear again from the persistent Oklahoman.

Mitscher's second big decision of 1911 came in November. In his last year at Annapolis, he had read a British book on aviation; he also knew that a few young enthusiasts were attempting to introduce aeronautics to the Navy. But it is doubtful that Mitscher realized then that aviation was the specialty for which he was most suited. It is also doubtful that he would have reached similar heights in the strictly surface Navy. It has been said that Lindbergh, Doolittle, Rickenbacker, Wiley Post, and Amelia Earhart were born to fly. In the same loose sense, so was Mitscher.

As the *Colorado* steamed toward the Philippines, he requested a transfer to aeronautics, which was approved on the ship and by the Pacific fleet commander; but the Navy Department was in no hurry. Naval aviation could have answered roster that second day of November, 1911, with three planes, six pilots, and a dozen or so enlisted men. The admirals had little time for flying-machine talk. Mitscher was advised to learn seafaring first; it was excellent advice, later events established.

Mitscher's next few years in surface ships were not memorable. He transferred to the armored cruiser *South Dakota* in 1912, bringing with him an ensign's commission. As a watch and division officer, he had his first real opportunity to handle men, and did well, but periodically the mulish streak would snare him. He was suspended from duty for ten days and confined to his room while the *South Dakota* was in Olongapo, Philippine Islands, for refusing to obey a sentry's order to halt. Later, he received a three-day suspension for rendering improper honors to a visiting foreign admiral. His reason was refreshing but not sufficient—he stated he didn't think much of the foreign admiral's navy.

As the *South Dakota* roamed Far Eastern seas, Frances Smalley, who closely resembled Gaby Deslys, a prominent actress of the day, received letters postmarked Woosung and Tsingtao and Yokohama; each, a little more fervent. However, none mentioned marriage. The ship finally reached San Francisco and Mitscher promptly received orders for more sea duty, on the gunboat *Vicksburg*. Then came the forthright proposal. Frances hedged, and a rather disconsolate, but not defeated, young ensign boarded the *Vicksburg* and got underway for Mexican waters.

When he returned, he took a month's leave and went to Tacoma to pursue his romance in person, plying Frances with bouquets, and every conceivable argument. It took almost a month, but he climbed back on a train for San Francisco with an engagement consent. There he learned that his next ship, the gunboat *Annapolis*, would be undergoing additional repairs, and he headed back for Tacoma, placing a call from the depot on arrival.

As she reports it, he said, "Frances, we will be married Thursday."

She held out for three days, and then, on January 16, 1913, they were married. They were together in San Francisco and in southern California for a few days before he sailed for patrol duty in Mexican and Central American waters. The *Annapolis* was one of the ships detailed to protect American interests during the revolutionary disturbances then occurring in that area. He was away eight months and Frances returned north—her persuasive, self-reliant new husband still somewhat of a mystery. She still wonders, she says, what there was about Marc that always made people do the things he wanted them to do.

The American warships lay offshore, deployed around Petosi, Nicaragua; Topolobampo, Mazatlan, and Pichilinque, in Mexico; swung to the hook in the thick heat and rolled sluggishly while cadavers drifted by. Mazatlan was the worst. Men on the American ships were quietly losing their minds.

When Mitscher arrived back in the States, his weight was down to a hundred and fifteen pounds and his jaws were sunken. He resembled a man who had been in prison rather than at sea. Frances hardly recognized him. The captain of the *Annapolis* was brought ashore and sent to a hospital, temporarily insane, and several crew members followed him. But two weeks later, Mitscher embarked in the U.S.S. *California* to revisit the same maddening millpond for another eight months. Meanwhile, he kept firing aviation applications at Washington.

During the five- or ten-day periods between ships for the next few years, Frances began to learn something about the complex man she'd married. It was not easy. For instance, when he said good-by it was always with finality. He never turned back, lingered, or waved, but walked rapidly to the gangway and disappeared within the ship. She learned not to stand on the dock and await another appearance.

She learned he had a trouble smile—a thin, chilling movement of the muscles around his lips. She learned that he was rather formal; he seldom removed his coat, even in the privacy of a hotel room or at home. He always awakened at dawn without benefit of an alarm clock, a habit she did not share or enjoy. She learned he disliked handling money and wouldn't argue or quibble with a salesman even when he knew he was being cheated. He was delighted when Frances purchased clothing for him, even hats, but reserved the right to select his own suits. He displayed so gentle a domestic nature that Frances was perplexed several times when she heard her husband had taken part in what amounted to street fights.

One night, Mitscher and Claude Gillette, shipmates again, were riding the hoot-owl interurban between Los Angeles and San Pedro. Several men on the train began pestering an unescorted girl. Mitscher hopped up and ordered them to cease, and was challenged. He asked the conductor to delay the trip a few minutes. Schedules weren't rigid, and the conductor set his brakes. The passengers filed out on the moonlit flats by the track. Mitscher removed his coat and derby hat, and pummeled the largest of the hoodlums with both hands, and then climbed back on the car, without comment, and it rocked and pitched peacefully on to San Pedro. Another time, several young men flirted with Frances, and Mitscher got out of the car, fists ready, and forced a retreat.

His sense of honor had no middle ground, no gray zone. Something was right, or it was wrong. A man was a gentleman, or he was nothing at all. In the purest, old-fashioned sense, *ladies* were on a pedestal; any female who was a notch below was to be ignored. Mitscher's profanity, even though softly spoken, was blistering and bountiful on occasion; but he never used it in the presence of a lady.

Frances began to see more of him when he went into destroyers. He served in the U.S.S. *Whipple* and the U.S.S. *Stewart*, both operating in the Pacific. However, during the first three years of their marriage, they were together less than three months.

Mitscher was now beginning to reject aviation. The Bureau of Navigation had consistently pigeonholed his requests. Naval aviation, however, was expanding; an Office of Aeronautics had been established and Pensacola, Florida, was designated as the location for a flying school. Smarting from the refusals, Mitscher argued the future of aviation with Lieutenant John "Stumps" Edgerly, an Academy classmate who had left Navy ranks to enter Army aviation (now a retired Air Force general). They sat, many times, at the bar of the New Palace Hotel, at 5th and Elm, San Diego, and discussed its military value.

Mitscher told Edgerly that though aviation might work for the Army, planes would never successfully operate with the fleet. Technical problems, he said, were too large in the Navy, and the battleship would always remain the striking weapon of sea power. This was one of the few times that Mitscher could have been accused of knowingly talking through his hat.

On July 7, 1915, the *Stewart*, accompanied by five other destroyers, sailed from Mare Island, California, under secret orders, and Mitscher was in charge of her engine room. At Bremerton, where the division put in for fuel and stores, he met

Frances and said he was going to make one final application
for aviation; if the Navy didn't approve it, he'd try for an engineering specialty. Several months previously, he'd been
promoted to lieutenant, junior grade.

As the destroyers sortied into the Juan de Fuca Strait, the
secret orders were unsealed. Japanese ships had been prowling
around Kiska for several months. The destroyers were ordered
to investigate. The weather was rough and cold and the destroyers slogged along, putting in at Seward and Kodiak. The
crew lived off the land, and it was not unusual to see three or
four quartered deer swinging from foredeck stanchions.

With almost five years of sea experience behind him, including heavy gunnery work, Mitscher had laid the foundation for
a surface career. There was not a Japanese vessel to be found
within two hundred miles of Kiska, and the division wallowed
back through the Bering Sea toward Bremerton, reaching port
September 7, 1915. Mail was distributed and the dignified
Lieutenant Mitscher suddenly ran down the deck, his usual
military bearing shattered by leaps and whoops.

"I've got my orders," several shipmates remember him shouting. "I'm going to aviation."

Then, with a package of venison steaks under his arm, he
went ashore to see Frances, who was ill with tonsilitis.

Within a few days they started for Pensacola and there
found a chiding letter from Stumps Edgerly, recalling those
hot debates at the bar of the New Palace when Mitscher had
declared Navy flying was a poor bet. Mitscher wrote Edgerly:
". . . change of mind is a wise man's privilege, and a woman's
whim, and I'm not wearing skirts."

CHAPTER

⚓ 4 ⚓

Flying on Wood, Wire, and Canvas

THE rickety planes at Pensacola were lashed together with bindings that included baling wire and plumber's tape. One pilot, the Marine Corps' first aviator, Alfred Cunningham, wrote the Navy Department:

> My machine, as I told you and as Mr. Towers [later Admiral Towers] probably told you, is not in my opinion fit for use. I built it from parts of the Burgess F and the Wright B, which are not exactly alike and nothing fitted. I had to cut off and patch up parts and bore additional holes in the beams in order to make them fit . . . something seems to vibrate loose, or off, a majority of the flights made. It is impossible to fly over a few hundred feet with a passenger. Lt. Arnold [later General H. H. "Hap" Arnold, of the Army Air Forces], of the Army, after seeing the machine and examining it, said that none of the Army fliers would go up in it. Will you kindly let me know what the prospects are for my getting a new machine?

Mosquitoes, breeding in the shallow creeks, whirred out through swamp laurel to attack mechanics who patiently spent four hours of repair work for each fifteen minutes of air time.

It was a monotonous circle of fly, sweat, and repair; then fly again. Naval Aviation, however, had advanced as far as that Florida beach-head and clung tenaciously to it.

Mitscher wasn't scheduled to report until October 15, 1915, but he came early to talk to the pilots and examine the aircraft hangared in a row of tents fronting the water. On the afternoon of October 13, he made his first flight. No one can recall who piloted the plane. It might have been John Towers, Patrick Bellinger, or Henry Mustin, each an illustrious birdman, or maybe Robert Saufley, another pioneer.

One night in the Pacific, Mitscher said he was positive the plane had been an AH-2 type. That particular Curtiss contraption more resembled a warped box kite than a flying machine. Wood, wire, and canvas, it had a pusher engine of 100 horsepower that vibrated as much as it pushed. Trundled down to the water on a plank incline, it sputtered, shook, and somehow flew. That night, he talked to Frances about it for hours. The "thing" had actually flown. Contrary to character, Mitscher accepted aviation, seemingly bought it without question, in the fleeting minutes the AH-2 june-bugged around Pensacola Bay.

Then he went aboard the armored cruiser *North Carolina*, Pensacola's station ship. The Navy preferred to have officers listed on sea duty even if they spent most of the time ashore. Actually, there was as much aviation activity on the *North Carolina* as there was on the beach. She had a catapult over the fantail, bridging her after-turret like a narrow-gauge railway, and in November, Mitscher stood on her deck to witness the world's first successful "cat shot" from a ship underway. Mitscher would also be on hand at every other major milestone in naval aviation until he died. It is impossible to write the story of Admiral Mitscher without also writing most of the history of naval aviation.

He was among the first thirteen Pensacola students. Some of

those present, either as students or as instructors, are today in aviation's hall of fame. Pat Bellinger, an instructor, was the first American to fly a plane in combat, and also participated in the first transatlantic flight; so did John Towers, also an instructor, and student A. C. "Putty" Read, both retired admirals now. And Henry Mustin, Spuds Ellyson, Chevvy Chevalier, Robert Saufley, Kenneth Whiting, John Rodgers, Al Cunningham, V. D. Herbster, and B. L. Smith, all hard-core aerial vikings, were at Pensacola. They were, in effect, naval aviation. The planes were fragile and cranky, but Mitscher was in fast company.

Lieutenant Kenneth Whiting was a ready-made idol. Taught to fly by Orville Wright, Whiting commanded the flying school. Impulsive and often in trouble with superiors, his daring overshadowed any reprimand. At the bottom of Manila Bay, Whiting enclosed himself in a submarine torpedo tube, ordered the outer end opened, and then swam to the surface, to prove a man could exit under water and live. Qualified to operate either submarines or aircraft, Whiting was a suave, handsome hard-drinking, high-flying New Englander who went aloft, he told friends, for the "pure, wholesome hell of it." Although their personalities clashed, Mitscher and Whiting became close friends immediately, and Whiting taught him a number of stunts with those bolt-and-wire caravels.

Offsetting dramatic Ken Whiting, and acting as a considerable stabilizer, was Lieutenant Henry Mustin, who had first gone aloft in 1911. Mustin was already thinking of "high speed aircraft, with machine guns and bombs; torpedo planes to use against enemy battleships; fast fighter planes to protect the slow flying bombers." [1] He commanded the air station and Whiting's flying school operated within that command. Serious and demanding, Mustin was a true mentor. Whiting fired

[1] Archibald D. Turnbull and Clifford L. Lord, *History of U.S. Naval Aviation* (New Haven, Yale University Press, 1949).

Mitscher's imagination and Mustin brought him to earth again. They are memorialized in aviation by Whiting Field in Florida and Mustin Field in Philadelphia.

The war in Europe, soon to spread to the Atlantic seaboard, was of passing interest at Pensacola, and there was little time for Mitscher to follow it. He flew, under instruction, almost every day. Shirt-sleeved, bareheaded, and booted, he sat on the leading edge of the wing of the pusher-engined biplanes; a strap across his thighs, another wide belt across his midriff. There were no cockpits in those flimsy Curtiss, Wright, and Burgess-Dunne machines.

(In World War II, when young pilots were present, Mitscher often described one method of instrument flying at Pensacola. The best instrument, he said, was a piece of string tied to a strut supporting the seaplane's center pontoon.

"If the string was blowing off to one side, you knew you were side-slipping; if it was blowing straight back to you, you knew at least you were still in the air. But if you ever saw that string dropping, you knew you would probably crash, sure as hell.")

He learned how to tear down and repair an engine, how to patch fabric and practically rebuild an airplane, which was occasionally necessary. He played poker now and then with Ken Whiting or relaxed over drinks at the homes of station personnel, but more often, Frances would read or sew while he sweated over a plane in a hangar tent until well after midnight.

Mitscher went about learning to fly slowly and carefully. He listened to Whiting and the instructors, sorted out the information, and then saturated himself with it.

The *North Carolina* steamed out of Pensacola on March 20, 1916, with five Curtiss planes on deck, bound for Guantanamo Bay, Cuba, and exercises with the fleet. If the young radicals had accomplished anything, now was the time to prove it, battleship officers said. The exercises were designed to "establish facts as a guide for future developments of aeronautics within the Navy without regard to pre-conceived ideas." [2] (The pre-conceived idea was exceedingly simple: Airplanes would eventually replace battleship guns.) The results were disappointing. It was during this period that Mitscher first entered the battleship versus aircraft controversy, which lasted for thirty years.

He was an observer on several flights during the maneuvers and spent the rest of the time with baling wire and pliers. Captain Mark Bristol, in making out Mitscher's fitness report for the period, noted the "student aviator's eagerness," and rated him "excellent."

It was now apparent that the United States would become involved in the European war. The pace was stepped up at Pensacola, and Mitscher was out of the house at dawn, seldom returning until after dark. Frances heard about crashes on the beach and in Pensacola Bay. But never a word from her husband about them.

The planes hit the beach or flew head-on into trees. One pilot cleared the beach but skimmed into an open hangar, lodging his wings against the framework, to descend embarrassingly by ladder. However, if Mitscher was involved in a serious crash at Pensacola, there is no record of it. Smashing a pontoon, wing, or propeller wasn't usually a serious matter:

Mr. Mitscher and Mr. Strickland [his passenger] had a queer accident Saturday. The N-9 porpoised, water struck, and broke the propellor and the propellor cut the pontoon off about midway the first watertight compartment, causing the machine to stand on end. Outside of the broken propellor and pontoon it wasn't damaged nor pilot or passenger hurt.[3]

The months passed quickly, and on June 2, 1916, at the age of twenty-nine, Mitscher won his wings.

[2] *Ibid.*
[3] Unpublished papers of the late Captain Kenneth Whiting, USN.

CHAPTER

⚓ 5 ⚓

Sea Aviator

NONE of the 1916 Pensacola graduates were youngsters and Mitscher, at twenty-nine, was almost completely bald. Heavy lines were beginning to develop in his forehead, and crow's-feet projected out from his eyes, probably the result of wind, water, and sun against the fair skin. At times, he acted and talked as if he were ancient. He thought flying was exciting but not glamorous. Only the Whitings made it seem glamorous.

Fitness report, April 1, 1916 to September 30, 1916:

Performance, 4.0. He has lost weight and has had stomach trouble due to hard work and hot climate. He is inclined to work to such an extent and such hours that his health is not excellent. He has not applied for leave since being assigned to aviation.—Mustin.

Mitscher would return to quarters, flop down in a chair and fall sound asleep. Mustin warned him to slow the pace, at the same time illogically making him engineering officer, the most unwelcome job on the entire station. His task was to keep the aircraft buzzing around the bay by nursing engines and coaxing more work from the already overburdened mechanics.

A few months later, Mustin and Mitscher separated for several years. Mustin received orders to surface duty and was relieved by Captain J. L. Jayne. To honor Mustin's departure from the air station, five Curtiss planes were sent up to fly formation. Pat Bellinger returned from an inspection tour in time to see two nose under on take-off; one hit the water after being airborne for a few minutes. Mitscher landed his aircraft on the shore with a split propeller, and the lonely fifth plane stayed up to continue the now ridiculous farewell. Mustin, probably wondering what he had accomplished in two years, trudged off the beach, leaving Mitscher to cope with his own destiny.

In April, 1917, the Navy Department sent an urgent wire to Pensacola. A pilot was needed to head the aviation department in the cruiser *Huntington*, scheduled to enter convoy duty in the Atlantic. Diplomatic relations had been broken off with Germany. Jayne had previously recommended Mitscher as fully qualified to command an aviation school or air detachment and promptly wired Washington that he was available. Frances was told it would be best for her to return to Tacoma.

The *Huntington*, commanded by nonaviator Captain Robison, had a catapult over the stern to fire off her Thomas Morse biplanes, and several kite balloons which were reeled out on a long cable. An observer, on lookout for subs, rode the careening kite balloons. She had the usual gun batteries. Mitscher had hoped for something better. His crew consisted of twenty men, of whom seven were pilots. They were all pitifully inexperienced, and the cruiser steamed around Pensacola Bay for several weeks while he attempted to season them.

Bellinger, in charge of experiments and the erection of all new aircraft, assigned a number of tests to the *Huntington*. Mitscher conducted more than a dozen cat shots, all successful. Then Captain Robison, who was very much interested in the newfangled air operation, came up with an idea. Instead of firing the plane off, he said, they could try lowering it from the side while going ahead.

Bellinger shrugged his shoulders and a crane soon began swinging the Morse into a ludicrous position—dangling over the cruiser's side. Crawling into the cockpit as the *Huntington* picked up speed and surged through the water, Mitscher yelled hoarsely, "I don't think this is going to work!"

Bellinger nodded, then turned to the Pensacola chief, Captain Jayne, who was aboard as an observer. "Do you want to stop it? We're going to have an awful wreck here in a minute."

"Let Robison go ahead," replied Jayne, "it's his ship."

Desperately Mitscher looked toward the bridge at Bellinger. Seeing no change in plans, he waved for the engine start, gunning the plane until it began to shake; then he waved again, and it was lowered swiftly toward the water. It touched in a shower of spray, the propeller chewing into the sea, and flopped over. There was nothing to release it from the cable; it wouldn't jog loose.

Mitscher's head disappeared in froth as wreckage scraped along the cruiser's hull. Meanwhile, Robison danced around the *Huntington*'s bridge, shouting orders; then the head bobbed up astern while the ship made an emergency turn and launched a whaleboat. Soaked and sputtering, Mitscher stepped back aboard. He had been dunked several times before at Pensacola, but never needlessly.

Only two years out of the surface Navy, Mitscher was already a confirmed "air" sailor. The chasm between the two branches widened daily. Extremists clashed both on paper and in person.

This was an operational learning period, and although he disliked the cruiser duty, it gave him an opportunity for a variety of work the air station couldn't offer. Most of it he did not enjoy. On the trip to Europe, he would be "piloting" the kite balloons. Washington had warned that the biplanes aboard the *Huntington* could not be used for antisubmarine

work patrols, since there was no practical method of recovery
except in a flat calm.

Meanwhile, Ken Whiting's advance guard had settled down
at Bordeaux to hunt submarines off the French coast. Mitscher
wanted to be with Whiting and the overseas contingent, and
complained bitterly to Frances that the war was passing him
by. He seemed distressed at the condition of the aircraft and
the long path ahead for aviation. He wrote Frances before the
Huntington sailed for Europe as flagship of Convoy Group 7,
a plodding collection of merchantmen and troop transports:

. . . We had admiral's inspection today and didn't do very well.
The men didn't seem to have much spirit or pep. Maybe too much
Pensacola. Maybe too much New York. I am looking very dignified with my two stripes [he had been promoted to lieutenant,
senior grade, on July 1, 1917]. You should be here to see your
lieutenant. Tomorrow the movie man shows the pictures he took
here and I will see how big a fool I look in the movies. But I don't
think I will see much of the cheery side of life as long as I remain
in aeronautics. We transferred ten wrecks to the yard and repaired
two. The other day Donohue smashed one of the remaining two
and we worked night and day to get it ready for admiral's inspection. Stone fired off with it today and smashed it again. So now we
have to repair it again. However, my spirits aren't broken, if the
planes are, and I have great hopes of someday reaching the ambi-
tion of my life. An aviation ship.

Mustin and Towers had talked about an aviation ship, with
a platform deck, as early as 1914, so Mitscher was not dealing
in idle dreams. Many Navy pilots had drawn crude sketches
of carriers on napkins and in school notebooks. Naval engineers
knew it would be comparatively easy to design a workable aircraft carrier. Proving to the white-maned man-o'-war admirals
that the carrier would also be a practical ship was a knottier
matter. Mitscher belonged to a small clique which opposed
converting a conventional ship by simply tacking on a flight
deck. Ideally, an aircraft carrier would have to be built from

the keel up, complete with hangar deck and machine shops, gasoline storage facilities and some means of flight control.

Paper-napkin renderings were nice for daydreams but the *Huntington* was a reality. Mitscher ordered the kite balloons reeled out each dawn as she steamed toward Europe. The planes had tarpaulins draped over them, and were inoperative. The erratic gas bags had no directional control except the slender steel cable attaching them to the ship's stern, and they were of negligible value for observation. The observer usually was too busy hanging on to his mount.

Mitscher had not trusted them since tryouts at Pensacola. One had broken loose with a man clinging to the ropes and floated up to about 12,000 feet. The captive passenger finally ripped the panel and the bag wobbled down, narrowly missing Santa Rosa Island. Nevertheless, Mitscher had to use them.

One morning, while Susie Hoyt, of the air detachment, was aloft, a squall blew in. The *Huntington* began to pitch violently and the wind force mounted, looping the balloon in slow spirals. According to his account, Mitscher saw that Hoyt had been knocked out. His body hung limply in the straps. A few minutes more and the basket would probably loop into the water. Hoyt's chances of escape were small and Mitscher telephoned the bridge, requesting that the ship be stopped. It was Hoyt's only chance.

"We're in a war zone. We can't stop the ship," replied Captain Robison.

The winch heaved slowly and the looping balloon edged toward the stern. Mitscher repeated the request, informing Robison that Hoyt was unconscious. Robison again refused and ordered Mitscher to cut the cable. As he spoke, the balloon was slamming into wave crests, then bounding thirty or forty feet into the air.

Bristling with anger, Mitscher finally yelled into the phone, "Captain Robison, for God's sake stop this ship." The balloon made one final plunge as the *Huntington* churned to a halt. Robison had submitted.

Crew member Pat McGunigal tied a line around his waist, dove into the tangle of fabric, and came up with Susie Hoyt in his arms. McGunigal was recommended for the Navy Cross.

As for the reluctant Robison, Mitscher said later, "He was doing the right thing, of course." One of the first laws of the sea, encompassing the greatest battleship and the scurviest tramp afloat, is never to risk a ship and her crew for the life of a sailor. The *Huntington* was an easy target that morning in late August, 1917 but no U-boat took a shot at her. Mitscher again stretched the old sea law to the breaking point many times during World War II and was lucky enough to get away with it.

Robison, realizing the strain of the moment, apparently held no brief against the stubborn little pilot for his actions, and for disobeying a direct order to cut the balloon cable. In fact, on the next fitness report, he said of Mitscher: ". . . he makes good decisions."

When Mitscher left the ship, Robison further stated on October 13, 1917: "When not engaged in aeronautical duties, he has acted as officer of the deck and as ship control officer. As head of the aviation department, he has accomplished much constructive work in experimentation and development." When Mitscher wasn't wrestling the balloons, he had tinkered with the catapults.

On arrival back in the United States, Mitscher was ordered to take command of the newly built Montauk Naval Air Station, on the tip of Long Island, about a hundred miles from New York City. German subs were moving westward in increased numbers. Still angling for duty in France, he was not in the least elated with the Long Island assignment.

His patrol territory stretched roughly from Fire Island Light to Nantucket Shoals. Dawn to sunset, the planes, each armed with a machine gun and a pair of bombs, flew off a stocking-shaped fresh-water lake named Fort Pond. Mitscher made a patrol two or three times a week and spent the balance administering the small command. Actually, he had more trouble with the crochety spinster who managed the inn where the pilots lived than he did with U-boats. In spite of protests, she kept turning off the heat, until finally Mitscher stripped the furnace of its valves.

It was during this bleak winter of 1917–1918 that Frances became enthusiastic about aviation. At Pensacola she had walked down to the beach many afternoons to watch the planes bounce across the water and struggle into the air. At Montauk, she asked to fly. Mitscher muttered something about regulations and heavy schedules, and the fact that the planes were not in prime condition.

Frances quickly reminded him that some of the other wives had been up. Indeed, she felt like an outsider in the clannish group at the inn. She couldn't talk about take-offs or landings, much less about how it felt to handle aircraft controls. He doggedly resisted each of her pleas.

Then a training blimp, manned by a French crew, visited Montauk. That evening the commanding officer of the blimp, as a matter of courtesy, invited her to take a flight. She accepted, hinting that it might be better to keep it a secret. Minutes before take-off the next day, Mitscher approached the mooring mast. "Under no circumstances will you go up in that blimp," he said.

Frances was furious as she saw the airship climb gently skyward. He weathered her wrath calmly, and without rebuttal, as they watched it pull for altitude. Suddenly, control trouble developed and the blimp upended itself, to hang suspended for a few dangerous seconds. Mitscher pursed his lips and pointed a finger toward the odd position of the airship. Then he turned, to hide his laughter, and walked rapidly away.

It was years before she broached the subject again, and not until 1944 would he permit her to fly even in a commercial aircraft. He considered planes completely safe for himself and for anyone else who cared to ride in them, but never were they safe enough for Frances.

From Montauk, Mitscher went to the air station at Rockaway, also on Long Island, where he stayed three weeks. Florida was next. He had again requested France, but the Bureau of Navigation was faced with a shortage of training personnel and denied his request. Frances didn't go with him to Miami. They were expecting a baby and Mitscher wanted her to be in Tacoma with her family. He still thought some miracle might send him overseas. Frances would be stranded in the east if there were orders to Bordeaux.

CHAPTER

⚓ 6 ⚓

In Command at Miami

WORD had already reached the Miami Naval Air Station that Lieutenant Mitscher was steady, quiet, thorough, and tough. Wearing the hot, uncomfortable high-collared Navy air uniform of that day, Mitscher published his orders in early March, 1918, and took over his first major command. Miami NAS, primarily a basic training unit, was the largest naval-air facility in the country with the exception of Pensacola.

It had been grubbed out of a mangrove swamp on Dinner Key in the Coconut Grove district south of Miami proper. When Mitscher arrived, there was still much to be done. Morale was shaky, and the efficiency rating of the station had been slipping. Washington had sent an investigator, and testimony of the pilots indicated that the executive officer, a wealthy westerner, now a millionaire sportsman, was to blame. The pilots thought the officer had used influence to get the coveted job.

Mitscher was not satisfied with gossip and investigation findings and spent a few days personally checking the performance of his second-in-command; then he went out to sample the man's flying ability. He saw him make an elementary turn improperly, and demanded his flight records. They were spotty indeed. In less than an hour, Mitscher relieved him of all duties, disqualified him as a naval aviator, and struck a final humiliating blow by ordering him back to Pensacola for additional flight training.

The pilots were stunned; many wondered if life wouldn't have been kinder under a continuation of the old regime. It was quite obvious that the new skipper meant to straighten out the kinks and run a smart organization.

There were problems, big and little. The station's machine-gun range was being built on Virginia Key, away from the residential area. Work on digging up a backstop and clearing the necessary land had been going slowly, prompting the gunnery instructor, Ensign Duncan H. Read, to visit Mitscher's office. "Why is it going slowly?" Mitscher inquired.

Read replied, "We don't have enough workers to do the job, Captain." [Regardless of rank, commanding officers of ships, stations, and certain units are addressed as Captain.]

Mitscher put on his cap and together they went to the range. He walked around it in silence, Read strolling beside him. Finally, Mitscher pointed to a group of men who were standing around the machine guns, gawking at the equipment.

"What are all those people doing?"

"They're training to be observers."

As such, they would operate bombsights, fire machine guns, and keep watch from the rear cockpit, and as rated men, they did not normally engage in manual labor.

"Starting tomorrow they'll observe mangrove swamp," said Mitscher crisply. "I'll get machetes for them," he added. In ten days, the range was completed.

At the weekly staff meetings he would sit silently for ten or fifteen minutes listening to comments or sea stories. There was plenty of talk, he soon concluded, but not enough flying. So he introduced early-morning flying operations, gradually moving them up until take-off time was three thirty in the morning; one night he kept them out until ten o'clock. The double-pontooned R-9 seaplanes droned around the station endlessly. After several weeks he put the weary pilots back on the routine schedule. But flying skill had improved remarkably.

The change at Miami was noticed in the naval district headquarters, where Rear Admiral W. B. Fletcher reported, in late April: "Results have been accomplished. A wide awake, active patrol has also been conducted in the Florida Straits." An important mission of the command was to keep German submarines at bay along the Key West–Cuba ship tracks.

At Saturday inspection Mitscher searched for dust with the usual white gloves. He had two royal palms planted near the entrance, and ordered his new executive officer to procure paint by the barrel to give the station a new face.

But Mitscher was rarely visible to the students. Remaining aloof from routine operations, he managed to establish an aura of special respect. Some students thought he was exceedingly frosty in view of the small amount of braid on his sleeves. Stiffly formal during the working day, he was discovered stuffing caramels in a keyhole of a fellow officer's cottage one night; another time he stole pillows from several cottages. The next day, perched on top of them, he expressed dismay that "vandals had been at work on the station." His infrequent displays of humor were always puckish and baffling.

He shared Miami with the Marines. In so far as official paper work was concerned, they were under his command, since he was senior officer on the station. However, the flying leathernecks were under the direct leadership of Captain Roy Geiger (the late General Geiger). As usual, the leathernecks were living rough. They camped in tents and flew their land-type aircraft from a disgraceful temporary field. Although he always had a soft spot for the flying Gyrenes, Mitscher delighted at twitting them at every opportunity.

For instance, friendly theft of Geiger's equipment went on for months with Mitscher's tacit approval. When Geiger complained, Mitscher listened solemnly and promised quick action. He accompanied him on a search and they discovered a gun, unmistakably marked USMC. Mitscher feigned surprise, though he knew the Navy had "borrowed" ten or fifteen Marine machine guns, and was most apologetic. As Geiger drove away with it, Mitscher said gravely to Read, who had accompanied them, "Now, Read, get it back in a few days!"

Mitscher's ability to allow, or provoke, the right amount of humorous relief first became evident in Miami. Any military command occasionally needs a good dose of levity lest it grow too pompous. Somewhere along the line Mitscher had discovered the application points and the right timing. This ability was helpful in World War II, when the air was often so tense a scratchy pen could cause two yeomen to square off.

In many ways, Miami gave Mitscher an unwritten examination in leadership. It had all the problems—human, mechanical, and even acts of God.

As the training program expanded, he kept in constant touch with Washington and Pensacola. He repeatedly asked for more instructors, maintaining that they couldn't do the proper job if overworked, that they couldn't give sufficient personal attention to the student pilots. For the benefit of planners in the Navy Department, he outlined procedures used in training the Miami students and suggested ways to improve the courses at other stations. The Bureau refused to grant him more instructors, but a letter was forwarded saying his ideas were excellent and had been incorporated into a flight-instruction syllabus.

If the teaching staff was inadequate, the aircraft were worse. The condition of the planes haunted him, and he lived in fear of wholesale fatalities. Once, as he watched the flight of an F-boat, used for primary work, it reached about a hundred feet and then thudded down on the water. Not concerned with what the careful purse controllers in Washington might think, Mitscher said, "Burn it!"

On the day five Miami planes crashed, Mitscher informed the operations officer that another wreck that week would result in punishment. Not for the pilots. Only the *operations officer* would be punished. The pilots puzzled over how he could hold the operations officer, who sat behind a desk, responsible for crashes that were occurring miles away. However, the crash rate dropped swiftly.

One of the pilots, Newton H. White (now a retired captain), said, "I didn't realize for many years that Pete was simply using the operations officer as a foil. All the while, he was really threatening us. But he was smart enough to do it without rattling us." Mitscher's talent for handling airmen, the talent that was the real instrument of destruction from the Marshalls to Tokyo, was beginning to develop.

He had something else to think about in the late spring. Frances was seriously ill in Tacoma. In fact, she was near death. For several days she lay in a coma. Checking constantly by phone, he performed his duties woodenly, shunned contact with officers closest to him, and would not share his worry or discuss it. The crisis passed; Frances lost the baby, and several weeks later wrote him that they could never have another. They had both wanted children, and Mitscher had several times told her about experiences he wanted to relate to his grandchildren. But in all the years of their marriage he did not mention the loss of the baby or the lack of children. It only drew them closer together.

By July, 1918, when Mitscher was promoted to lieutenant commander, Miami was at peak capacity, and running smoothly. The summer and fall passed quickly and uneventfully but the month of December, 1918, was a nightmare. The flu epidemic, still raging in Georgia and Alabama, had slipped into Dinner Key. Mitscher paced the floor, slept fitfully, and looked helplessly about him as man after man was carried or staggered into sick bay.

With more than two hundred ill, he used one of the school buildings as an additional hospital and sent an urgent wire to Washington for medical supplies, doctors, and nurses, but the pool was already overtaxed. Frances had recovered and come east. She cooked and worked in the hospitals while he attempted to keep the air station in a semblance of order.

Then Mitscher began to sniffle and sneeze. Frances stuck a thermometer in his mouth. It registered a slight fever. The next morning she pleaded with him to stay in bed, but he lunged out, rocky and delirious. She attempted to get him back under covers. Finally, he locked the bedroom door and a few minutes later she saw him run out in his white dress uniform although a thunderstorm was drenching Miami. A doctor cornered him on the station and forced him into bed. Six days later, however, he was up and in command again. His slight build was deceptive; he had a tremendous constitution.

The ravaging epidemic and the signing of the armistice lowered morale; the reserves began clamoring to go home. Mitscher sympathized but still had to maintain operating manpower until Washington ordered a cutback. The situation was explosive. He flew over to Pensacola to discuss the reserve release and on his return a junior officer dashed out to the plane to inform him a mutiny had occurred.

On the way to the mess hall, where the "mutineers" had been imprisoned, Mitscher learned the details. A group of enlisted men had come in late from duty, missing dinner. Served platters of cold sandwiches, they had responded with catcalls and shattered dishes. The executive officer had then burst into the mess hall shouting, "You'll eat 'em and like 'em!" Met with another storm of catcalls, he'd locked the mess-hall doors and summoned the master-at-arms.

Mitscher strode up and brushed aside the cluster of men at the door. He ordered the men within released at once, and a full meal prepared for anyone wanting it.

Later he gave the executive officer a tongue-lashing. He said that never again, so long as he commanded, did he want any man deprived of a hot meal, or of the right to complain. When Mitscher was detached from Miami, in February, 1919, after receiving orders to the historic Transatlantic Flight Division, Admiral Fletcher wrote: "He organized the station and carried it on successfully as both a training station and patrol station. He is an officer of force, decision, and ability."

Lieutenant Commander Mitscher of Miami NAS was not unlike the wiser, wizened, and still tough air admiral of the Marianas.

CHAPTER

⚓ 7 ⚓

The "Nancys"

THE American public was informed that the Navy's transatlantic flight would be a routine venture. "To see if it could be done," said Secretary Josephus Daniels. Few people were fooled. The real reason, of course, was to claim for the United States, and the Navy, man's first transocean flight.

Mitscher's orders placed him in charge of training and detail for the division, and he was promised one of the four planes scheduled to make the flight. However, on a night late in March, 1919, the NC-1 was crippled in a storm after breaking loose from her moorings and the NC-2 had to be cannibalized. The flight was reduced to three planes. It was a bitter blow to the Transatlantic Flight Division, and worse for Mitscher because there would be no aircraft for him to command. He was junior to the other three candidates.

Mitscher had followed the progress of the NC construction almost from the day—August 23, 1917—when Rear Admiral David Taylor, the Navy's Chief Constructor, routed a memo to his top aeronautical engineer and designer, Commander Jerome Clarke Hunsaker. "It seems to me," Taylor said, "the submarine menace could be abated, even if not destroyed, from the air." He wanted a flying boat capable of crossing the Atlantic, a boat that could live in a rough sea as well as in the air.

So, out of necessity, the NC boats were born. "N" for Navy; "C" for builder Glenn Curtiss. They were nicknamed Nancys. The best engineers in the Navy, Hunsaker, Holden C. Richardson, and George Westervelt, nursed them from drawing board to flight trials. Hunsaker and Richardson were the main contributors. In World War II, the layman gaped at the size of the B-29. The old NC V-bottomed flying boats were almost as large. They had an upper wingspan of 126 feet and an overall length of 68 feet. Four Liberty engines combined for a thrust of 1600 brake horsepower. It was a lot of airplane for those canvas-back years.

Mitscher had discussed some of the early Nancy problems with the design group and offered advice. According to Dr. Hunsaker, who resigned from the Navy in 1926 and is now Head of the Department of Aeronautical Engineering at the Massachusetts Institute of Technology, one of his suggestions, made at a crucial moment in the post-test Nancy evaluations, "changed a very doubtful project into a relatively sure one." After the flight trials of the NC-1 in 1918 it appeared that the boat, with a gross weight of some 28,000 pounds, could not get off the water reliably. Mitscher suggested adding a fourth Liberty engine, to be placed behind the middle of the three engines mounted as tractors—pulling engines—but reversed to act as a pusher. Hunsaker sharpened a pencil and filled several pages with figures. No one had thought about a pusher engine for the Nancys. It would work, he decided, and also stretch out the range.

Hunsaker dictated a letter approving the proposed alteration on behalf of the Navy. But Mitscher was more interested in flying than in engineering. He felt only a little better when, shortly after the loss of the plane in March, Captain N. E. Irwin, the Director of Aviation, informed him he could still make the flight as a pilot. Vying for billets was strong. Lieutenant Richard E. Byrd, soon to be acclaimed for polar explorations, was bidding for an assignment, and was already in the division designing navigation instruments. But Byrd had been overseas and Irwin refused to budge from his ground rule: No overseas veteran could make the flight. Byrd did develop the bubble sextant for the project, an instrument still used by aerial navigators.

Mitscher stayed in Washington until late April, and then reported to the station at Far Rockaway, Long Island, New York. Franklin D. Roosevelt, Assistant Secretary of the Navy, arrived on the scene to check progress. F. D. R. had maneuvered White House sanction for the flight. He poked around the flying boats and talked to Towers, Bellinger, Read, and Mitscher, who had all reported to the station. Mechanics clambered over the wings and boat hulls, paying scant attention to commissioning ceremonies of NC Seaplane Division One. Senior officer Towers read his orders and made the plane assignments. Towers took the Nancy 3 as his flagship, awarded Bellinger the Nancy 1, and assigned Read to Nancy 4.

Mitscher, next senior on the Nancy 1, was executive officer; plane commander Bellinger would navigate. Mitscher would share the piloting with beefy Lieutenant Louis T. Barin. Harry Sadenwater was assigned as radio officer. The crew was rounded out with Machinist Rasmus Christensen and Chief Machinist's Mate C. T. Kesler. Pat Bellinger was thoroughly satisfied with his personnel.

In four years of aviation, Mitscher had gained a reputation as a conservative airman—"a safe pilot, always." He could stunt and knew most of the tricks, but there wasn't a pilot in the Navy who could remember Mitscher going up to "wring a plane out" just for the heady joy of it. Co-pilot Barin was a wringer, but one who mixed daring with skill. The genial, barrel-chested former acrobat had hand-built two planes, flying them successfully, before he qualified as a Navy pilot in 1916. They made a good combination—Mitscher's conservatism and quick, positive judgment, Barin's daring and rugged strength.

With commissioning formalities over, the Navy became impatient. Two British flying teams were already in Newfoundland awaiting favorable weather to make a west–east crossing. But while the Navy Department fidgeted, the NC-1 crew fought trouble. A mysterious hangar fire the first week in May converted the right wing of the Nancy 1 into a crisp tangle. The only wing the Curtiss engineers were able to supply at once had more area than the original member, but they slapped it on anyway.

Mitscher and Barin taxied the Nancy 1 around Jamaica Bay for several hours on May 6; then Bellinger signaled to take her up. It was the first time either of them had been at the controls of a plane that large. She lifted from the water but flew lopsidedly, and Bellinger finally motioned to set her down again. It took the combined strength of Mitscher and Barin to keep her on even keel. They worked most of the night in an attempt to balance her and on May 7 they tested her again. Then Bellinger told Towers he was ready to go. Nancy 3 and Nancy 4 also reported flight readiness.

CHAPTER

⚓ 8 ⚓

NC-1—Down at Sea

THE morning of May 8, 1919, was dismal. But planning and testing were complete. Hunsaker could lay down his slide rule. Weary Curtiss workmen could leave their dope rooms and hope for a full night's sleep.

Towers scanned long-range weather reports from Washington, while Bellinger, Mitscher, and Barin had a short workout with Nancy 1 and then brought her back to the marine railway to be hauled out. Nancys 3 and 4 were perched on the ways and waiting. At 0930, Nova Scotian forecasts came in. Towers said, "Well, boys, let's go." Captain Irwin passed out four-leaf clovers, and the crews boarded the flying boats.

At 0957, engines turned up; then Nancy 3 slid down the ways and circled slowly outward across the bay. Nancy 1 was next and Nancy 4 followed close behind. For a few hundred yards they taxied ahead. Then Towers, standing in the open forward cockpit of Nancy 3, waved his arm and the throttles opened. They roared forward. On the beach, a small chilled crowd set up a din. Read's 4 was planing and soon lifted. Nancy 1 thundered as Mitscher poured gas into the Liberty quad. Nancy 3 made a wide left turn and set the course for Halifax,

Nova Scotia, 540 miles away. Then they all disappeared into the murk.

Frances had last seen Marc early that morning when he left their apartment in Brooklyn; now she stood nervously in Times Square waiting for the news flash on the *New York Times* bulletin board. Soon a boy ran out and tacked a small piece of paper up. The NC boats were away, and her own personal drama of waiting and wondering began. She says that she never consciously entertained the idea of receiving a telegram of official regret. But the long, empty hours, to be repeated so many times in later years, nevertheless affected her profoundly.

By noon, Nancy 1, making about 70 mph, was abeam of Montauk NAS, Mitscher's first shore command, but the passing was not observed. He was too busy. The boat was still sluggish, still off balance from the borrowed wing. Mitscher and Barin struggled to keep her stabilized, while Bellinger, in the forward cockpit, checked charts and kept lookout for the destroyers stationed across the ocean on the flight line.

Several miles away, Nancy 3 was running smoothly. With Towers in her forward cockpit was temporary passenger Richard E. Byrd. But Read's plane soon reported engine trouble and landed on the water a few miles off Chatham, Massachusetts. The air got rougher as the remaining two flying boats moved east. Nancy 1 dug into the bumps, shivered and bounced, and roared on. As the sun lowered, the coast of Nova Scotia rose gaunt and blue in the distance. At 1858, Nancy 3 settled on the water in Halifax harbor; ten minutes later, Mitscher glided Nancy 1 in. Weary from fighting the big, unbalanced boat over five hundred miles, they went aboard the U.S.S. *Columbia* for dinner, sleep, and rubbing alcohol.

Bellinger was satisfied that they could solve the stability problem, and in the morning they tackled the wing. Mitscher dumped ten and a half gallons of water into the wing-tip float on the light side. The Nancy 1 then balanced satisfactorily. At dawn on May 10, preparing to get underway again, Barin slipped and fell on the wet deck. He plunged a hand through the canvas and suffered a severe sprain. With Barin a one-armed pilot, Mitscher did practically all the flying to Trepassey, Newfoundland. The air was even rougher and colder than on the Nova Scotian leg. As they approached Trepassey, they spotted icebergs, but skimmed in without mishap.

The tender U.S.S. *Aroostook* radioed to the States: DRIVING THROUGH A FORTY MILE BREEZE SEAPLANES NC1 AND NC3 MADE THE PUSH FROM HALIFAX TO TREPASSEY WITH BRILLIANT SUCCESS. Morning papers in New York and Chicago hinted that transocean history was in the making.

But Towers, knowing the capricious North Atlantic weather, had the *Aroostook* send a qualifying message: PUBLIC SHOULD BE PREPARED FOR FALSE STARTS WHEN TWO NC BOATS LEAVE TREPASSEY HARBOR AS AN EFFORT WILL BE MADE TO TAKE EXCESS FUEL MAKING GETAWAY FROM CHOPPY SEAS DIFFICULT.

The two NC boats became three once more when persistent Read brought the Nancy 4 into Trepassey on May 15. The division was again at full strength. At the weatherman's nod the planes would fly. All else was ready. The bridge of ships was strung across the Atlantic at about fifty-mile intervals to act as floating markers, to obtain weather data, to shoot star shells, and to serve as emergency rescue craft in case of forced landings.

In the late afternoon on May 16, the NC-4, with a new engine, bounced out on take-off and climbed into the sky that was already darkening around the edges. Towers was off at 1806. But Nancy 1 behaved badly. A heavy ground swell rolled off the entrance to Trepassey Bay and she reacted violently, pitching and bouncing along. Mitscher forced gas to the engines and she got up to about 35 mph and hung there frighteningly. Spray shot forty feet into the air as she staggered across the waves, unable to fly. Then she slowly began to step up; finally, planing speed was reached and the lurching, bucketing ride ended. She lifted, dripping water from her hull, and was away at 1809. Next stop, the Azores.

Mitscher was wearing two pairs of long woolen underwear, covered by his regulation forest-green uniform. Over it all he wore a leather flying suit with a hood, fur-lined boots, and heavy, fleece-lined gloves, with wide gauntlets. A hunting knife was strapped on his hip. He wore goggles and a helmet with built-in earphones for communication with Bellinger and Radio Officer Sadenwater.

Bellinger stood in the bow, occasionally kneeling to check position on the dimly lit chart spread out on the deck. His station was about eight feet ahead of Mitscher and Barin. When the phones were inadequate, Bellinger passed notes back or crawled through the narrow tunnel to the pilots' cockpit and squatted beside them to discuss progress. His knees were bruised from the frequent tunnel journeys.

The instrument panel in the cockpit was uncluttered. Mitscher and Barin had only to check direction, altitude, speed, and inclination. Several clocks were on the panel, also gas and water meters (the Libertys had radiators, similar to those of automobiles). Compasses were set before them, behind a stumpy windshield. Below and to the rear was the radio officer's compartment, cozily inside the hull; behind that, the mechanics had a compartment.

There was a dim glow inside the pilots' cockpit from the instrument panel. A more cheerful light was cast by the twelve exhaust ports of the engines, where blue flame blended into red metal. In the period before moonrise, a period of complete darkness, they all watched intently for the destroyers. Bellinger searched the horizon ahead in a semicircle while Mitscher and Barin peered to each beam. As they droned over the station ships, a star shell would burst and light up the sky:

Another fifty miles. On course. All okay. Nancy 3 and Nancy 4 were somewhere nearby, but the planes had separated and were proceeding independently. Mitscher was spelled at the controls every half hour by Barin.

At 0221, May 17, Sadenwater radioed: "Cape Race Radio from NC-1. . . . All well here and we are in commercial radio communication. Good morning, Cape Race, from NC-1."

The moon came up; they flew on through the chill night. The weather was perfect, which meant, above all, that they could see the horizon. They drank coffee and munched on sandwiches, and at dawn the flight was still peaceful. Several hours later a patch of gray came into the horizon. Bellinger carefully surveyed the line where sky met sea. There was something false about it. Then he realized he was staring at a fog bank, a deadly and false horizon. Simultaneously, he felt the Nancy 1 climbing. He'd previously arranged with Mitscher to take her up when low clouds or fog were sighted. Mitscher leveled her off at about two thousand feet as they droned over the fog.

Radio direction-finding equipment, supposedly the key to the success of the flight, was almost worthless. Static created by the forty-eight spark plugs of the Libertys made clear reception impossible. They steered by that ancient mariner's instrument, a simple compass card floating in alcohol. They had no blind-flying instruments. They wouldn't have known how to use them, anyway. Without horizon, they all had the same fear—a spin. They wouldn't know when the plane went into one, and they couldn't correct the condition even if they did know, for there was no line on which to stabilize vision.

Bellinger was a human instrument. Fog tumbling and rolling about him, he was the first to feel the motion when the plane began to slip. Each time it slid off to the side, Bellinger signaled and Mitscher and Barin banked to bring her back. The compasses swung right and left. Once, the compass cards rotated violently. Mitscher was being seasoned further in a school of flying where a strong hunch frequently had to serve as a navigation aid and the seat of his pants as a bank-and-turn indicator.

"Lord knows what we were doing. Probably going into a spin when the compass rotated," Bellinger guesses. "Actually, it was due only to the good judgment of Mitscher and Barin that we didn't spin into the sea."

The fog enveloped the plane completely. While Mitscher flew, Barin would clean off the instruments and compasses and then reach over and wipe Mitscher's goggles. Then the procedure would be reversed as Barin took the controls. At 3,500 feet they cleared the fog. Splotches of sun were visible. But within twenty minutes the thick mist trapped them again.

Perhaps they were on course, but with only their compass as a guide it was more likely that they were veering off to one side of the Azores. They were lost.

Bellinger leaned back and yelled, "What do you think about trying it low?"

Mitscher nodded and shoved forward. The fourteen-ton plane headed downward in a long slope, her engines eased and purring. Mitscher leveled at 300 feet; then dropped her to about 100. The swirling mist was solid. Then 75 feet. Bellinger shook his head. It seemed hopeless. They ran at 75 feet, dangerously low over the water; too low to recover in an emergency. Then the fog lifted partially. Visibility was now about a half mile, but there was no sign of the destroyer marker line; nor could they spot land. They had no idea of where they were.

For a moment they discussed the situation. Finally, Bellinger said, "Let's put her down and get a radio check." Mitscher agreed. Bellinger went forward for the landing.

The water, as it rushed past below, looked calm and smooth. But the fog, which had already marred the transocean plan, was about to finish the job. The Nancy 1 lit, bounced and trembled, slowing to a drift. Within a few seconds, it was apparent she would never fly again. A wave had hit the horizontal stabilizer and snapped its control wire. Choppy seas instantly began battering the plane.

At 1140 (Washington time) Sadenwater sent a message from the Nancy 1: SOS SOS SOS XNC 1 LOST IN FOG X ABOUT POSITION 20.

"That calm, smooth water," Bellinger recalls, "was rough as hell."

The destroyers *Phillip*, *Water*, *Harding*, and *Dent*, on the end of the guard line, wheeled out of position and steamed at high speed toward the weak radio signals. A little later, Frances heard the news.

Bellinger threw over the sea anchor, a canvas, cone-shaped drogue, to keep the plane headed into the swells. The line carried away. Mitscher fashioned another sea anchor from a large bucket, by punching holes in its bottom with his hunting knife. He carried that same knife with him for the rest of his life, both at sea and in the air, handy in case he needed to cut himself away from parachute shrouds or fouled lines. The jury-rigged drogue worked and the Nancy's bow swung head-on into the waves again. Sadenwater remained at his radio down in the hull.

"Get on life preservers," Bellinger shouted.

As he spoke, the right wing tip and float broke off and drifted by. The edge of the lower left wing was in the water. Sadenwater kept sending his SOS signals. Mitscher swung down to the lower wings, crawled out, and slit the fabric, creating a free nonresistant passage for the water flow. He cut his hand and Bellinger began to bandage it, wondering, he said later, if they were all going to be shark food. Already they could see fins circling the battered plane.

At last Sadenwater joined them, and there they perched, three men to each upper wing, to await rescue. In midafternoon their luck turned. The S.S. *Ionia*, a Greek tramp, out of Hampton Roads to Gibraltar, chanced on them and made the pickup.

At 2255 (Washington time), the U.S.S. *Harding* radioed: X CREW OF NCI SAFE ON GREEK SHIP IONIA X.

Frances relaxed; and then realized that Marc's personal defeat was almost as bad for him as being adrift.

Jack Towers was also down, somewhere off the islands, and unreported. Eventually his plane, the Nancy 3, functioning as a surface craft, backed into Horta after fifty hours of battling winds and waves. The NC boat hulls were sound.

Read flew on without mishap to Portugal, then to Plymouth, England. The Nancy 4 claimed for the United States man's first transatlantic flight. Alcock and Brown did it again in June; Lindbergh did it solo and nonstop eight years later. But the Nancy was first.

The unsuccessful Nancy 1 and Nancy 3 airmen went on to England by ship. Along with the jubilant Read's crew they were feted in London. Mitscher met the Prince of Wales and the Minister of War, the Honorable Winston Churchill; Paris was next. Then they embarked on the ex-German transport *Zeppelin* to return from Europe, and arrived in the United States on June 27, 1919.

Frances missed the yacht sent out to meet the *Zeppelin*, but finally greeted her husband at Hoboken that night. The Nancy fliers, except Mitscher, posed for photographers on the dock, while he whisked Frances off to their apartment, scrupulously avoiding the newsmen. He felt all attention should be directed to Read and the NC-4 crewmen.

Mitscher received the Navy Cross, a commendation letter from the Secretary of the Navy, and sundry honors from nonmilitary organizations, as did all the other Nancy fliers, but he appeared to be embarrassed by his honors. The flight of the Nancy 1 had been a failure, although the plane was capable. The navigation was the culprit. But neither Mitscher nor Barin felt the bitter ending was due to avoidable error on Bellinger's part.

For years afterward Mitscher seemed contemptuous of the flight, saying: "It only proved one thing. Any damned fool should have been able to figure that out. Radio direction-finding equipment wouldn't work because of vibration and static."

Mitscher's main contribution to the Nancy plane adventure was the addition of the pusher engine, which helped take Read to Plymouth. And it is safe to guess that not more than one pilot out of every fifty in Task Force 58 knew that Mitscher had participated in man's first successful attempt to fly the Atlantic. The Admiral, in practicing his religion of pilot rescue during World War II, knew how it felt to be down at sea.

The Navy versus Billy Mitchell

MITSCHER soon rejoined Henry Mustin, who had been promoted to captain, and reported to the comfortable old *Aroostook*, from which Mustin flew his flag as Commander, Air Detachment, Pacific Fleet. Several weeks later, Mustin sent him to an Army field to learn land-plane flying. Under air pioneer Major Barton K. Yount, Mitscher rounded out his training as a pilot. Still monitoring Mitscher's career, Mustin had arranged for the Air Detachment duty, and Mitscher was glad to return to Henry's calm, sound guidance.

A senior squadron commander, Mitscher also commanded the detachment of air forces at the Fleet Air Base, San Diego. Under the system whereby an officer sometimes wears several hats (each command is a "hat"), and has authority for different decisions under each hat, Mitscher had charge of the seaplane squadrons operating from the *Aroostook* and also the planes at the air base. Jack Towers was there, as chief of staff to Mustin, and ran the detachment when Mustin became ill. Lou Barin had come west to command one of Mitscher's squadrons.

In Pensacola and at Miami, Mitscher had tried to harden himself to death. Men had been killed at both places; some were friends of his, though none close. Then one morning, Barin sat in his plane awaiting take-off. The method of controlling airfield traffic was simple—you dodged. A student pilot came in low, and the thrashing wooden propeller chewed through Barin's cockpit. Mitscher helped extract his mutilated body from the wreckage. The death plunged him into despair and brought on a safety campaign at San Diego. Any pilot who was careless or pranked risked a court-martial. He was a pallbearer at Barin's funeral and then bought Lou's automobile, a Haynes, knowingly paying Barin's mother far more than it was worth.

It was the first car the Mitschers owned. On lieutenant commander's pay, at the time, he could afford both a car and a maid. Frances hadn't learned to cook, and was active socially. Life was gay for young naval officers in the early twenties, and Mitscher reluctantly went to the parties around North Island, mostly to please Frances. He still didn't dance and hadn't cultivated a taste for polite parlor chit-chat. A duck blind or fishing rod suited him perfectly when he wasn't flying.

During this period naval aviation was making a slow transition from totally seaplane operations to use of both land and sea types. The *Langley* would soon be ready for planes with wheels, and pilots were needed for them. They were jockeying war-weary Jennies, DH-4's, and Sopwith-Camels. Mitscher was delighted when the new Vought VE-7 arrived on the scene, but turned sour when the Navy sent out seventeen Loenings—stubby single-wing aircraft with jumbo Hispano-Suiza engines. The pilots took one look and grimaced. There was too much engine for the airframe. Then Mitscher stepped into the cockpit of the first Loening on the line and taxied out—he tested all new types before the other pilots flew them. The little plane darted off the runway and San Diego's airmen watched the sky as he paced her. He brought the plane in for a smooth but "too hot" landing, and hopped out, shaking his head. Shortly after his test hop two officers were killed in Loenings, and eventually, Mitscher recommended to Towers that the planes be destroyed. Washington agreed, and the burn pile roared. There were other times when Mitscher would climb into the cockpit of a plane and then refuse to take it off the ground.

Despite recurring tragedies, these were the roaring air twenties. James Doolittle crossed the country in twenty-one hours; an Italian squadron flew around the world. Byrd winged over both poles. Lindbergh landed at Le Bourget. The *Langley* joined the fleet, and the *Saratoga* and *Lexington*, almost too dazzling for the eyes of Navy pilots, steamed up beside her. The comparative progress in that ten-year period has never been excelled and probably never will be.

Above this explosion of energy, certainly the cause of some of it, sometimes overshadowing all of it, was the biting, relentless voice of General William Mitchell. An aviation fight was inevitable and Mitchell knew how to fight. He wanted a separate air force, divorced from both Army and Navy; he wrote off surface fleets as practically obsolete and questioned the need for large foot armies, speaking out in his own service, in Congress, in the newspapers, and wherever he could buttonhole a listener. In the summer of 1921, in bombing tests off the east coast, obsolete German and United States ships were pitted against aerial bombs. Like Mitchell, few navy airmen had any doubts about the outcome. The ships were sunk.

The Navy was in no position at this time to defend itself against advocates of a completely separate air force, for it was deep in family trouble. Members of naval aviation, prepared for a rosy future after World War I advances, were suddenly reminded that surface sailors still dominated; the battleship was still supreme. The matter of promotion was raised. How could a pilot, devoting all his time to aircraft, possibly fit into the unrestricted command framework of the

Navy? How could he make admiral if he didn't know how to fight fleets of surface ships? Mitscher joined the family war and made a number of personal enemies among the staunch surface advocates.

Later, on October 6, 1925, at a Morrow Board hearing on this subject Mitscher said:

Give the high commands, for the time being, to officers who have had general rotation of duty and the young naval aviation officers can eventually build up to command the carriers and aircraft tenders, then go to senior commands.

Let the surface officers have it . . . until such time as aviation has demonstrated its importance to the fleet and has replaced certain important units of the fleet. Whether that will ever happen I do not know but I believe it will.

Many surface officers thought that the carriers and seaplane tenders should be commanded by surface officers. Mitscher thought that idea was ridiculous; he wanted men who envisioned larger wings rather than bigger gun barrels; he wanted personnel experienced in aviation matters, "who know, and will appreciate and can advance the viewpoint of the flying man."

With little desire and no talent for political wrangling, either intra-Navy politics or the faster Capitol-hill brand, Mitscher entered the Washington arena in May, 1922, as commander of the Naval Air Station, Anacostia, a post he held for five months. During the final sixty days he was busy preparing the Navy's speed team for the National Air Races at Detroit. He was nonflying captain of the unit. The Army won the big race, the Pulitzer, but the Navy triumphed in the Curtiss Marine Trophy contest. Again in 1923, Mitscher captained the Navy's entry at St. Louis. Famed speed pilot Al Williams was one of his fliers. This time, the seagoing airmen swept the races.

One night during the training period, Frances heard him

thrashing around in bed. He mumbled unintelligibly for a few seconds, then said distinctly, "Lads, lads, you know I wouldn't ask you to do anything I wouldn't do myself." Then the nightmare apparently subsided. Frances lay awake for several hours wondering what the man who told her so little had asked his pilots to do, hoping also he wouldn't fly in the races himself. She didn't inquire the next morning or later. Mitscher still preferred her to think about other things than his job and his flying, and still chided her if she became too interested.

After Anacostia, he reported to an organization that had not existed when he went to the Pacific coast in 1919. It was the Navy Bureau of Aeronautics, formalizing aviation within the Navy. Billy Mitchell's pressures had helped create the Bureau of Aeronautics, and a shrewd, immensely popular and brilliant man headed it. He was Rear Admiral William A. Moffett, a surface sailor realigned to air thinking. Moffett had pipelines to Congress, a flair for stealing headlines, and the ability to launch a counterattack against Mitchell without the usual planning conference. Naval aviation was fighting for its life; so was the surface Navy, though many battleship adherents didn't realize it for a long time.

Mitscher once said, "Mitchell was fifty years ahead of his time." He felt the Army airman wanted to fight today's battles with day-after-tomorrow's aircraft. For one of his contentions, that of battleship vulnerability, Mitchell had heavy backing within naval aviation, and his pleas for more air-power funds were welcomed. It was not until he pressed for a single air force, depriving the Navy of its air arm without reducing any responsibilities, that Navy pilots turned against him. The fallacy of Mitchell's opinions on navies was clearly demonstrated in World War II.

Mitscher dealt in aircraft capabilities, in finding the right planes for the forthcoming carriers. He made many trips to factories in Garden City, Long Island; Philadelphia, and Baltimore to study and test such odd, now forgotten types as the SS1, the MO-1, the XS1, and the VO-1. But a good portion of his day was allotted to assisting Moffett and his deputy, Captain A. W. Johnson, in the somewhat larger matter of the struggle for naval aviation survival. Mitscher was a comparatively silent partner, passing ammunition to Moffett and Johnson, who were in the vocal forefront. Mitscher maneuvered behind the scenes, often briefing the two spokesmen, whose aviation experience was meager. He was usually handy to analyze and advise when Mitchell had issued a public statement.

As Johnson later described it, Mitscher might say: "Mitchell's right, we can't argue that point," and the point wouldn't be argued. Or if he thought Mitchell wrong: ". . . dammit, he knows better than I do that we haven't got a plane in sight that good."

"Nobody knew better than Pete Mitscher the capabilities and limitations of aircraft. Mitchell didn't recognize the limitations," Johnson said later.

Although the long daytime hours were spent in turmoil, Mitscher could and did relax occasionally at night. He would meet the young men who passed through the Bureau of Aeronautics (many of them admirals now) at informal parties around Washington, his personality undergoing a complete change, the barren office façade melting quickly.

At the parties, Mitscher would insist gaily, "Call me Pete!" And a high-balling, singing, grinning Pete he was until the next day. He is remembered for many hoarse renditions of his favorite, "Carry Me Back to Ol' Virginny." He would get just a touch into his cups, never more than a good glow. Generally a bourbon man, he always handled liquor with respect. Old hands like John Dale Price, later a vice admiral, respected

Mitscher's party informality and watched newcomers with glee when, the next morning, they invariably tried to carry the previous night's first-name routine into the office.

The new pilot, still warm with the memories of a gay, convivial Mitscher, would usually come bounding into work: "G'mornin', Pete."

Mitscher would clear his throat and peer about bleakly, the light-blue eyes sweeping the corners as if to locate this fellow "Pete."

"What did you say?"

"Good morning, *Commander* Mitscher," the new pilot would stammer.

Mitscher would sometimes work for an entire day without uttering more than a few sentences. Harry Cecil, the Cash Cecil of the Annapolis debacle days, who was in flight division, could draw him out, and occasionally there would be a sudden, inexplicable chuckle to break the silence. Mitscher did smile, in fact was provoked to hearty laughter, over the sometimes startling actions of Admiral Moffett, like the day Moffett announced the airship *Shenandoah* would go to the North Pole. The resulting publicity stole newspaper space for several editions. Captain Johnson, astonished at Moffett's action, said weakly, "Not a single cell of the ship has been built."

Moffett snapped, "It'll be completed! And go there!"

Again, in September, 1923, Moffett purposely held up the first flight of the *Shenandoah* to coincide with the Army's bombing tests on the U.S.S. *Virginia* and the U.S.S. *New Jersey*; again, it diverted attention. At times the fight over control of military aviation was completely ruthless, but it concerned the honest differences of opinion of essentially honest men on both sides, then as now, and aviation thrived on the rivalry.

Mitscher, writing in the Naval Academy Class Bulletin in 1924, and transmitting views of the Navy Department, which he had helped formulate, said:

The Navy Arctic Expedition will have as its mission the exploration of the North Polar region and the scientific investigation and establishment of a transpolar route.

To carry out these missions two vessels with mooring masts will be used together with six aeroplanes, with 2400 miles radius, and the USS *Shenandoah*. One surface ship, with three planes, will work from the vicinity of Nome, Alaska, and the other surface ship will work from Spitsbergen . . . the *Shenandoah* will leave Lakehurst . . . and reach Nome in early July, 1924.

Air mail planes are flying in temperatures of forty below zero daily during the winter. Why not an air route from England to Japan via the Arctic Ocean? Three hundred years have been expended in the exploration of the areas shown on the maps. Aircraft can do the work of discovery in a few hours time. . . .

It might appear that Mitscher was enthusiastic over the Arctic plans for the *Shenandoah*. Actually, however, he did not trust the gas-filled giants; he wanted wings under him. But he labored over polar charts and sought information on engine operations in sub-zero weather, planning to go along as pilot of one of the reconnaissance planes. In the end, the plans for the expedition, first announced before the *Shenandoah* even existed, collapsed entirely when she broke apart in midair over Ohio, unleashing another barrage from Billy Mitchell.

In Washington there were so many boards, both congressional and military, meeting to investigate aviation that officers sometimes showed up at the wrong hearing and suddenly realized they should have been two corridors down. Mitscher testified before most of them over a two-year period, including the Eberle Board, the Rodman Board, the Lassiter Board, the Lampert Committee, and the Morrow Board. In a typical day's testimony he covered Army-Navy air missions, shore establishments, aircraft procurement, pilot training, pilot promotion, and usually the views of General Mitchell.

While this fight occupied headlines, the controversy over the role of aviation personnel within the Navy smoldered on, and sometimes led to open conflict. Captain Harris Laning, later a vice admiral, skipper of the U.S.S. *Pennsylvania*, requested that Mitscher be ordered to the Pacific fleet to assist in drawing up doctrine on aerial control of gunnery. He cited Mitscher's experience and ability. Mitscher was anxious to go and thought he had ideas that might make spotting doctrine easier. But in a letter dated September 22, 1924, Admiral E. W. Eberle, Chief of Naval Operations, replied stiffly: "While Lieutenant Commander Mitscher has contributed to the aviation point of view . . . it is believed personnel now in the fleet should be competent to revise doctrine."

A few days after Eberle's rebuff, wearied of bickering and the periodic Mitchell outbursts, Mitscher requested duty as a naval attaché in "any country." Harry Cecil was in Rome, away from the torment. Thoughts of a comparatively easy embassy job, a chance for the Mitschers to travel—which they had not done—attracted him. It was the only time he asked for duties which would separate him from the planes and pilots, and the request was promptly turned down by Moffett. Mitscher was glad, later, that Moffett did so. Moffett's next summation of him said pointedly: ". . . he has been kept ashore here because his services cannot be spared and because there is no one available to replace him."

Mitscher went to the field at Anacostia at every opportunity, preferring to either observe or personally participate in the various Bureau of Aeronautics tests under his cognizance. Navy planes were having trouble with a "flat spin," and would often rotate to the earth like an oak leaf in an autumn breeze. Lieutenant Ralph A. Ofstie, now a vice admiral, was sent to the west coast to determine the causes of the spin. He returned and reported to Mitscher that the tail surfaces should be expanded; then he offered to demonstrate how to effect recovery from the spin. Mitscher said he wanted to go along, "so you can show me what it's all about."

On May 13, 1925, a Boeing biplane was rigged out with cloth streamers on the struts to indicate wind flow and show the plane's reactions. At 4,000 feet over the capital, Ofstie deliberately put it into a spin, which quickly went flat. The plane spiraled earthward and Ofstie began to point out the wind flow shown by the various streamers. In the front cockpit, Mitscher took notes as the careening laboratory tumbled down. He nodded again and again as Ofstie's gloved hand traced the trouble. At about 2,000 feet, the experiment completed, Ofstie attempted recovery. The plane didn't respond. It whined, whistled, and whirled. Ofstie was too busy to check on Mitscher's state of mind but believes his passenger was calm, and had full confidence they would pull out.

Seeing the trees on Hain's Point approaching at express speed, Ofstie slammed the stick back, cramming it deep into Mitscher's stomach, to level off before they hit. The plane was demolished. Frances read about it in the afternoon paper, and later her husband came home, limping and bruised, mumbling something about a "rough landing." Mitscher did not rebuke Ofstie because the experiment ended in a crash, but complained vociferously about the power with which the lieutenant had slammed the stick into his belly.

Between planning, committee hearings, and occasional experimental flights like the one with Ofstie, Mitscher frequently journeyed to Fort Tilden, New Jersey, where the Army was working out antiaircraft defenses; he was also busy with ordinance conferences and engineering conferences. His duty-order file in the Bureau of Naval Personnel is several inches thick, and doubtless many side trips and conferences have not been noted. Retired Admiral DeWitt C. Ramsey has called Mitscher "a walking encyclopedia of aviation." The tour of duty in the Bureau of Aeronautics in the twenties added many pages.

The climax was his presence at hearings of the Morrow

Board, named after its chairman, Dwight W. Morrow. Convened to study the best means of developing and applying aviation to national defense, its distinguished members included Senator Hiram Bingham and Congressman Carl Vinson. Mitchell's attacks had brought the controversy to a point where decision was necessary, and the board sat in judgment. Mitscher was called before it on October 6, 1925. Others to testify included Mitchell, Moffett, and Orville Wright. With the exception of the group conducting 1949 hearings on the Navy–Air Force B-36 controversy, the Morrow Board was the most important body ever assembled to discuss military aviation.

Senator Bingham asked Mitscher: "Have you known of any acute dissatisfaction among personnel of the Navy Air Service?"

"Yes, sir!"

"To what do you attribute it?"

". . . the naval aviation officer feels that aviation has assumed a fixed and important position in the general scheme of warfare, particularly naval warfare, and must be considered carefully as to its offensive values as well as its defensive values. He feels that it is important enough to be commanded by personnel who know, and will appreciate, and can advance the viewpoint of the flying man. He feels that experienced aviation men should have administration of the training of aviation personnel and the detail of aviation personnel. He feels that aviation development of the Navy presents a career, and that once he takes up aviation he should be permitted to follow the general aviation line throughout his life. He feels that Navy aviation presents a new problem not quite similar to any of the past problems of naval experience."

This was an opportunity, perhaps the best ever afforded to the still small band of pioneers, to make it plain, once and for all, that naval aviation was durable, and had plenty to contribute. Mitscher's comments, and the comments of the other professional aviators, were directed not only to the members of congress but also to the senior admirals.

As the hearings expanded to the larger issue of total air power, Mitchell's case for a united air force, without special aviation to carry out sea-power missions, crumbled. Mitchell took the case again to the press and was finally summoned for court-martial. On December 7, 1925, Mitscher was a prosecution witness at the trial. Mitchell's temporary promotion to brigadier general had been lifted months before, and he stood trial as a colonel. After his conviction, the cleavage between the air services began to mend slowly, but it has never completely healed.

Mitscher left the Bureau in the spring of 1926 with two glowing appraisals by Admiral Moffett. ". . . his knowledge of aviation, in theory and practice, is unexcelled by any officer in the Navy." So reads a fitness report that was exceeded only by Moffett's next one, in May, 1926, in which he advised promotion boards: ". . . I consider this officer without a superior in his knowledge of aviation, sound judgement, ability and clear thinking."

CHAPTER

⚓ 10 ⚓

First Aircraft Carrier

"COVERED WAGON" was a well-chosen nickname for the *Langley*, the Navy's first carrier, which had been converted from the collier *Jupiter*. A flight deck supported by steel box girders covered her yawning holds, and she still had coal-dust particles in her when she was sunk in 1942. On a typical morning late in May, 1926, several hours out of San Pedro, California, the *Langley* steamed in search of wind.

Mitscher, ready to fly, waited for Captain Charles Jackson to find it. Covered Wagon's engines could generate but 14 knots, and since 21 or 22 knots of wind, across the deck, were needed to launch planes, Jackson spent much of his time chasing stray puffs of air; then the breeze freshened and Jackson directed her bulk into it. Admiral DeWitt Ramsey remembers Mitscher waddling out to the VE-7, his parachute pack bumping him with every step. The stem-winder biplane bore down a portion of the *Langley*'s 536 feet of flight deck at 45 mph and began climbing, then banked out to orbit as engineers from the Bureau of Aeronautics readied the arresting gear.

As the catapult had posed problems in firing aircraft off cruisers, the arresting gear—a system of cables to slow the forward motion of landing aircraft—presented trying moments for the carrier. The *Langley* had been the testing ground for dozens of variations in arresting gear since 1922. Mitscher headed back and made the approach, angling down to the deck, in the groove. Just above stalling speed, he cut the motor, the tailhook grabbing for the cables. The plane bounced, slewed crazily for a second and swerved off to one side, fighting her pilot every inch of the way. The gear obviously needed more adjustment, and the engineers went back to work. Occurrences of this sort were routine, and Mitscher made five or six more trials that morning.

The *Langley* served as a test platform for both pilots and equipment. Many of today's top Navy air officers qualified for landings and take-offs on her ten-inch planks. Aboard for carrier qualification at the time were Ramsey, John Dale Price and Gerald Bogan, all flag officers in World War II.

As head of her aviation department, in charge of flight operations, Mitscher stayed on the flight deck or on the bridge near Charles Jackson or Frank McCrary, who was to be her next skipper. When a pilot made a sloppy landing, Mitscher would bound out to admonish or encourage him, whichever was needed. With the *Saratoga* and *Lexington* near completion, the *Langley*'s most important mission was to provide qualified pilots for the bigger, faster carriers. This day, typical in the *Langley*'s life, was typical also in Mitscher's life for the next six months. Although this was his first tour of carrier duty, he had had so much time in the air that it was easy for him to learn the new techniques. When he departed, Captain Frank McCrary, filing the required report to Washington, added a footnote: "I consider his opinions the most valuable of any officer in the service."

During the summer, Oscar Mitscher died of pneumonia at the age of sixty-five. Although there had been little contact between them since Mitscher entered the Academy, he had remained devoted to his father, and Oscar, in turn, had lived to see his son establish a professional naval career.

Meanwhile, the *Saratoga*, first United States ship to be launched as an aircraft carrier, was being completed at the American Brown Boveri yard, Camden, New Jersey. Ken Whiting had orders as her executive officer and Mitscher came along as air officer, again responsible for operating the planes. This was in November, 1926. The Mitschers took an apartment in the slum district of Camden.

"Why in the world did you pick this place, Marc?" asked Frances, surveying the shabby surroundings.

He replied sheepishly, "It's only a few blocks from the ship-yard."

He spent so much time hovering around the *Saratoga* work-men that Frances felt he might as well have been at sea. He personally examined almost every piece of equipment that had anything to do with the launching, landing, or operation of the aircraft. By fall, 1927, the *Saratoga* was ready, and her com-missioning pennant was hoisted on November 16.

Mitscher brought a UO-1, a Chance-Vought fighter, down on the *Saratoga*'s deck on January 11, 1928, for the first land-ing. When she joined the fleet, Captain Harry E. Yarnell, later an admiral, was skipper; Whiting was her executive officer. Mitscher, as air officer, was charged with planning operations, getting the planes off deck on schedule, and supervising the flight-deck and hangar-deck crews. Roughly five hundred men were under his direction at one time or another during these operations. He stood on a small platform on the *Saratoga*'s bridge, giving instructions as plane handlers trundled aircraft into position or shoved them to the elevators. Mitscher knew the lines of authority and seldom usurped powers or responsi-bilities. At the same time, he jealously guarded his own. For a time, some junior officers thought Mitscher too unquestion-ing of his seniors' desires, especially Yarnell's. Later, they discovered he could take decisive exception if the issue was of consequence to him, as in one interchange with Ken Whiting. As a deckload of planes was being sent skyward, Whiting suddenly grabbed the mike from Mitscher and began giving orders to the launching officer.

Mitscher took off his headset, and handed it, with mike, to Whiting. "We can't both be air officer, Commander," Mitscher said coldly to his old and dear friend, who had inadvertently pricked a most sensitive area. "I request my detachment immediately." Whiting blinked and sputtered in confusion; then he realized he had negated Mitscher's authority, and passed the mike back apologetically.

Carrier operations were new; the pilots were inexperienced, and Mitscher fretted about them. He was unable to get away from the feeling that he should fly every plane himself. When the *Saratoga* was anchored off Long Beach, California, he sent Lieutenant Frederick W. Pennoyer, later a vice admiral, on a round-trip seaplane flight to San Diego, a hundred miles away over open water. Several hours before sundown, Mitscher was notified that Pennoyer was overdue. He came out of his cabin at a run, shouted for a whaleboat and a coxswain, and chugged away from the *Saratoga*'s side, heading for San Diego on the route Pennoyer would most likely follow on his return flight. It probably did not ever occur to Mitscher that he could have assigned the search to a junior officer.

As the boat tossed along, he sat in the stern sheets busily calculating Pennoyer's gas consumption and checking a chart. Just before sunset, Mitscher conned the whaleboat up to the drifting plane. Squatting on the stern sheets, he called over: "Planes don't fly long without gas, Lieutenant Pennoyer." Then he sat in complete silence on the ride back to the *Saratoga* with his rescued bird, who had run out of gas thirty miles short of the ship.

In one operation, Mitscher set a carrier record which stood

for several years. He co-ordinated the work of the plane handlers and pilots so that they could take aboard four squadrons, about eighty aircraft at the time, stow them in the hangar deck, and then fly them off again in less than an hour. The operation involved landing the aircraft, getting them to the elevator, whisking them below, parking them, and then reversing the whole procedure. As carrier aviation began to expand, with an influx of new, young pilots, the name of Pete Mitscher became a byword within the flattop fleet.

In early carrier planes the throttle was located on the right-hand side of the fuselage and the pilots landed from a right-hand pattern; consequently, paddle-waving landing signal officers (LSO), always took a position on the starboard side of the flight deck, near the stern. Then new carrier planes were produced, with the throttle on the left, and Mitscher advocated placing the LSO to match the new position of the throttle. Accustomed to seeing the LSO to starboard, the pilots protested. Mitscher didn't argue, but on the next day's operations, there were two LSO's on deck—one on the right, and another on the left. Finding the LSO on the left far more useful, the ship's air group capitulated, and soon the right-hand LSO was discarded.

By 1929, Mitscher's ability both as a leader and as a pilot was unquestioned. However, in the opinion of some senior officers, he lacked "educational requirements." His record was void of graduate work in tactics and strategy. Actually, Mitscher had been too busy flying to attend the War College; too busy training, planning, developing, and learning—all for air power. Moreover, in 1929—as in 1946—he was not particularly impressed with the sacrosanct institution at Newport, Rhode Island, which is practically mandatory for officers who have set sights on an admiral's flag. Had there been any emphasis on naval aviation at Newport, he might have made an effort to attend, but the study courses were designed almost exclusively for surface fighting. Mitscher was content to learn tactics and strategy in practice.

On October 1, 1929, Mitscher returned to the *Langley*, this time as her executive officer. Captain Arthur B. Cook, her skipper, received a presidential letter of commendation for the *Langley*'s battle efficiency in which the inspecting officers singled Mitscher out as deserving special credit for the "smart and efficient way the *Langley* has performed her duties." Cook recommended Mitscher as fully qualified to command the *Langley*. It was a nice gesture, but Mitscher still had but two and a half stripes; he was still a lieutenant commander after twenty-five years in the Navy. Commanding the *Langley* was a captain's job.

CHAPTER

⚓ 11 ⚓

Lean Years

MITSCHER's jump from junior-officer level to senior, with gold braid for his hat brim, was made in the fall of 1930. At precisely 1010, October 1, 1930, he entered an examination room in the Navy Department to sit before a board considering his appointment to the temporary rank of commander. He was examined on international law, general and military law, strategy, tactics, and communication. He had brushed up on these subjects while aboard the *Langley* and passed without too much trouble. The board noted that he had not attended the War College but recommended promotion anyway

Although assigned to desk work in the Bureau of Aeronautics, he made several proficiency hops each month. Most of them were routine, but on February 24, 1931, streaking in for a landing at Anacostia in a Vought Corsair, he came in too fast and ended with the plane's tail pointing skyward, the engine burrowing into Anacostia sod. He crawled from the wreck unscratched. It was embarrassing, of course, especially since aircraft were not expendable under any circumstances.

The depression's gloom had settled over the Navy, and an economy drive was on. Some nonaviators saw an excellent opportunity to reduce expenses by eliminating flight pay, which amounted to a 50-per-cent addition to the regular salary. Although Moffett built a backstop against this move, bitterness between air and surface personnel flared up once more. Mitscher and Cash Cecil, together again, and Charles Pownall, who was to command the carriers in the early days of World War II, made a concerted effort to soothe feelings and narrow the breach between surface sailor and airman. Occasionally, some pilots would launch a spirited campaign to establish an autonomous naval-aviation organization, but Mitscher, apparently realizing that the only success lay in closer co-operation with the battleship, cruiser, and destroyer sailors, went quietly about the Bureau of Aeronautics discouraging any attempts for separation. These ships would provide surface protection for the carrier task groups.

At this time Mitscher, as a part of his business, was beginning to worry about Japan. It would be a gross exaggeration to say that in the early thirties he was predicting a war with Japan. Nevertheless, being in charge of aviation plans, he was confronted with some rather startling facts from the Far East.

The Japanese had entered naval aviation in 1912; their first carrier, the *Hosho*, was commissioned in 1921, a year before the United States sent the *Langley* into the fleet. In 1930, the Japanese had 284 naval aircraft. Intelligence reports indicated Japan was also making advances in aircraft production and had plans for more carriers. Mitscher knew the Japanese were copying some features of the *Lexington* and the *Saratoga*.

He worked on the aviation section of the war plans kept in readiness against attack. Britain was the only naval-aviation power in the Atlantic, and it was not likely that she would open hostilities against the United States. Quite simply, that left Japan. The Orange Plan, dealing mostly with the Pacific area, covered both combat estimates and aircraft industrial mobilization.

Original estimates, as worked out by Mitscher and his staff in the early thirties, proved close to the number of planes and bases needed in the first years of World War II. He concentrated on small planes of the dive-bomber type, also of use for fighter-intercept missions. His plans asked for increased attention to the development of heavy industrial capacity to produce this type of plane, which proved its worth at Coral Sea, at Midway, and in the Marianas. He also favored immediate and greater carrier expansion, stressing speed and maneuverability, the pillars of successful fast-carrier task-force operation.

Moffett wholeheartedly supported the main points of Mitscher's readiness plan for naval aviation, but even Moffett's conference-room generalship, aided by concrete facts drawn up by Mitscher's staff, failed on numerous occasions. One noon hour, returning from hearings of the General Board on carrier characteristics, where Moffett was fighting a losing battle on some aspects of carrier development, Mitscher said disconsolately to Hugh Goodwin, "One of the troubles with this Navy today is that a lot of the admirals think that some of the other admirals are still a bunch of kids." Moffett had just lost a round to his seniors on the General Board.

Mitscher's realization of this truth—a junior, in the eyes of his senior, never grows up—was actually a statement of the condition that had plagued naval aviation since 1914. During this period, the "synthetic" aviators, unjustly maligned at times, were born. They were men who qualified for aviation either as pilots or as observers, late in their career. A quickie course at Pensacola enabled them to be assigned to aviation duties. Admiral Halsey was a synthetic; so was Vice Admiral John Sidney McCain, who later alternated duty with Mitscher in Task Force 58. Naval aviation had grown faster than its officer corps. The Navy was not inclined to jump comparatively junior officers, such as Mitscher, to the rank of captain or rear admiral, but aviation billets requiring senior rank had to be filled. The synthetic method was selected. Also, many officers who held the rank of captain realized that to compete professionally in future years, an aviation qualification would be highly desirable.

By Pearl Harbor, only two of the aviation old-liners, Patrick Bellinger and John Towers, had reached flag rank. To pilots who had suffered the starvation years and flown the jury-rigged planes, the synthetic represented another volley from the battleship guns, and was symbolic of most of the ills of naval aviation. The abilities of such men as Halsey and McCain were not questioned. It was the apparent denial of the top air command plums that hurt.

CHAPTER
⚓ 12 ⚓
The End of the Dirigibles

ADMIRAL MOFFETT had kept his faith with the airships and firmly believed that the Navy had a bright future in the slow, majestic, silvered dirigibles. He predicted aerial carriers which could launch groups of planes at high altitudes; airships capable of transporting huge cargoes and many troops. But the dream seemed never to reach reality. One after another, the ships were destroyed.

He was delighted when Mitscher and Cecil, two of the most outspoken rigid airship critics, halfheartedly agreed to go with him on the *Akron* for a short flight out of Lakehurst. Cecil had qualified as an LTA pilot in the twenties but apparently was not very enthusiastic about airships when it was decided that both Mitscher and Cecil could not be spared from the important work in progress at the Bureau of Aeronautics, they flipped a coin. Mitscher lost, and declined Cecil's offer to step aside.

On the night of April 3, 1933, the *Akron* arose from her mast at Lakehurst and headed out to sea. In addition to Moffett and Cecil, she had aboard sixteen officers and fifty-five crewmen. It was a routine flight, to calibrate radio instruments. Moffett went along for pleasure and observation. Thunderheads were on the horizon as she left the New Jersey coast but meteor-ological forecasts mentioned no real danger. In the vicinity of Barnegat Light, she encountered a vicious local squall. The *Akron* rode it until her rudder-control cable snapped, then she wallowed helplessly in the raging wind and finally dropped tail-first into the white-capped sea.

In the early morning, the phone rang in the Mitschers' apart-ment on Connecticut Avenue, and Frances saw the curious smile of trouble as her husband answered it. "The *Akron*'s down," he said quietly, and then went to the Navy Depart-ment to read the dispatches and be in direct communication with Lakehurst.

Cash Cecil and Bill Moffett were gone. The people who meant the most to him were slipping away. Of the few old and close friends, only Ken Whiting remained. Harry Cecil had been a part of his life since his days at the Naval Academy. It had been a quiet, strong friendship. Significantly, no one can remember any amusing stories about the relationship of Mitscher and Cecil, although they'd flown together, pilot and co-pilot, worked together, and partied together. For a few days, there was a faint hope. With Frances, he visited Harry Cecil's wife several times each day.

There is no better illustration of Mitscher's emotional con-trol than these visits. Frances would watch him as he ap-proached Isa Cecil's door. His face would be blank, his eyes dull and pained. As his hand touched the knob, she could see a pause, then a forced change. He masked his grief behind a warm, confident smile. The mild blue eyes were radiant; he talked to Isa reassuringly. Finally, Isa would return his smile.

Then, as he departed, and the door closed behind him, Fran-ces could see the mask disappear instantly, as if a hand had suddenly passed over his face to reinsert the truth.

CHAPTER

⚓ 13 ⚓

Flight to Pearl Harbor

By summer, 1933, Mitscher was thoroughly seasoned in aeronautics administration; by this time his flight log recorded over 3,000 hours in more than fifty different models of planes. Seemingly, he had done all the kinds of flying possible in naval aviation, but he did lack experience in large patrol planes.

Although the old Nancy planes were designed primarily for patrol, his time with them had been limited to the transatlantic flight; therefore he'd persuaded Moffett, some months before the *Akron* crash, to endorse a request for assignment to flying boats. Mitscher was ordered to the Aircraft Squadrons, United States Fleet, as chief of staff to Rear Admiral Johnson, who operated from the tender U.S.S. *Wright*—the same Alfred Johnson he had worked with in the Bureau of Aeronautics during the twenties.

Several days after Mitscher reported, he told the staff, with Johnson's approval, that he wanted the planes to fly, not to float their pontoons in a slumbering lagoon.

A mass flight from Norfolk, Virginia, to Coco Solo, Canal Zone, was proposed. Mitscher readied six P2Y boats, twin-engined, long-range aircraft, manufactured by Consolidated.

The *Wright* then set off for the Canal Zone, and on October 8, 1933, Lieutenant Commander H. E. Halland brought them into Coco Solo to set a formation-flying record of 2,059 miles.

Mitscher suggested flying the P2Y's from the west coast to Pearl Harbor. The Navy Department agreed, but advised transporting them to San Diego by ship, then flying them to San Francisco, then on to Honolulu. Such a flight had never been made.

Data indicated that the P2Y's couldn't possibly make the leg from San Francisco to Pearl Harbor, 2,400 nonstop miles without refueling.

"If we can start from San Diego and get the gas consumption down, then I know they'll go to Hawaii," Mitscher said. Then he informed the mechanics and pilots that the boats would henceforth consume only 53 gallons per hour instead of 62. By using a stingy mixture and making shorter take-off runs they did reduce the consumption of the P2Y boats to only 53 gallons per hour.

In the first week of January, 1934, he went again to Johnson. He wanted to make the flight himself. An earlier attempt by Commander John Rodgers had failed, and Mitscher did not want to risk another failure. But as chief of staff, he couldn't go as a pilot without risking accusations of lack of confidence in the squadron commander, Lieutenant Commander Kanefler McGinnis. To avoid ill feeling, he told McGinnis he would accompany the flight as an observer; officially he was listed as an assistant pilot. Only a few people, at noon on January 10, 1934, knew that Mitscher was in the lead plane as the flying boats taxied out of Paradise Cove, made a rendezvous over the foggy Golden Gate, and aimed at Pearl Harbor for the first mass-formation flight over the Pacific.

The flight must have brought back memories of the NC-1. Ships were strung out below, and they encountered fog a hundred miles out and flew by instruments most of the way. Supernumerary Mitscher sat in the cockpit beside McGinnis for the entire 2,399 miles. The only piloting he did was as relief to McGinnis. When the planes passed over Makapuu Point, Oahu, twenty-four hours and sixteen minutes out of San Francisco, Mitscher made ready his exit. The flight was a success.

Ringed with a lei, he disappeared among the milling welcomers. There was hardly a mention of his name in connection with the flight. Frances met him, having come out previously by ship, and the Mitschers apparently vanished from Honolulu. Actually, they were visiting friends; but the subject of his connection with the epic transpacific jaunt was a closed matter. The San Francisco–Honolulu flight proved to the commercial companies that overwater passenger flights to the islands were within reach, and in a short time, Pan American Airways planes were on a regular run.

After the flight, Johnson and Mitscher went to Midway Island to look over possible seaplane-base sites, then pioneered naval aviation in Alaskan waters. The flying boats were busy, and Mitscher was rapidly filling in the gap in his own career.

Ken Whiting, who now commanded the *Saratoga*, then claimed Mitscher as his executive officer, and arranged for orders. Rear Admiral Johnson detached him reluctantly: ". . . a driving personality that gets results without incurring dissatisfaction. A natural leader of men though personally retiring and shunning publicity. Commander Mitscher was largely responsible for the success of the flight of VP 10 from San Francisco to Pearl Harbor."

Mitscher was still thinking about the danger of Japan, continuing to base his arguments on the fact that the Japanese were building a naval air arm. He didn't clutter up the thesis with economic factors or grand strategy, but stayed strictly within his own field—combat readiness. Some of the *Saratoga* pilots thought Mitscher was fooling either them or himself.

Aside from his insistence on this baffling contention, they found him to be almost entirely unchanged. He knew the *Saratoga* stem to stern. At sea, the easiest period for an executive officer, he maintained high efficiency on the *Saratoga*. At anchor or alongside the dock, always a troublesome time for an executive officer, he stayed where he could easily be located. Off duty, his favorite place was his own cabin, where he usually could be found reading a detective novel, most likely one with fast action. He seldom got annoyed when he was interrupted, and would elevate his glasses, offer his solution to whatever problem was presented, probably without checking the voluminous manuals that any executive office maintains, and return immediately to the cop-and-robber story. He was not the "busy" type of executive officer who dashes about the ship with a pad and pencil to ferret out inadequacies of ship or crew. He passed such duty to junior personnel.

As often as possible, he would steal a few hours away from ship duties for flying. On the morning of August 28, 1934, he took off on a cross-country flight in a Vought Corsair from the *Saratoga*'s utility unit. Aviation Chief Machinist's Mate R. J. Munkittrick was crewman. Heavy rain closed in near Gwin Island, Virginia, and Mitscher made a forced landing in a cow pasture. They squatted beneath the wing for several hours until the weather cleared. The pasture was wet but suitable for a carefully executed take-off. Mitscher opened the throttle and they rolled forward. Nearing take-off speed, he caught a blur of movement dead ahead and jerked the plane into the air. It hung for a second, and then the left wing crashed into the limb of a tree and the plane flipped over on its back.

His official report said: "It was necessary to pull the plane into the air at nearly stalling speed to avoid hitting a colored woman and a little child who were running toward a herd of cattle." Mitscher and Munkittrick walked away with nothing more painful than an assortment of bruises. Somehow he seemed to have a charmed life. He had been in a half dozen or more crashes and yet exhibited no scars.

Mitscher was drawing more and more within himself, wasting fewer motions, wasting no words. No one, not even Frances Mitscher, or his family, has ever understood why he talked so softly, and said so little. But, as one *Saratoga* officer recalled, "If you didn't hear him, you had better damn sight ask someone who did." There were times when he preferred not to say anything at all. At the Bluejackets Ball for the *Saratoga* in late 1934, Captain Whiting made a short speech to the ship's personnel; then Mitscher, duty bound, mounted the stage. His lips moved—that much is absolutely certain—and he looked intently at the crowd before him. Then he left the stage, to the polite applause of his audience.

Frances whispered, "Nobody understood a word you said."

Mitscher twinkled back, "I didn't intend anybody to understand it." He had nothing to say to them.

C H A P T E R

⚓ 14 ⚓

Prelude to War

REAR ADMIRAL ERNEST J. KING dictated a letter on April 17, 1935: "It is requested that Commander Mitscher be assigned duties as head of the Flight Division of the Bureau of Aeronautics. The request is made because of pending legislation on cadets, personnel and training. It is essential that a naval aviator of extensive experience and proven judgement be charged with these responsibilities."

Ernest King was, in many ways, the perfect naval officer—expert seaman, gunner, and administrator; tough, honest, and a disciplinarian, winning loyalty by sheer strength of character. He was not content with any command until it was the best afloat or ashore. A few days after memorial services were held for the *Akron* dead, back in the summer 1933, King had succeeded Moffett as the chief of the Bureau of Aeronautics. He'd qualified for aviation in 1927 at the age of forty-nine.

The paths of Mitscher and King had crossed several times, but without great effect. Neither man had attempted to encourage friendship, and Mitscher had already made up his mind about King. "He's too cold," Mitscher once remarked. Mitscher thought the stern, tall Ohioan could not understand the frailties of human nature; he felt King believed all other men were essentially compounded of his own granite, that they only needed firm direction to bring out their best. At the Bureau of Aeronautics there was not the slightest pretense of cordiality between Mitscher and King. There was, however, a clear mutual respect from the very moment Mitscher returned in the late spring of 1935.

It was not unlike previous tours of duty there. The same problems existed: the need for more planes, more and better personnel, and the ledger item which would make both possible—more money. Mitscher was now head of the Flight Division, which included operations, training, personnel, aerology, and aerial photography. He concentrated on justifying the need for additional funds for personnel and training. The Navy received better treatment before Congress than it had expected, and King, before departing for other duty, noted of Mitscher: ". . . a personality that inspires confidence and loyalty. Quiet, forceful, tactful, conscientious, steady and practical. An asset to any organization." This, from King's pen, was high tribute. But to the last day there was not the slightest pretense of cordiality between King and Mitscher.

Then in 1937, Mitscher was ordered to command the U.S.S. *Wright*, mother to the seaplanes in the Pacific. Although this was the first ship command for Mitscher, he had been with the *Wright* enough to know her strengths and weaknesses in a seaway. The four early years in cruisers, gunboats, and destroyers had given him knowledge of the basic skills of seamanship. Later duty in the tenders and carriers had equipped him to pilot either aircraft or seagoing vessels. He had docked both the *Langley* and the *Saratoga*, no mean feat in a strong tide with the wind kiting up under the mammoth flight decks and driving against the high sides.

He took the *Wright* from San Diego to Alaska, tending the patrol planes and taking part in fleet exercises. King, by now

Commander Aircraft, Battle Force, was conducting a much-needed reorientation of the fleet in this area, which resulted in the need for more flying by the patrol planes. The pilots balked and expected fellow-airman Mitscher to sympathize with them and cast his lot against the "battleship" admiral. But King was also air-minded. Mitscher surprised them by not only praising King's program but making efforts to go far beyond it, although he had no actual command of the aircraft. In the summer of 1938, the *Wright* was awarded the coveted big white "E," for efficiency in engineering, to paint on her stack. Before that, she was cited for "smartness and efficiency in advance base exercises."

Mitscher became a captain in 1938, adding a fourth stripe, and shifted duty to command of Patrol Wing One. He remained in the *Wright*, although no longer responsible for her operation. His responsibility was now the forty-odd planes and five hundred men of Patrol Wing One. Lieutenant Commander Alfred Melville Pride, later a vice admiral, was Mitscher's chief of staff. Pride had been in aviation almost as long as Mitscher, having served under him at Miami and flown planes off turret platforms on the *Arizona* and the *Nevada*. He had invented the *Langley*'s arresting gear. He had enlisted as a machinist's mate in World War I and was deeply interested in aviation engineering. Pride was but one of the non-Academy naval fliers whom Mitscher took personal interest in.

There were times, however, when Mitscher completely baffled the ruddy-faced New Englander. He disturbed Pride by going to great lengths to soften general courts-martial of several officers. The cases were clearly drawn, the offenders definitely guilty. Pride felt they should receive the maximum penalty. But Mitscher believed that, given the chance, they would straighten out. He had never tolerated deliberate neglect of duty, nor would he permit an inefficient officer to remain on his staff for more than a few weeks. However, punishment for an honest mistake, even though it appeared honest only to him, was always meted out with temperance.

Many of the Patrol Wing personnel brought problems to him. Sometimes there were domestic troubles, more often Navy problems. Then his tongue would loosen and he would become suddenly talkative, discussing the problems with Pride for as much as an hour. But ordinarily, Pride would have to carry the conversation as they ate in the small flag mess of the *Wright*.

The flying boats stayed in the air. In 1938 and 1939, newspapers occasionally carried a few paragraphs about another mass flight record being broken. Mitscher scheduled the long overwater hauls and could be found in the cockpit of the lead plane, his large, freckled hands on the controls, the hunting knife, relic of the Nancy flight, strapped to his left hip. On January 10, 1939, in a Consolidated flying boat, he led a formation of forty-eight planes from San Diego Bay southward along the Mexican coast and across Nicaraguan jungle to a safe landing at Coco Solo—the largest group of planes ever to fly 3,000 miles. Then Mitscher ordered them back into the air, this time to San Juan. A week later, they were off on another cruise.

By June, 1939, Mitscher was back at his old stand at the Bureau of Aeronautics. The atmosphere had changed. Europe was on the verge of war. President Roosevelt, in his message to Congress in 1938, had asked for a 20 per cent increase in naval strength. The Bureau of Aeronautics was no longer a tatterdemalion organization; it grew each day. After the long years in planning and flight divisions, Mitscher returned as assistant chief of the Bureau.

In early September, after Hitler drove into Poland, Roosevelt declared a limited emergency and the Navy moved quickly for ships, personnel, and aircraft. A few days after the proclamation, Rear Admiral Johnson had planes flying neutrality patrols over the ocean. Mitscher concentrated upon procuring aircraft and upon the health of the industry that would have to provide them. Personnel would be useless without the planes. The assistant chief's job, one of vital importance in those last hours before the war, placed him deep in administrative matters. It was a tiring period.

In August, a stocky reserve commander, Luis de Florez reported to the Bureau. He had invented many oil-cracking processes and was widely recognized throughout the petroleum industry. Mitscher, who had met him during World War I, often described him as "that crazy inventor." He had never known another man like him.

One of the ablest engineers in the world, de Florez had flown airplanes when Mitscher was still on gunboats. In 1912, as an M.I.T. student, he had written a scholarly thesis on aviation, and that same year he learned to fly. A volatile man, full of new ideas, he observed Navy regulations only until they interfered with his own schemes.

Mitscher gasped when de Florez said, quite sincerely, "Let's call ten thousand engineers into the Navy." His thinking was on the scale of Niagara Falls and Hoover Dam, in terms of thousands of planes instead of hundreds.

He was speechless when he learned de Florez had invaded the solemn Bureau of Naval Personnel and called upon them to bring the horde of engineers into active duty, more than the Navy had uniformed in over a hundred and fifty years of existence. But he realized that the "crazy inventor" had solid ideas, and supported him.

"But you've got to do things the Navy way, Luis," Mitscher reminded him.

De Florez tried and couldn't. Mitscher sent him on ten days' leave, hoping that a period of reflection would change his tape-cutting tactics. De Florez couldn't change. When pressures became hot, and heavily braided admirals up the line showed annoyance, Mitscher moved his office down the street, out of the Navy Department. But never out of the Navy. De Florez was too valuable and Mitscher knew it. Mitscher's early faith in de Florez later paid large dividends.

Even though war was imminent the feeling of skepticism toward the role of naval aviation—as an untried weapon—still persisted in many quarters. World War I had not proved anything; surface gunnery had been fighting naval wars for centuries. A way of life, like the Navy, is not changed overnight.

A new draft of the Operating Force Plan, which described the missions of various elements of the fleet, was being prepared. In this plan, the flying element had always been listed as the "Naval Aeronautical Organization." Mitscher saw the first draft and noticed that the title had been changed. He interpreted this as an attempt to eliminate the distinction of naval aviation.

When he was told that Admiral Harold Stark, Commander in Chief, United States Fleet, had ordered the change, Mitscher refused to believe it. It seemed impossible that, on the eve of war, the turret gun would still dominate Navy thinking. However, Mitscher was extremely jealous of the advance of naval aviation and brooked no minimizing of its importance, no matter the intent.

Some of his friends remarked that he seemed unusually tired during this period. One explanation was the deluge of work that combat preparations had sent into the Bureau. More important, probably, was the fact that he was a seagoing aviator, unhappy out of his element. In early May, he received a promise of commanding the U.S.S. *Hornet*, being finished at Newport News, Virginia. The carrier *Hornet* was the seventh ship so named. The first was a sloop, mounting ten nine-pound cannon. *Hornet* No. 7 lived the shortest, most illustrious life of them all.[1]

He came aboard in early July as chipping hammers still pounded at rough welds, and she was still showing red lead,

[1] An eighth *Hornet* was launched in 1943.

amid the confusion that could be expected in any fitting-out period. After taking several turns around her, he went on a month's leave, the longest rest of his entire career. The Mitschers lolled on the Virginia Beach sands, and for the first time, he didn't seem particularly sensitive about exposing the high-hued tattoo. He shook off the Bureau of Aeronautics pallor, played golf and bridge, and enjoyed himself, then reported to his ship.

She was green, with a green crew, not a novelty in the Navy in 1941. A majority of her junior officers had never seen a carrier, much less steamed past a sea buoy in one. Under a warm October sun, with four thousand spectators looking on, Navy Secretary Frank Knox welcomed the *Hornet* into the fleet. November was hectic as Mitscher readied her for sea, and a shakedown cruise.

George R. Henderson, the *Hornet*'s executive officer, was a graduate of Mitscher's command in the *Wright*, and best known for his work in seaplanes, in which he held nine world records. He had also had flattop experience in the *Lexington* and the *Langley* and had been with Mitscher on the transpacific hop. Like Mel Pride, Henderson had come into the Regular Navy from the reserve during World War I. Mitscher had taken him aboard the *Wright* as navigator after he was refused that job on the *Yorktown*.

The *Yorktown*'s executive officer had said, "I don't think Henderson has the background. He came in through the Naval Reserve."

Mitscher overheard the remark and immediately sent for Henderson, saying, "I'm taking command of the *Wright*. I want you to be my exec." While he was interested in Henderson, he was as much interested in rebuking the *Yorktown* officer.

But Mitscher had never been particularly concerned with a man's background if he could produce, and he usually chose men who could. Apollo Soucek, the *Hornet*'s air officer, was also a record breaker. In 1930, Soucek went to 43,166 feet to set a new world altitude mark for land planes; he'd flown from the decks of the *Saratoga*, the *Lexington*, and the *Langley*. Youngest of Mitscher's key men on the *Hornet* was a forty-year-old Tennessean, the navigator. Frank Akers, an electronics specialist, was the first pilot to make a blind instrument landing aboard a carrier. Mitscher's varsity team did not lack in talent or experience. All the *Hornet*'s principal officers later reached flag rank. The *Hornet*'s main battery, of course, was her air power. The planes and pilots assigned to her made up Air Group Eight, consisting of four squadrons of special-purpose planes, each with specially trained pilots. Under the air-group commander, Stanhope C. Ring, was a squadron of fighters commanded by Lieutenant Commander Patrick Mitchell, VF-8, commonly called "Fighting Eight"; a squadron of dive bombers led by Lieutenant Commander Robert R. Johnson, VB-8 ("Bombing Eight"); a squadron of scouts led by Lieutenant Commander Walter Rodee, VSB-8 ("Scouting Eight"); and a squadron of torpedo planes led by Lieutenant Commander John C. Waldron, VT-8 ("Torpedo Eight"). There were seventy-seven planes in all.

By the first week in December, 1941, the *Hornet*, inside and out, was beginning to take form and personality. During the frequent wardroom conferences, Mitscher avoided criticism of the departments that reported slow progress. Instead, he looked long and quizzically at the officers in charge.

"It was worse than a reprimand," Akers said later.

On Sundays, with the ships swinging at anchor in Hampton Roads, tied along the piers at the naval base, or clustered in Portsmouth's Navy yard, Mitscher usually devoted himself to golf. He shot in the low nineties, occasionally as low as eighty-eight. The Mitschers and the Hendersons were on the course at the Norfolk Yacht Club early on December 7. The morning was brisk, but pleasant, and Mitscher shot his steady game into the low nineties. About noon, they came off the greens.

They were lunching in the club when an ensign, his face white and drawn, walked up to the table. The ensign had been sent by Soucek, who was senior duty officer on the *Hornet* that day, and had an envelope in his hand. Mitscher opened it and read the note from Soucek.

"Pearl Harbor has been bombed; we're at war with Japan," Mitscher said, and motioned for the check.

PART TWO

⚓ ⚓
⚓

From Tokyo to the Solomons

CHAPTER

⚓ 15 ⚓

Hornet

ON DECEMBER 8, as the smoke thinned over Oahu, and the wreckage of the fleet was exposed, it became apparent that little but the aircraft carriers stood between Hawaii and the Japanese warships sailing each tide from Sasebo and Yokosuka. The *Enterprise* and the *Lexington* were at sea; the *Saratoga*, at San Diego; the escort carrier *Long Island* was in Bermuda; the *Hornet* was at Norfolk; the *Ranger*, the *Yorktown* and the *Wasp* also were in Atlantic waters. Keels for ten more had been laid but it would be months before launching and more months before they would be ready for service.

Mitscher had REMEMBER PEARL HARBOR painted in huge block letters on the *Hornet*'s stack, and at daybreak on December 27, she stood out to sea, following the curling white wakes of the *North Carolina* and the *Washington*. Reaching the Gulf of Mexico, Mitscher parted company with the battleships and commenced shakedown, testing everyone and everything from the whistle to his nerves. There were engine and gunnery trials, and constant launching and landing of aircraft. The *Hornet* was operated at full pace even on Sunday mornings, a period usually reserved for church except under actual combat conditions. Mitscher would send down regrets to Chaplain Edward Harp, requesting divine services be canceled, and then order planes launched.

One afternoon during the shakedown an incident took place which was not extraordinary in carrier operations, but which caused Mitscher to demonstrate his attitude toward his men—and toward the work of command. Flight operations were under way. The *Hornet* scudded along with over 35 knots of wind over her flight deck. One by one planes took the landing signal officer's cut and came to a twanging, jolting halt. As always, Mitscher watched each landing closely. One young pilot in the dive-bomber squadron had taken three successive wave-offs.

Finally, Mitscher stepped toward Apollo Soucek. "Who is that?"

"That's Mr. Gee, Captain." Gee was twenty-one-year-old Ensign Roy Gee. Soucek remembers that Mitscher gave him a sour look and turned his attention again to the noisy flight deck. Gee took two more wave-offs. By then, all the other planes were aboard, and Soucek was beginning to sweat. Mitscher was obviously getting angrier by the minute. The *Hornet* was being delayed. Soucek knew it was not a case of incompetence, for Gee had made thirty carrier landings. After the seventh wave-off, Mitscher stalked over to Soucek's platform.

"Commander Soucek," he said harshly, "what is the matter with that man? If he ever gets aboard, I want to see him."

Finally, on either the ninth or tenth approach, Gee went straight into the groove, at perfect height, took the cut, and made a perfect landing. The *Hornet* hauled around on her base course, and Soucek ordered Gee to report to Mitscher. According to Soucek, the conversation was brief. "Can't you fly?" Mitscher asked.

"I won't do it again, Captain."

"You're damned right you won't do it again," Mitscher exploded. "At least, not on my ship. You're not even going to fly off this ship again."

It was the first time Soucek had ever heard Mitscher raise his voice; he had never seen him in such a state. But several mornings later, at the close of a conversation about another matter, Mitscher asked Soucek, "Is that young Mr. Gee still grounded?"

"Yes, he is."

Mitscher looked out from under the bushy brows. "Don't you think he's had enough?"

"Captain, we've been barking a lot. It's time to bite. If you let him fly, it's no punishment. That goes for the rest of these pilots, too."

The next day, Mitscher again mentioned Gee's case, and Soucek again advised that punishment not be shortened. On the fifth day, when the carrier was preparing to go north, Mitscher said to Soucek, "He's had enough. Put him back on flying status."

Soucek had guessed all along that Mitscher would campaign for Gee's flying freedom, and Gee eventually rejoined his squadron.

On the *Hornet,* as on the *Wright,* Mitscher was gently criticized for a too lenient approach in handling his men. Although at Captain's Mast he often served out brig and bread and water to the older hands, he understood the problems of a new sailor. He frequently eased punishment because of extreme youth.

"Most of these men never saw a ship two months ago. It's an easy way to break their spirit," he told Henderson.

At dusk of the final day of January, 1942, Mitscher had Thimble Shoals Light, at the entrance to Norfolk harbor, safely abeam; he anchored in Hampton Roads to await the arrival of Captain Donald B. Duncan, from Admiral King's staff. He had been alerted that Duncan was on the way but had no idea what King's representative, a veteran naval aviator, wanted to discuss. Duncan was received aboard on the afternoon of February 1. A brisk, all-business officer, he went immediately to his subject.

"Can you put a loaded B-25 in the air on a normal deck run?" he asked.

"How many B-25's on deck?" Mitscher wanted to know.

"Fifteen."

Mitscher made a rapid calculation on the *Hornet*'s flight-deck spotting board, a scale replica of the ship's flight deck. Henderson peered over his shoulder as he worked out plane positions.

"Yes, it can be done," Mitscher said finally.

He didn't question Duncan, at the time, as to why an Army bomber would be operating from a carrier.

"Good," said Duncan, "I'm putting two aboard for a test launching tomorrow."

The *Hornet*'s log for February 2, 1942, records, without indicating the nature of her mission, that at 0536 fires were lit under Number 6 boiler and by 0900 she was ready for sea. The two bombers were aboard. Mitscher ordered one to be spotted well aft; another forward, in the actual spot where the first plane of the contemplated fifteen would have to be.

As the *Hornet* steamed out, a light snow began to fall. A pair of destroyers, the *H. P. Jones* and the *Ludlow* were ahead, wide-angled on each bow. Submarine danger was always present off Norfolk, but the *Hornet*'s 22 knots made her a difficult target.

The largest Navy planes to operate from a carrier had a wingspan of 40 feet; the two Army bombers spotted on the deck had spans of 67 feet and were 53 feet long. They normally required 1,200 to 1,500 feet of runway for the take-off. *Hornet*'s deck was 780 feet long, and the bombers could use a little more than half that space to get airborne. Duncan had already concluded that it could be done, but he wanted Mitscher's verification, and he wanted to see the planes actually launched.

At about 1300, they stood bundled up in foul-weather gear on the port wing of the bridge. Mitscher ordered flight quarters. The engines on the bombers were turning up, and he swung the *Hornet* head on into the raw, wet wind; the destroyers maneuvered into plane-guard positions to effect rescue if the aircraft faltered.

The first B-25 sped down the deck and lifted easily into the air with space to spare. Mitscher glanced at Duncan and smiled. Their calculations had been correct. As the second test was hurried along, there was a sudden interlude. A lookout reported a submarine; a thin spire had been sighted breaking through the dirty gray water. Mitscher suspended flight operations and turned the *Hornet*, opening fire with his five-inch stern guns. The *Jones* and the *Ludlow* plunged toward the wavering object, hurling depth charges. Then the *Ludlow* signaled: "Submarine is a sunken merchant ship."

Mitscher laughed. "Very realistic drill," he said to navigator Frank Akers. "Send them a 'well done.'"

The second B-25 was launched at 1530, and the *Hornet* steamed back to port. Duncan was now satisfied that the bombers could take off from the *Hornet*'s deck. He left for Washington to report his findings.

Somewhat puzzled, Mitscher, Henderson, Soucek, and Akers discussed the odd circumstances of Duncan's visit. Duncan had said the tests were being run to determine the take-off capabilities of a B-25. That could have been done ashore. Also, Duncan had allowed space for at least fifteen bombers. If the *Hornet* were to be used to transport bombers to an outlying Army Air Force base there would be no need for launching procedures. Cranes could transfer the planes to the shore more easily. Mitscher decided that the *Hornet* was about to be used for an extremely interesting mission, certainly one involving the B-25's. He wouldn't hazard a guess on the target.

"The less you know, the better," he told his staff, but he was annoyed that he had not been taken into Duncan's confidence. However, the readiness to carry out orders unquestioningly was strongly ingrained in him, and the annoyance was only passing. That he remained curious was obvious to his officers.

Less than a dozen men in the United States knew of the plan, conceived by submariner Navy Captain Francis Low, to bomb Tokyo. Admiral King and General Arnold, Chief of the Army Air Corps, had received White House agreement for it. The selection of the *Hornet* to deliver fifteen bombers to within four hundred miles of the Japanese coast had been made for two reasons—her immediate availability, and Ernest King's belief that Mitscher, if it was humanly possible, would get the Army planes safely to the take-off point and launch them properly.

Without the slightest knowledge of the plan, Mitscher was ordered to be ready to sail on about March 1. His orders routed him through the Panama Canal to San Diego, thence to the combat zone and into the operational control of Admiral Chester Nimitz, Commander in Chief, Pacific. Then for thirty days he fretted, while last-minute repairs and modifications were made.

CHAPTER

⚓ 16 ⚓

Doolittle's Raiders

MEANWHILE, at Pensacola, Lieutenant Henry L. Miller, a Navy carrier-pilot instructor, was handed orders for temporary duty at nearby Eglin Field. He was told to train Army pilots to take off in the least possible distance, to simulate carrier take-offs with B-25's. Miller too was puzzled.

Among his students was Lieutenant Colonel James Doolittle, and Miller's training diary records Doolittle's attempts at mastering the short-runway procedures. The difficulties are reflected by the mistakes he made in a typical session in Plane No. 2266: on the first take-off—a bad start, jerky procedures; on the second take-off—the nose up and down twice; on the third take-off—another bad start, the nose wheel cocked. Even such an experienced pilot as Jimmy Doolittle found the Navy brand of flying a problem. Finally, Miller noted: "Procedure O.K. He's got the dope."

If Doolittle, one of the world's truly great fliers, was having difficulty, the other pilots, the youngsters with perhaps one fiftieth of his experience, were having even more. They'd been accustomed to a mile of runway. In the end, however, they too mastered the new technique. Meanwhile, Mitscher was at sea, driving the *Hornet* westward, unaware of the strange enterprise being conducted at Eglin. Just before midnight on March 3, the Assistant Secretary of the Navy for Air, Artemus L. Gates, a World War I Navy pilot, had boarded the *Hornet*. With him was Captain Luis de Florez.

De Florez was all over the *Hornet,* investigating everything he saw. He roamed through the engine rooms and crawled into every machinery space; one day, dashing up a ladder, he slammed into Mitscher. De Florez drew aside and apologized.

"Luis," Mitscher said, "can't you ever light?"

But Mitscher was delighted that de Florez was along. Luis was one of the few men who completely fascinated him. De Florez wanted to fly off the *Hornet*'s deck in a torpedo bomber and got permission from Lieutenant Commander John Waldron, skipper of Torpedo Eight. It did not occur to him to ask Mitscher. Waldron gladly sent him aloft, but on landing the plane crashed into a safety barrier and de Florez received a nasty bump on his forehead.

Gates and de Florez got off at Panama. At San Diego, the *Hornet* shuttled in and out of port, qualifying additional pilots. At the end of the first day's qualification runs, Mitscher was dismayed. Three youngsters had crashed attempting to get aboard; the *Hornet*'s flight deck was scorched from burning gasoline. One of the pilots had piled up a few feet away from the island. Then a visitor arrived to take his thoughts off the green pilots. He was Captain Duncan.

The door to Mitscher's cabin was locked. "Pete, you're going to take Jimmy Doolittle and fifteen Army bombers to hit Tokyo."

All Mitscher said was: "That's fine."

The plan unfolded. On March 31, the *Hornet* docked at the naval air station at Alameda, across the bay from San Francisco. The channel was not completely dredged and Mitscher slid her through mud to reach the pier. Sixteen B-25's, just in from Sacramento, were hoisted aboard. Whenever he could, Mitscher assisted shipboard rumors that the bombers were being transported to Pearl Harbor.

In Washington, Admiral King wrote a personal message, dated March 31: "I hope and expect that the first war operation of the *Hornet* will be a success. I am confident that it will be in so far as her officers and crew—under your able leadership —can make it so. Good luck and good hunting."

Thursday, April 2, at 1018, the *Hornet,* in company with the cruisers *Nashville* and *Vincennes,* the oiler *Cimarron,* and the ships of Destroyer Division Twenty-two, slipped through the Golden Gate, outbound. The bombers made a ridiculous pattern on her flight deck—sixteen albatrosses perched on a soapbox. Their wings hung over the *Hornet's* sides; her own planes were below in the hangar deck. When the mist hid the coast of California, Mitscher picked up the microphone of the ship's speaker system. His announcement was concise.

"This ship will carry the Army bombers to the coast of Japan for the bombing of Tokyo."

There was stunned silence, then the *Hornet* reverberated with cheers. In his Action Report, Mitscher said, "Morale reached a high peak." The *Hornet's* blinker light flickered the message to all ships in the group.

Lieutenant Henry Miller was on board to make a demonstration flight with the sixteenth B-25, to prove to the Army pilots that it *was* possible to fly off 31,000 pounds in less than 500 feet. Up on the flight deck, he and Doolittle studied the lashed-down planes. Scanning the clear portion of the deck, Doolittle said, "It looks awfully small to me."

"This'll be a cinch, Colonel," said Miller. He pointed to a tool box on the deck about 150 feet out ahead of the first bomber. "That's where I used to take off in fighters," he said.

Later, Mitscher told Miller he didn't know whether he could give him enough wind for the proposed demonstration flight that afternoon.

"We've got plenty of wind, Captain," answered Miller. About 30 knots was being clocked. "We won't have any bombs and it'll be lighter than the other planes. Why, I taught these guys how to take off in 300 feet and I'll have about 395 feet to take this one off."

"Well, hell, then, we'll take this extra plane!"

"Captain, will you let me off at the next mail buoy?" asked Miller, who had been chasing around the country for weeks, mostly on telephonic orders. The Navy didn't know his whereabouts half the time. In addition, he'd come aboard with little more than toothpaste and shaving cream.

Then Mitscher requested Doolittle and Soucek to come to the bridge and suggested keeping the extra plane for the Tokyo mission. Doolittle was skeptical. He thought a demonstration might give his pilots a needed morale boost. There would be no doubts in their minds if they saw Miller actually take off.

Mitscher said, "They've got to fly them all off anyway, no matter whether this one takes off or not. This way, you've got an extra plane."

"Suits me," said Doolittle, and Soucek nodded his approval. The plane stayed aboard, and several weeks later, Arnold, King, and others in the know were surprised to learn that sixteen planes bombed Tokyo.

The operations order, issued by Nimitz, said simply: "Bomb Tokyo area with Army aircraft now aboard the *Hornet*, using high explosive and incendiary bombs. Select military objectives as practicable. Direct bombers to proceed to friendly territory in China after the bombing."

Admiral Halsey was commander of the task force; Rear Admiral Raymond Spruance commanded the supporting ships. Until Doolittle was airborne, the Navy was in command. If the task group was attacked, the decision on the strike would be up to Mitscher. He could shove the B-25's over the side if he so desired.

Mitscher relinquished his bunk and cabin to Doolittle; his mess to the Army pilots. Actually he lived in his sea cabin on the bridge level in any case. Doolittle spent much time on the bridge chatting with the man the Navy had chosen to take him out. They got along well.

On April 13, Task Force 16, with Halsey padding around the bridge of the *Enterprise*, poked above the horizon, and the two forces welded into one. The *Enterprise* provided air cover (CAP) and search facilities for the *Hornet*, which could not launch its own planes. The task force proceeded slowly, the destroyers unable to maintain speed in the heavy seas; the oilers, straining to churn up 16 knots, also retarded the pace.

Occasional squalls beat the seas into long, spiraling humps. Sometimes the *Hornet* rose and fell two hundred feet. Japanese medals, formerly the property of shipyard workers and some of the *Hornet* sailors, were attached to the bombs. A note on one said: "I don't want to set the world on fire—just Tokyo." Mitscher pinned a pompous medal on a five hundred pounder. He was optimistic about the mission. As the *Hornet* toiled toward the range circle, Chaplain Harp asked, "How are we going to make out on this deal?"

Mitscher replied confidently, "The mission has to be successful. The whole war does. Japan is such a young nation technically. They can't compete with us in technical know-how. Every way, we have the edge on them." Later, there were times of death and destruction when such words seemed hollow, but Mitscher never changed his estimate.

The bombers were respotted on the *Hornet*'s deck on April 16 with the tail of the last plane hanging over the ship's stern ramp. On April 17 the ships' fuel tanks were topped off. The oilers and destroyers were detached and left behind, while

Hornet, Enterprise, and the cruisers began the high-speed run to the launching point.

On the morning of April 18, Mitscher was awakened just after 0300. The radar had picked up unidentified targets, and he sent the ship to general quarters at 0411. Doolittle raced to the bridge. The targets, "objects" they were called, went their way; so did the task force, a trifle jittery now. At daylight the *Enterprise* launched search planes. Ensign J. Q. Roberts sighted an enemy patrol vessel.

The operation cocked itself automatically. The Navy couldn't take the Army any closer to Japan. Doolittle conferred with Mitscher and the cruiser *Nashville* steamed out to sink the hapless patrol ship. Admiral Halsey, from his bridge on the *Enterprise,* signaled: LAUNCH PLANES X TO COLONEL DOOLITTLE AND HIS GALLANT COMMAND GOOD LUCK AND GOD BLESS YOU.

Mitscher aimed the *Hornet* into the 18-knot wind; *Hornet*'s speed was 22, making 40 knots over the deck to launch the aircraft. Spume lashed angrily over the ship. Doolittle waved good-by. Bending into the man-made gale, Mitscher saluted him, and Apollo Soucek, drenched from spray, clothes plastered against his body, got on the bull horn to direct them. The launching officer twirled his checkered flag over his head, imploring Doolittle to rev up faster, faster, faster.

As the engines howled, the flag flashed down, and Doolittle dropped his feet off the brakes. The B-25 surged down the deck. The others followed at 3.9-minute intervals. Mitscher was afraid of a crash and was amazed that they all got off safely. As each plane got the flag-drop, Mitscher's thin shoulders, and his arms, instinctively worked. He still punished himself by "flying" every aircraft on a carrier take-off.

At 0920, with the last bomber away, the ships turned to rejoin the rest of the task force. Mitscher ordered his own air group spotted for action in case the enemy should attempt to retaliate. By 1100, word was received of the Tokyo raid, and *Hornet* again rang with cheers. Mitscher noted, however, that after the news of the success, "a majority of the men and officers were quite surprised no further action was contemplated." The Doolittle launching was over, and Mitscher was anxious to get on with a Navy job. In *Hornet*'s Action Report to Commander in Chief, Pacific, he wrote: "It is believed that attacks should be made as frequently as possible, or raiding missions, to keep up morale and action exhilaration."

Tactically, he urged the use of submarines in the event of another such raid and suggested sending U-boats ahead of the raiding task force to clear sea lanes of enemy vessels that might warn of the attack. Today radar picket submarines are deployed in this manner.

Later, there were charges that the Navy endangered the success of the mission by forcing Doolittle's launching before the selected take-off point was reached. To these criticisms, Mitscher answered: "We had to launch them. We weren't where we wanted to be. We gave them extra gas. It was all a calculated risk. We couldn't risk them [the carriers] after the fishing boats had been spotted."

To critics of the entire mission, some of whom believed it to be fruitless, Mitscher answered: ". . . it paid big dividends since it threw the islands into a panic and forced them to keep a large defense force at home, instead of sending them as intended to support the proposed invasion of Australia."

Hornet returned to Pearl Harbor on April 25, her first war mission accomplished. To inquisitive shipyard workers, she had simply been out on a routine war cruise. Such was the secrecy that her log book makes no mention of the B-25 trials or of the Army fliers being aboard until the exact minute of launching. President Roosevelt announced that the Doolittle planes had taken off from "Shangri-La." Months later, due to security leaks in Australia, the public learned, as did Frances Mitscher, that the carrier *Hornet* was Shangri-La.

Action in the Solomons area, bloody and indecisive, had been mounting, and intelligence warned of heavy Japanese forces in the Coral Sea. The *Hornet* sailed again, headed for a battle that was already hot. It was the first major naval engagement in which no shots were exchanged by surface vessels. But Mitscher missed it. It was joined before the *Hornet* could reach the Coral Sea. The carriers *Lexington* and *Yorktown* took on the Japanese without her. The *Lexington*, smoking, holed and shattered, was so badly damaged she had to be destroyed by our own forces, on May 8. The Japanese lost the carrier *Shoho* and suffered severe damage to other units. Their advance southward was checked for the time being.

Hornet steamed back to Pearl Harbor, still untested in conflict, and Mitscher was informed he had been selected for rear admiral. It was thirty-eight years since he first took a Navy oath. He accepted flag rank on May 31, 1942, and his blue, two-star insignia fluttered from a *Hornet* halyard.

Except under rare circumstances, such as these, a rear admiral does not command a ship. He commands groups or types or units of ships or sometimes planes or bases. However, *Hornet*'s new prospective commanding officer, Charles Perry Mason, had not had sufficient time to be "shaken down." So Mitscher, as an admiral, sailed in command of the *Hornet*. Mason was, of course, an intensely interested observer. He reminded Mitscher, "Take good care of her. This is my ship."

The destination was the sea and sky around Midway Island, 1,080 miles from Honolulu, where another major battle was shaping.

C H A P T E R

⚓ 17 ⚓

Carrier Operations

FLIGHT-DECK operations never lost their fascination for Mitscher. In talking about them, he was unusually mellow, often flowery. He once described an aircraft carrier as the "most exciting apparatus on earth." The operations of a carrier have been likened to a circus performance and to the dance because of the grace and co-ordination demanded. In fact, the activity of the plane handlers on the flight deck is often termed a "ballet."

The sounding of flight quarters on a big carrier casts a spell that seems never to lose its power in repetition. Pilots who are not manning planes, or required to be in the ready rooms, are often to be found lining the island railings, "flying" each plane off and sweating out each landing as incoming aircraft hurtle into the imaginary groove. Even greenhorns twitch and lean with "body english," as if playing a gigantic pinball machine, as the planes seek to get aboard safely.

Like any other ship, however, everything reduces to a routine, although a carrier's routine is usually more active than that of any other type of combat ship and is more apt to be interrupted by the unexpected.

A typical plan of the day in combat might include:

0400: Reveille for Air Department
0430: Launch CAP (combat air patrol)
0500: Flight quarters for pilots and aircrewmen
0600: Launch Flight One (fighters)
      Launch Flight Two (bombing strike)
0800: Launch Flight Three (target air observer—CAG)
0900: Recover Flights One and Two
0930: Recover CAP
1100: Launch Flight Four (photographic mission)
1200: Launch Flight Five (bombing strike)

And so on until dusk. As the war stretched out, and more carriers became available, duties were divided so that in each task group, carriers rotated combat-air-patrol (fighter-cover) duty; or, when such specialization became possible, night-fighter carriers would furnish all-night fighter cover, and rest during daylight.

In World War II, there were certain phrases, identifications, and trade words peculiar to carrier aviation. Some of them still exist. The *Hornet*, for instance, carried an air group composed of squadrons of VF—fighters, VB—bombers, VSB—scout bombers, and VT—torpedo planes. Just as the officer of the deck was called the OD, many other important jobs were reduced to the ignominy of initials. CAP meant, and still means, "combat air patrol"; CAG stands for "Commander, Air Group"; IFF denotes "identification, friend or foe"; TBS, the high-frequency short-range radio system used for "talk between ships." An unidentified or enemy plane is always a "bogey"—pronounced *beau-ghee*. The bogey is never "shot down"—it is unceremoniously "splashed." "Tally-ho" warbling out of the combat-information-center (CIC) loudspeaker or in the earphones of the fighter-director officer (FDO) meant that our intercepting fighter planes had sighted the enemy.

It was mumbo-jumbo to the beginner, but in practice it was a simple and effective shorthand.

The *Hornet* did not have a flight-deck catapult so all planes were flown off. They moved, one by one, to a spot usually abreast the island structure, locked brakes, applied full power, and then when the officer standing on the deck forward of the wingtip gave the go-ahead signal, the pilot released his brakes and roared down the deck into a 35-knot wind created by a combination of the natural wind and the ship's forward motion, and took off before reaching the end of the deck. Another plane would follow in fifteen or twenty seconds.

Upon returning to his ship, the pilot first entered the lower landing circle, a pattern of aircraft circling to make an approach. When he started on the down-wind leg on a course parallel and opposite to that of the carrier, he flew at about 250 feet altitude. Once abeam, the pilot gradually turned into the wind and on the carrier's heading. When the plane was about 100 yards astern and about 20 to 30 feet above the flight deck, flying at not more than 10 knots above stalling speed, with the aircraft nosed up, the landing signal officer (LSO) took over to direct the pilot aboard by visual signal or, if his approach was faulty, give him a wave-off. The timing of the whole sequence, air to ship, or ship to air, was split-second, and the pilot was but one among a hundred or more who made it work.

CHAPTER

⚓ 18 ⚓

Air Group Eight

"In accordance with Commander in Chief Pacific Operation Plan 29–42, the Hornet got underway from Pearl Harbor, 28 May 1942, recovering the Air Group at sea, at 1630, the same afternoon," begins the *Hornet*'s Action Report for the Battle of Midway. As was usual, her aircraft had been stationed ashore when the ship was in port. They flew out to roost when she was a short time out of Pearl Harbor. Minutes after the planes were aboard, the speaker system blared throughout the ship:

"This is the captain. We are going to intercept a Jap attack on Midway."

That settled any doubts in the minds of the *Hornet* pilots. Not all of Torpedo Eight was aboard. Six new Grumman Avengers, part of VT-8, were based on Midway. The *Hornet* pilots had been training for months, long before the ship got her final coat of paint, but not one was blooded. Their total average flying hours were somewhere around 285 each. Routine training was conducted enroute, and most of the aircraft, in addition to combat air patrol, were scheduled for daily exercises. The force steamed on to a rendezvous with Rear Admiral Frank Jack Fletcher's Task Force 17.

Mitscher bantered with his officers and squadron commanders. He was in high spirits. There was horseplay and he joined in. Sam Osterlough, the ship's doctor, had brought aboard a crate of fresh grapefruit at Pearl Harbor, and kept the fruit locked up in his sick-bay refrigerator. Chaplain Harp and Waldron connived to steal it and Harp made a clean getaway during GQ one day. But Osterlough suspected and put him on report. Mitscher convened a mock trial, taking great delight in calling the chaplain's attention to the ways of the wicked.

But beneath the banter there was uncertainty as each turn of the screw brought them nearer Admiral Nagumo's enemy carriers. On June 1, Mitscher wrote out a message for Commander Henderson to read over the bull horn: "The enemy are approaching for an attempt to seize Midway. This attack will probably be accompanied by a feint at western Alaska. We are going to prevent them from taking Midway, if possible. Be ready and keep on the alert. Let's get a few more yellowtails." Although some skippers, through oversight or intent, kept their crews in suspense, Mitscher tried to inform every man of what might be hanging beneath the next cloud.

The next day, at 1400, the *Hornet* task force kept its rendezvous with the *Yorktown* northeast of Midway. Admiral Fletcher assumed tactical command of the entire American defensive force, but Nimitz, back in Pearl Harbor, still called the strategical signals. Halsey was ill, and Rear Admiral Raymond Spruance had taken over Task Force 16, in which the *Hornet* rode.

As the hours passed and the ships hid under the low overcast of a weather front, guns were checked and aircraft engines tuned. Mitscher, who had remained on the bridge since leaving Pearl Harbor except for cat naps in his sea cabin, pored over charts and all but memorized each word of each important dispatch. Cool, steady Walter Rodee talked to his scouts; Waldron drilled his pilots on torpedo tactics; flyers played poker, or drowsed in the ready rooms. Above the task force, CAP orbited endlessly.

Jack Waldron, who never called a torpedo by its proper name, preferring such affectionate names as "weenie" or "pickle," was a skinny, savage professional. He had given a mimeographed message to each of his torpedo pilots:

> Just a word to let you know I feel we are all ready. We have had a very short time to train and we have worked under the most severe difficulties. But we have truly done the best humanly possible. I actually believe that under these conditions we are the best in the world. My greatest hope is that we encounter a favorable tactical situation, but if we don't, and the worst comes to worst, I want each of us to do his utmost to destroy our enemies. If there is only one plane left to make a final run in, I want that man to go in and get a hit. May God be with us all. Good luck, happy landings and give 'em hell.[1]

That morning, June 3, the pilots and air crews were up at 0100 for breakfast and briefings. Mitscher slept for perhaps a half hour during the night; most of the time he stayed on the wing of the bridge, staring out into the night, his thin jacket drawn close around his neck against the chill air.

What was on his mind? We can only guess. Certainly he realized what the dawn would bring to the pilots. Coral Sea had been an air fight. But he was too old, his reflexes too stiff, to slug it out personally with a Zero or drive a torpedo plane so low that it would spin a web of spray before thrusting its missile out. Neither would he be concerned with the over-all strategy or tactics of the battle, for Nimitz, Fletcher, and Spruance would decide that. Mitscher's concern was the *Hornet* and Air Group Eight.

[1] Griffin, Alexander R., *A Ship to Remember* (New York, Howell Soskin, 1943).

Air Group Eight was ready. There was brash, brawling Gus Widhelm, and the nice guy, Stan Ring, and the man who was, in many ways, a reasonable facsimile of Mitscher himself, Jack Waldron; all of them actually knew little about aviation or war. They were going into battle for the first time.

Former Navy pilot Frederick L. Gwynn recalls:

As to what it felt like to be sent into danger as a pilot, I can remember one variation on the theme of admitted fear characterized in World War II. To get off a carrier deck, one does have a lot of mechanical preparation on deck and a never-failing audience, which means that the beginning of every strike involves fulfillment of Walter Mitty dreams. I'd say the actual take-off forced one into some self-confidence and bravado, unlike the infantry situation where no one was watching. Furthermore, as I found when I became a squadron exec, one would rather be sent than do the sending and then have to write the letter home.

Mitscher had done everything he could. From the time the air group had first swarmed aboard off Norfolk in December, he'd overseen their training, advised the squadron commanders, and primed them for battle. Now his job was to carry them in, launch them, vector them to targets, and finally protect his ship so that it would be there when they returned.

CHAPTER

⚓ 19 ⚓

The Battle of Midway

THE wind gauge on the *Hornet*'s island mast floated lazily around to record but 4 knots early on June 4. The sea was flat and still off Midway, and as the horizon turned from gray to pink, CAP sprang off the deck and went up to circle the task force. Mitscher had sent the *Hornet* to GQ an hour before sunrise.

At about 0530, a Catalina flying boat radioed: "Many planes heading Midway." The pitifully inadequate group of Marine, Navy, and Army planes on the tiny island took off to intercept. While the enemy struck at Midway, unaware that an American carrier force was closing them, Nimitz was preparing to spring his trap.

Shortly after 0700, while Army B-17's were unsuccessfully attempting to damage the enemy from 20,000 feet, the *Hornet*'s fighter pilots were called to deck; then the scout bombers were manned. Finally, Waldron's torpedo planes were ready. Hitting fast ships at sea is a job for planes that go in low. Then Mitscher spoke into the bridge microphone: "We intend to launch planes to attack the enemy while their planes are still returning from Midway. We will close to about a hundred miles from the enemy's position."

Ring, Rodee, Johnson, Mitchell, and Waldron ran up to the bridge for final instructions. Waldron told Mitscher he would take the torpedo planes in and get hits. The exact words of the brief conversation did not seem important at the time, but the *Hornet* bridge officers do remember that Mitscher touched the lean, fierce fighter on the shoulder. Then Waldron went below to the flight deck to man his plane with the big ¡torpedo tucked inside. The sharp pop of starting cartridges echoed across the flight deck; then the acrid fumes of exhaust swirled into the wind.

There was a cloud-flecked sky as Soucek gave orders to send the *Hornet*'s stingers off. The fighters, Grumman Wildcats, were first; Rodee's scouts in the Dauntlesses followed; then Johnson's divebombers, also in Dauntlesses; and lastly Waldron's heavy-bellied torpedo planes.

It took almost an hour for the launching and Mitscher bent over the railing, occasionally giving an order, and following each plane off with his eyes. Once the last torpedo plane was airborne, Mitscher was practically out of touch with the fight. Radio silence was maintained. Squadron commanders were in charge, with Stanhope Ring, as senior, over them. Mitscher could not contact, advise, or assist. He would have to wait until they got back to find out what happened.

Last-minute teletype instructions to the *Hornet*'s air group placed the enemy at a distance of 155 miles. The fighters and bombers climbed to 19,000 feet, flying at 125 mph. Waldron stayed below a layer of cumulus clouds, nursing his planes along at 110 mph. They breezed through the morning without knowledge that Admiral Nagumo had changed the course of his carriers and was retiring. When the bombers and fighters reached their supposed position, Nagumo and his carriers were not in sight. Stanhope Ring kept the air group traveling southwest.

But Jack Waldron, down below the blanket of clouds at

1,500 feet, unmindful that his fighter cover was not above, rolled the torpedo squadron northward on a strong hunch. He found Nagumo and the carriers *Hiryu, Akagi, Kaga,* and *Soryu.* What Waldron then did has been called foolhardy, but it was also heroic. He rode his torpedo planes in against the carriers without fighter protection; full into the ack-ack and whirling Zeros, hoping to deliver his weenies and pickles. Waldron presented fifteen solid targets to the Japanese gun gallery. Ensign Gay was shot down and hid beneath a floating seat cushion. He witnessed the Battle of Midway from that bobbing box seat and was picked up later.

The *Hornet*'s bombers and fighters were running low on gas. But planes from the *Enterprise* and the *Yorktown* arrived to convert three of Nagumo's carriers into flotsam. The *Hiryu* sent her planes after the *Yorktown* in retaliation. Meanwhile, back on the *Hornet,* Mitscher stirred about the bridge uneasily. He knew little or nothing of what was going on. Communications had been spotty all morning. Action reports seeped in, but nothing to indicate any decisive combat. Some of the planes had run out of gas and crash landed in Midway's lagoon; others had regassed at Midway. Survivors of the *Hornet*'s snipe hunt banged down on deck to regas. They didn't need to rearm. They hadn't fought. Mitscher pushed on, holding an easterly course at high speed to land his planes. The first wheels hit the deck at 1320. Rodee's scouts and part of Bombing Eight fluttered in. Then they waited for the fighters and for Torpedo Eight.

Ring and Rodee went to the bridge to tell Mitscher they hadn't seen the enemy and knew nothing of Waldron. Then Quillen, the rear gunner in Ensign White's dive bomber, reported that he thought he had heard Waldron's voice on his radio:

What I heard was Johnny One to Johnny Two. I am quite sure it was Lieutenant Commander Waldron's voice as I have heard him on the air a number of times. I also heard him say, Watch those fighters. Also, See that splash. Also, How'm I doing, Dobbs? Also, Attack immediately. Also, I'd give a million to know who did that. . . .

And then there was silence. Thus they died, all except one. Fifteen planes, each with pilot and crewman.

Japanese planes were attacking the *Yorktown*. Soon a column of smoke reached into the northwest sky. Some *Hornet* fighters were over there trying to ward off the blows, and got three Zeros. The *Yorktown* was mortally wounded. One *Yorktown* pilot wobbled toward the *Hornet* and crashed down in a grind of ripping metal, his machine guns peppering the island structure. Minutes later, the officer of the deck reported to Mitscher: five dead and twenty wounded. With Fletcher's Task Force 17 flag burning in the *Yorktown*, Rear Admiral Raymond Spruance took local tactical command. A Japanese submarine finished the *Yorktown* later.

Spruance signaled Mitscher and the *Enterprise* to get the *Hiryu*. Her planes had destroyed the *Yorktown* and could do the same to the *Enterprise* and the *Hornet*. At 1803, Mitscher launched sixteen bombers to join the *Enterprise* striking group. *Enterprise* pilots got there first and laid into the enemy carriers. The *Hornet* bombers circled at 20,000 feet while nine B-17's attempted to bomb the *Hiryu*'s escorting battleships, missing by a wide margin. Then VB-8 pushed over into their dives, releasing bombs at low altitude for hits on a battleship and a heavy cruiser. The *Hornet* had finally drawn blood.

As more action reports drifted in, Mitscher informed the *Hornet* crew, "Four Japanese carriers are afire. Direct hits have been scored on their battleships and cruisers."

It was growing dark, and the *Hornet*, blacked out, soon blended into the night. How could her surviving bombers find the flight deck? Two planes angled toward the task force.

Then others droned up. None of the *Hornet* pilots had qualified in night carrier landings.

"Turn on the truck lights," Mitscher ordered. The dim red
beacons shone out from her masthead but the planes passed
over. Mitscher knew the pilots could not possibly spot her
deck. "Let's give them more light."

Two search beams climbed into the air over the *Hornet;* a
string of lights outlined the flight deck to port.

Henderson said, "Captain, there must be subs here."

"The hell with the subs," Mitscher said, straining to glimpse
the aircraft as they approached and finally landed.

He had thought Stan Ring was lost. Then Ring came up to
the bridge, sweaty and haggard. The surviving pilots gathered
in the wardroom and pantry, happy to be alive, but the joy
was tempered by concern about the still unreported torpedo-
men.

Mitscher ordered Dr. Sam Osterlough to the bridge, and
Sam came up with his pockets bulging and clinking. "How
are they?" Mitscher asked.

"Some are a little shaky."

"Give them each a bottle and see to it personally that they
get to bed."

Osterlough, on the way to deliver his "packages" to the
pilots, stopped by Mitscher's cabin, pulled one of the two-
ounce bottles of brandy out of his pocket, and placed it on
the desk.

By now, it was obvious that Torpedo Eight was not returning. It appeared the *Hornet* had lost at least twenty-five aircraft and almost double that number of pilots and crewmen.
The day's operations had not been good, but the bombers had
partially recouped in the sunset attack. There were five bodies
in readiness for burial from the gun accident. Luck had been
very bad.

As the *Hornet* quieted down, and her crew sprawled out

to sleep for a few hours, Mitscher talked to Henderson on the wing of the bridge. "If we keep operating singly we can lose all the carriers," he said. At flight quarters, each flattop steamed out into the wind with her escorts, sometimes disappearing over the horizon. "That [the destruction of the *Yorktown*] wouldn't have happened if we were operating in a group so CAP could protect the entire force and each ship give support in anti-aircraft fire."

Mitscher's desire for more group operation had been over-ruled several times. It was argued that ships the size of carriers could not be operated in close formation. He brushed aside that argument. "Maybe the *Yorktown* will convince them," he said tiredly to Henderson. Then he went below to the hangar deck, where at 0110 services were held for the victims of the accident.

Meanwhile, Spruance had ordered a retirement to the east instead of maintaining his position or steaming westward. The wisdom of this move will be argued for a long time, since it enabled the remaining Japanese ships to open the distance. In his Action Report Spruance declared he based his decision on lack of information about the enemy and the risk "of a night encounter with possibly superior enemy forces." He thought another enemy carrier might be lurking nearby. However, Mitscher, Henderson recalls, felt that the task force should have steamed westward in pursuit of the Japanese.

On June 5, Mitscher launched twenty-six bombers for a strike against the still burning carriers and battleships. The planes found only oil slicks to mark the major ships but attacked a destroyer leaving the scene. Once again, they roared back over the task force in darkness, and once again, Mitscher lit up the *Hornet*. Out of gas, they sputtered in.

On June 6, search planes fanned out to find the remnants. Running low on gas, Gee landed on the *Enterprise*, and un-aware of his relative inexperience, the *Enterprise* sent him off on a long-range search mission. After a few hours he spied some ripples on the mirrored ocean and went down for a better look. Soon Gee relayed word that two groups of the Japanese fleet had been located. The pilot Mitscher had grounded in January thus vindicated himself completely.

Mitscher launched twenty-six bombers again, along with eight fighters. At 1150, *Hornet* planes attacked two cruisers and a destroyer. The cruisers *Mogami* and *Mikuma* were sunk by dive bombing. A few weeks later, the pilots of *Hornet*'s VB-8 were nicknamed "The Bombing Fools" because of their low-altitude drops.

A little later that day, when the planes had returned and were being rearmed for a second strike, the *Hornet*'s radio intercepted a message from a Japanese admiral saying he was being attacked (by *Enterprise* planes). The *Hornet*'s planes made the second shuttle to the fleeing enemy, and then came home for a rest. The Battle of Midway was over.

It is believed that since early afternoon of June 4, Mitscher, over and above the sound of battle and command decision, thought of little besides Torpedo Eight. Until Ensign Gay was snatched from the sea on June 5, there was still hope that perhaps all fifteen empty chairs in the wardroom would be filled again. Mitscher did not discuss at any length the loss of Torpedo Eight or his own feelings about Waldron until much later.

Frances Mitscher, who now lives alone in a modest little house not too far from the ocean in Coronado, California, said, "Admiral Mitscher was convinced that the squadron commander knew he was going to die. The tragedy of this brought him great personal grief."

In the Action Report to Nimitz, in which he nominated the entire squadron for the Medal of Honor, Mitscher wrote:

Just prior to launching he [Waldron] had reported to the commanding officer for final instructions and had stressed the point that his squadron was well trained and ready and that he would strike his blow at the enemy regardless of consequences. His grim determination to press home an attack against all obstacles, his foreknowledge that there was the possibility that his squadron was doomed to destruction with no chance whatever of returning safely to the carrier, impressed all present with the remarkable devotion to duty and the personal integrity of an officer whose pilots asked only that they be allowed to share in the dangers and disastrous fate sure to follow such an attack.

The report clearly reflects Mitscher's pride and profound admiration. Waldron was his type of man. The references to "devotion to duty" and "personal integrity," character traits which Mitscher held high, were repeated in almost phonographic fashion in other appraisals which he wrote throughout the war.

As Gay's account unfolded, and other data began to clarify the battle, it appeared that neither Waldron nor any of his pilots actually made hits on the carriers. Mitscher scoffed at the idea and for the next three years vainly tried to get the Medal of Honor for the entire squadron, refusing to believe that Torpedo Eight had been needlessly wiped out. When the war was over, a survey committee established that Waldron's squadron had sacrificed themselves without damaging the enemy. Even then, Mitscher declared the medal should have been awarded for the sheer heroic effort of their action. Besides, the torpedo planes diverted the attention of the enemy fighters and allowed the *Enterprise* bombers to come in undetected. The Torpedo Eight pilots were finally granted the Navy Cross posthumously. However, Mitscher took this as a personal defeat and often spoke harsh words about the Washington board that decided combat awards.

At the memorial services for Torpedo Eight and the other *Hornet* dead, held on Sunday morning, June 7, Chaplain Harp (later the Navy's Chief of Chaplains) read Owen Seaman's poem "Victory." Several hours later Mitscher requested a copy, and it remained in his possession until he died.

As the *Hornet* returned to Pearl Harbor, it was evident that Mitscher felt depressed for reasons beyond the loss of the pilots and crewmen. Although he congratulated the crew and announced a "well done" for all hands, he felt that the *Hornet*'s performance had not lived up to his expectations. He also felt that he had personally failed to deliver.

In 1947, a Naval War College strategical and tactical analysis of the Battle of Midway called attention to the *Hornet* air group's failure to sight the enemy fleet and turn north. It said: "The commanding officer should insure that flight leaders are properly briefed." However, Stanhope Ring, later a rear admiral, maintains that Mitscher properly briefed the flight leaders and gave them every scrap of information that was available on the *Hornet* bridge.

Oddly enough, after all the furor of Midway, a pair of binoculars caused excitement as the *Hornet* approached Pearl Harbor. Binoculars were, of course, scarce, well-guarded instruments in that early summer of 1942. During the fighting, a lieutenant had lost his pair on the bridge. The ship was searched thoroughly. Both Frank Akers, custodian of all navigational gear, and Mitscher were worried. When the *Hornet* reached port, and liberty was granted, Naval Intelligence searched all the pawn shops in Honolulu to make certain they had not been slipped ashore. A few days later they were found behind the settee in the chart room.

Akers said, "I think I'll wait a day or two to tell the lieutenant about it. Maybe he'll remember next time not to be so careless."

"No," Mitscher said. "Tell him right away. He's worrying about them. There's no use his worrying when we've got a war to fight."

CHAPTER

⚓ 20 ⚓

Shore-Based

As EARLY as May 16, before the Battle of Midway, Mitscher had learned he had been tapped for shore-based aviation, but he continued to hope he might be sent instead to a carrier task group, where he thought he belonged. However, Nimitz had already made his few task-group assignments, and Mitscher lacked seniority.

So, assuming his new rank of rear admiral, Mitscher reported as Commander, Patrol Wing Two, an administrative outfit with a multitude of chores, based in Hawaii. He definitely thought he had been shelved, one of two known occasions during the war when he decided Washington had abandoned him in a noncombat job. Sometimes, it appeared to his staff that he believed he'd perch on that self-hewn "shelf" for the remainder of the war. At such times, he was unmistakably pessimistic about his future in the Navy.

Part of the blame for the rear-area Hawaii assignment he placed on the *Hornet*'s performance at Midway, although there is little to justify his assumption of responsibility for this. Also, it was another indication to him that he was still not "in grace" with the senior Washington team.

Patrol Wing Two was an unexciting flying-boat organization dug in on Ford Island and at Kaneohe. Mitscher made his headquarters at Kaneohe, about twenty miles east of the tireless salvage operations on the battleships. The paper work was endless and boring, and he eyed the "In" basket ruefully, slighting details for his golf clubs on many afternoons, leaving the wing in the capable hands of his chief of staff, Commander Ring—the Stan Ring of *Hornet*'s air group. Mitscher had pulled Ring ashore with him.

In addition to refilling the patrol-pilot larder in the South Pacific, conducting a daily six-hundred-mile reconnaissance search and an inshore patrol of cruiser-based seaplanes, manning several outlying radio stations—and much more of the same—Mitscher was responsible for a vast chain of living quarters and for managing hotels in Honolulu for fleet recreational purposes.

He became angry when he was shown the nonaviation duties that had been unloaded on the command. According to Henderson, after checking off the piddling housekeeping chores assigned him, he wrote to CINCPAC (Admiral Nimitz, Commander in Chief, Pacific) through COMAIRPAC (Admiral John Towers, Commander Aircraft, Pacific): "To my mind, these are not the functions of a patrol wing." He succeeded in slicing off most of the nonaviation responsibilities, but not without meeting resistance.

He had his own ideas on patrol-squadron operations. He felt patrol squadrons should be highly mobile, versatile units, capable of getting into action quickly and operating with a minimum of supplies in an advanced combat area. First, he consolidated both wings at Kaneohe, where there was more room to operate; then he set about priming the flying boats, Consolidated Vultee's faithful Catalinas—the Black Cats—for combat; then he began prodding Admiral Towers to transfer the planes to the South Pacific.

There, the Solomons battles were raging. Marines had landed on Guadalcanal and were clawing out advances. There was also air fighting, and surface battles were waged almost nightly, some reminiscent of such fine beam-to-beam brawling as took place between the *Bonhomme Richard* and the *Serapis* off Flamborough Head.

Mitscher took a detour before reaching Guadalcanal. On December 23, 1942, he received orders to the South Pacific as Commander, Fleet Air, Noumea, the administrative unit for Halsey's air force, including both shore-based planes and flying boats. He arrived at Ile Nou (Dubouzet Island), about twenty miles from Port Noumea, on the southern tip of New Caledonia, on New Year's Eve.

The South Pacific was a great leveler. During the first week at Ile Nou, he was mistaken for one of the grizzled Navy chiefs who also inhabited the command area. The duty officers in headquarters sent a messenger to awaken a junior officer for a phone call. It was two or three in the morning and the messenger, a young Marine, fouled up his directions and invaded Mitscher's Dallas hut, rapping the sleeping Admiral on the back. Blinking and confused, Mitscher turned over.

"You're wanted on the phone, sir!" said the messenger.

He gazed at the youngster for a few seconds, then muttered, "Be damned if I'm going to answer the phone, private."

The private went back to headquarters, reporting he had been unable to find the officer concerned, but did rout out "a grouchy chief."

"Which tent did you go into?" the OD inquired.

The private pointed. The OD gasped in horror and prepared himself to take a reaming in the morning. But Mitscher, next day, chuckled over the incident, saying that identification with a Navy chief was not dishonorable; observing also that the South Pacific was not, under any circumstances, a place for stuffy admirals.

His method of operation in welding a staff into an efficient team was clearly visible at Ile Nou. Mitscher disliked yes-men, shrinking violets, and garrulousness. He wanted positive people on his staff, and usually eliminated officers who had to qualify their every statement. He preferred idea men, especially those who would contest him when they thought their ideas were better than his own, for though he expected loyalty, it was not to be blind loyalty. His own word for it was "support": Mitscher made it plain he expected his staff to support him—in the office, on the flying field, or in the thatch-roofed officers' clubs, where backbiting was sometimes a sport. And he let it be known he'd go to bat for them. At a conference on the mining of Kahili harbor, still firmly in Japanese hands, Lieutenant Commander John T. Hayward, who had come out with him from Kaneohe, was drawn into heated debate with an admiral on how the mission was to be conducted. Hayward had already made careful plans, and knew they were nearly foolproof. Finally, Hayward stood up stiffly, addressing the interfering admiral, "I can't do it that way. If you want it done your way, you'll have to get somebody else."

Mitscher then rose in disgust, glared at both Hayward and the interloping flag officer, and said, "Now, dammit, let's shut up all this talk and mine that harbor!"

As Hayward was leaving the conference, Mitscher beckoned him. "You knew you could do it your way. You knew I was backing you. Why did you have to go and argue with him?"

In late March, Stan Ring joined Mitscher at Ile Nou as chief of staff, replacing an officer who was hard of hearing. Mitscher would give a *sotto voce* order, and the fellow would have to go to someone else to find out what had been said. Mitscher stubbornly refused to raise his voice one decibel, so there was nothing to do but make a change. With Ring arrived Commander William A. "Gus" Read, a banker in civilian life and

one of four brothers who had served as naval aviators in World
War I. Read, assigned to operations, had been with the Admiral at the Bureau of Aeronautics in 1940. Also at Ile Nou
was cheerful Lieutenant Everett Eynon, the flag secretary—
staff Jack-of-all-trades. Both Read and Eynon were associated
with Mitscher for most of the war.

Mitscher did not collect people, in the precise meaning of
the word, but he made certain he was surrounded with persons
he liked, trusted, and respected. As he moved around within
the Navy, the same faces seemed to move with him. However,
personalities within the Mitscher household varied greatly.
Whereas constant visitor Luis de Florez effervesced, Read's
periods of silence often matched those of Mitscher himself.
There were interesting counterbalances on all his staffs, and
evidently they were not there by coincidence.

CHAPTER

⚓ 21 ⚓

Guadalcanal Command

On February 8, 1943, General Alexander M. Patch, USA, declared Guadalcanal secured. The Japanese had been defeated there. They had executed a skillful but costly evacuation and still held plenty of land elsewhere in the Solomons. At the time, the most important enemy positions in the northern Solomons were airfields on Munda Point, New Georgia, and at Kolombangara, both within easy striking distance of Guadalcanal. Some of the most furious air battles over the Solomons were yet to come.

Mitscher flew to Guadalcanal to command all aircraft in the Solomons, acquiring Navy, Marine, Army, and New Zealand Royal Air Force pilots and planes. His code name was Air Mica; his title, abbreviated, was COMAIRSOLS. Above him was horseshoes partner Vice Admiral Aubrey Fitch, COMAIRSOPAC (Commander Aircraft, South Pacific), who in turn answered to Halsey. Two or three junior admirals had quaked at the prospect of going into Guadalcanal, but Mitscher welcomed the assignment. As COMAIRSOLS his would be strictly a combat job. He relieved Rear Admiral Charles P. Mason, who had previously succeeded him as captain of the *Hornet*.

"I knew we'd probably catch hell from the Japs in the air. That's why I sent Pete Mitscher up there. Pete was a fighting fool and I knew it," said Fleet Admiral Halsey in April, 1953.

Tons of equipment lay rusting in stream beds, twisted hulks of transports and cargo ships stretched from Cape Esperance south along the shore, and the Japanese bivouac areas were deserted and maggoty. It was a dead island. Over it, in the air, the struggle was savage.

Three fields were in operation and a fourth under construction. Operating from them was a conglomeration of Corsairs, Avengers, Wildcats, Army P-38's, Catalinas, Army bombers, New Zealand RAF planes—anything with wings. On the day Mitscher arrived, there was a rousing air battle. "We were still fighting that same damn battle the day I left," he later told war correspondents.

Shortly after his plane touched earth, four Wildcats over the Russell Islands locked with fifteen to thirty Zeros. Within a few minutes after he'd greeted Rear Admiral Mason, eight Wildcats sped off Henderson Field to assist. They came back on the short end of the score—four losses against three kills. At lunchtime, radar picked up bogeys and fifteen fighters were scrambled to engage them at twelve to twenty thousand feet. This time, the Solomons command fared better, knocking down thirteen Japanese while sustaining two losses. By the end of the day, Mitscher was thoroughly convinced he'd walked into a tropical tiger pit.

This constant pressure had taken a severe physical and mental toll. Some of the depression of the foot troops, after their tremendous battles against Banzai charges and the fetid jungles of Guadalcanal, had leaked into the air command. A dangerous lethargy was creeping in; even gripes over tent living and muddy foxholes, where the Solomons pilots crouched nightly during air raids, were beginning to subside.

Mitscher sent to Halsey for galley equipment, huts, mess

plates, and decent shipments of food—war supplies as vital as
ammunition. Gasoline was scarce and the supply of aircraft
parts was outrageously inadequate. Several planes, in an emergency, had been fitted with wooden wheels which lasted for
one take-off and one landing. In the first week of command,
Mitscher paid more attention to living conditions and logistics
than to threatening the Japanese. After tackling those problems, he devoted his attention to personnel. When he discovered that several squadron commanders did not want to
fly, he fired them and opened the exit wide for timid souls who
wanted to remain out of the fight.

Everett Eynon had come out with him from Ile Nou, and
within a few days, Mitscher called for Stan Ring and Gus
Read. Ring was made deputy chief of staff for operations,
teaming with Lieutenant Colonel Frank Dailey, USMC, and
Commander Read became assistant chief of staff for administration. The chief of staff's job was held by Marine Brigadier
General Field Harris. Fighter and bomber commands were
divided between the Army Air Force and the Marines. Under
these two there was a separate bomber command, fighter command, strike command, and intelligence section.

With his organization shaping up, Mitscher set Ring to work
on broad plans to punish Munda, Kahili, and Vila, Kolombangara, with all the bombs that could be mustered. Meanwhile, the Japanese were hitting back, almost every night.
"Condition Red"—under attack—had become so much a part
of the dark hours that foxholes were used as much as cots. The
pilots, hot and tired from long hours in the cockpit, would
skid to a stop, eat dinner, and then hope for a rest, only to be
alarmed out of their tents by the clanking of a tire iron against
an empty shell casing.

To stop the night raiders, Mitscher decided to try the combination of a P-38 and a searchlight. One night soon afterward,
when a bogey was spotted, fighter director control vectored

a P-38 toward it; then the searchlight speared out and caught the prowling enemy plane in its beam. The P-38 dived and made the kill. It was the first enemy night attacker knocked out over Guadalcanal. The atmosphere changed. The raids still continued, but the sleep-laden eyes didn't blink quite so helplessly.

The night raids were troublesome, but Mitscher welcomed daylight attackers. Here again, the fighter-director system, with its near-perfect communications between ground and air, worked beautifully. Mitscher liked the enemy to come right over Henderson Field. An occasional visiting correspondent would be perplexed by this desire for attack on the home field. Mitscher explained it: "If an attacking plane is attacked over his target, even though he has only a limited supply of gas, he must fight back until his reserve is used up. Our system is to keep the Jap plane engaged until his reserve is used up, then chase him out to sea and run him into the ocean."

Operations headquarters was in a Quonset hut by the Lunga River, which ran steeply off the mountains. Behind it was a duplicate operations center in a dugout, part concrete, with palm-tree logs and sandbags, for use when raids were on. Mitscher would enter the dugout five or ten minutes before each raid and come out at the same interval afterward. Because the Japanese were usually prompt for their 0200 performance, he always asked to be awakened for that show and would sip coffee and chat with the duty officers.

For the first few weeks Mitscher lived in a 10-by-15 canvas tent by the Lunga; then he moved into a quarter-section Dallas hut. At first, his desk was the top of a foot locker. His usual headdress was a sun helmet, but he refused to join the tropical-shorts brigade. Shorts might have been cooler, but they also exposed more expanse for malaria mosquitoes.

In April there was rain, rain, rain. Sometimes three inches would fall in a morning and they would have to wade to meals,

sloshing and slopping in the mud. The Lunga was in full flood
and huge tree trunks tumbled slowly in the froth. April was
also the month of Spam—fried, cold, chopped, disguised, and
despised. There was no fresh meat or vegetables. His job as
COMAIRSOLS was rough, dirty, and dangerous.

CHAPTER
⚓ 22 ⚓

The Interception of Admiral Yamamoto

APRIL 7 was a busy day. Mitscher launched early strikes of Flying Fortresses against Kahili and Ballale, then sent fighters and dive bombers against Vila and Rekata. The strikes at Rekata had just been launched when coast watchers reported a hundred Zeros on the way to Henderson. Reports kept filtering in until radar picked up the big raid. An interception was made some distance from Tulagi. Marine First Lieutenant James E. Swett, of Fighter Squadron 221, Marine Air Group Twelve, led a four-plane division into a formation of fifteen enemy bombers, splashing three. With friendly ack-ack bursting around him, he took on six more, and shot down four. Then he went down with engine trouble, undoubtedly caused by American flak, and was plucked from the sea off Tulagi. Seven enemy planes in one sortie! Meanwhile, other AIRSOLS interceptors were splashing dive bombers and Zeros, thirty-eight in all. The Japanese pilots disengaged.

When confirmation of Swett's exploit was received, Mitscher told Read to prepare a letter recommending the young Seattle

Marine for the Medal of Honor, which in due course was awarded him. Swett was the first Medal of Honor winner from any of Mitscher's commands. Before the war ended, Mitscher recommended five more for the award, and four received it.

In mid-April, a dispatch came from CINCPAC informing Mitscher that the supreme Japanese naval commander, Admiral Isoroku Yamamoto, would be at Kahili, the enemy airfield on Bougainville, on April 18. It gave Yamamoto's time of arrival and the type of plane he would fly in.

Such knowledge came from the intelligence officers listening in on radio messages sent by the enemy. Naval communications cryptographers had broken both the Japanese diplomatic and military codes. The moment the "top secret" message clicked out of Imperial headquarters, it was the focus of extraordinary interest. Admiral King was informed, as was Secretary Knox. President Roosevelt knew of it, too. Mitscher's orders were: "Nail Yamamoto."

Staunch air-advocate Yamamoto had led the Japanese fleet against Pearl Harbor; he had commanded it in the Battle of Midway. Mitscher had heard, by then, that some of the Doolittle fliers had been tortured by their captors; he knew also that the AIRSOLS pilots had not fared well in Japanese hands. It was obvious to those around him that he considered this an opportunity that must not be lost. He told General Harris to draft a plan to shoot down Yamamoto's plane. The plan would have to be nearly perfect.

Harris summoned Commander Ring and they made preliminary time and distance calculations. Next, Colonel Ed Pugh, of fighter command, was brought in to discuss the type of plane needed for the attack. Then a larger conference was held, including Lieutenant Colonel Aaron Ward Tyer, of the Army Air Force, several Army fighter pilots, Commander Read, and Lieutenant Colonel Sam Moore, Pugh's assistant. All conceivable holes were plugged. Read, who did not know about the broken codes, suggested that, since the information about the Yamamoto visit might have been picked up from gossip in Rabaul and therefore be unreliable as to detail, the surest method might be to strafe the small boat in which the admiral would ride after landing. Harris said such an idea had been considered and dismissed.

Then Harris, accompanied by Ring, Read, and several others, went to Mitscher's tent with the plan. He studied it carefully, removing his spectacles and twiddling them between his thumb and forefinger, as was his custom when weighing a decision. At last Mitscher jabbed the end of the frame into his mouth, the usual sign that his mind was made up, and okayed the plan. Admiral Fitch approved it for Halsey, and Washington was informed.

The Army had P-38's—Lockheed Lightnings, which were heavily armed twin-tailed, twin-engined fighters with a long range. They would be perfect for the job. Major John Condon, a Marine, plotted the course for the attackers. The distance from Henderson to Kahili, by direct line, was 300 miles. Condon proposed to route them away from the normal route in order to avoid enemy search planes, a flight of 400 miles. The intercepted timetable for Yamamoto's visit was explicit. Mitscher could envision failure only if the Japanese were late, and the enemy's reputation for punctuality was reassuring on that score.

Colonel Pugh assigned the job to eighteen Army P-38's under Major John Mitchell. Six of the best shots were selected as trigger men. The remaining twelve planes would provide cover for the trigger section. Mitscher had said: "Destroy the target at any cost." That meant even ramming Yamamoto's plane if necessary, according to Sam Moore.

On the humid, cloudy morning of April 18, the Lightnings warmed up on the strip at Henderson Field. It was Sunday. Only a handful of men on Guadalcanal knew the real target.

Mitscher rode over from his camp in a jeep, and stood on the apron to watch them go.

One trigger man blew a tire on take-off; another had fueling failure. That left four. Captain Thomas Lanphier commanded the trigger section. To Bougainville, at 250 mph, they drove low over the water to avoid visual or radar detection. A few minutes away from intercept time, Lanphier went to 10,000 feet; Major John Mitchell's cover section soared on up to 20,000 feet.

At 0933, they roared over the coastline of Bougainville in precision formation. At 0934, right on schedule, two twin-engined aircraft were spotted down low. They were Japanese "Bettys." Lanphier ducked under a Zero and got Yamamoto's plane at treetop level; the other Betty was knocked down, too, and a third was downed later. By 0938, Admiral Isoroku Ya-mamoto was dead, and Vice Admiral Ugaki, Yamamoto's chief of staff, was critically injured.

Gus Read and Stan Ring drafted the wording of the Admiral's victory dispatch:

POP GOES THE WEASEL X P 38S LED BY MAJOR JOHN W MITCHELL USA VISITED KAHILI AREA X ABOUT 0930 SHOT DOWN TWO BOMB-ERS ESCORTED BY ZEROS FLYING CLOSE FORMATION X ONE SHOT DOWN BELIEVED TO BE TEST FLIGHT X THREE ZEROS ADDED TO THE SCORE SUMS TOTAL SIX X ONE P 38 [Lieutenant R. K. Hine] FAILED RETURN X APRIL 18 SEEMS TO BE OUR DAY X

Mitscher added the last sentence as a personal aside to Hal-sey. On that same date in 1942 they had launched the Doolittle fliers for the Tokyo raid.

Halsey replied happily: X LOOKS LIKE ONE OF THE DUCKS IN THEIR BAG WAS A PEACOCK X

Knox, King, and Nimitz were jubilant, but the Japanese only fought harder. Several weeks later, an enemy pilot named Takesho was shot down and on his body was a letter from his mother: "It is a pity we lost the worthy admiral. Please revenge for his death."

For several weeks thereafter, Mitscher sent planes over Ballale and Kahili in order to make it appear that Yamamoto's death was purely happenstance and thus prevent the Japanese from realizing that their codes had been broken.

Although the enemy was harassing his territory day and night, Mitscher continued to build up his existing fields and press the completion of the bomber base, Carney Field. Meanwhile, he was hitting the enemy at Munda and Vila, and beginning to soften up Buin and Kahili as a prelude to the invasion of New Georgia. When the enemy retaliated, Mitscher had the uncanny knack of guessing the right number of planes to meet them. In theory, he had about three hundred aircraft but only one third of these were operational at any one time. Losses were mounting and replacements were slow. Weather and faulty navigation caused more casualties than combat. He began sending up weather planes to obtain advance warning on approaching fronts. Strike by strike, and bomb by bomb, Mitscher's planes gradually eliminated the air threat to Guadalcanal, Espiritu Santo, and Noumea.

Together with better combat results went a marked improvement in reconnaissance, photography, and rescue operations. When Mitscher asked: "How many are down?" he also wanted a reply to: "How many did we pick up?" The "Dumbo" planes—flying boats on rescue missions—were as important as the fighters. After one attack, seven Henderson pilots were scooped from Rennel Island waters.

He was quick to protest when trigger-happy ships of our fleet took potshots at his pilots, although it was virtually impossible, on many occasions, to tell friend from foe. One night he flew over Munda on a reconnaissance mission and passed near an American task force, mainly cruisers with escorting destroyers. The task-force commander shot first and asked later, as he should have done. But Mitscher was furious. When he landed he told General Harris, "If they're going to shoot, they can shoot me down." He sent a message to Rear Admiral Walden L. Ainsworth advising him that he was going to make a flight and would be over Ainsworth's ships. It was a rough night, and Mitscher piloted the PBY low over the force. The guns, of course, remained silent. But the flight did serve as a cautionary reminder.

In any tri-service command, conflict is inevitable. Mitscher had disagreements with the Army over the need for long-range search patrols. He knew the results were negative 90 per cent of the time, but the other 10 per cent was of deep interest to him. The Army preferred to load up with bombs and hie away on purely offensive missions. Feeling between Navy and Marine pilots on one side and the Army flyers on the other was strained on many occasions during the first six weeks of Mitscher's command. For instance, Army squadrons were bound by instructions from Washington which the field commanders could not change regardless of the tactical situation. One such order was that pilots could fly only one day in four. The result was that Navy and Marine pilots bore the brunt of extra flights and flew about twice as often as the Army pilots. Resentment was inevitable.

But usually the conflict was over something rather petty. In May, a pilot of Lieutenant Colonel Tyer's squadron shot down an enemy plane in a difficult attack. Mitscher told Commander Read to inform Tyer he wanted to recommend the pilot for a Navy Cross.

But Tyer said bluntly to Read, "I'll turn in my suit before I'll recommend one of my men for a Navy decoration."

Read went back to Mitscher, who wrinkled his forehead in dismay. "Get word to Tyer I'd like to talk with him," he said softly.

The Natchez flier, a West Point graduate and topnotch combat pilot, sought Read out several hours later to apologize. "The Old Man said he felt we were all on one team," Tyer said. "He said he wanted it to be known that when somebody does something we all appreciate it. He said he wasn't giving orders of an administrative nature to another command and had previously recommended a New Zealander for a Navy Cross. Of course I'll do it."

Some days later, another Army pilot, named Blondie Ryan, turned in an exceptional piece of work. Mitscher asked him what decoration he wanted.

"The Navy Cross, Admiral," Ryan said. He got it, and the team spirit began to settle over the airfields on Guadalcanal. Mitscher also demonstrated his appreciation in a way that was even more welcome than decorations. He ordered fifty or sixty cases of whisky—it tasted like radiator draining but it was still whisky—from Espiritu Santo. Whenever a squadron had a good day, he'd send over a case with his compliments. The whisky was stored in the operations headquarters. On the first night, two cases were stolen. Bottles were found behind the Marine camp.

Eynon informed Mitscher, who squinted intently over his glasses for a few seconds. "Okay," he said, then continued to do the paper work in front of him. The guilty parties had expected a full-dress investigation, it was learned later. No more whisky was stolen.

Once, one of Mitscher's pilots, back from a mission, flathatted over the field while the Admiral watched. He called the grandstanding pilot in, worked him over profanely, then said, "All right, son, now let's sit down and have a drink."

CHAPTER

⚓ 23 ⚓

Last Days at Guadalcanal

THE pilots' legend of Pete Mitscher began building there on the edge of the jungle. His method of command kept them off balance, but they were delighted by it. If they found it difficult to fathom the thinking behind his unorthodox approach, King, Nimitz and Halsey did not. They knew it simply as leadership. Perhaps his method is most successful in the intimate command structure of aviation, or the submarine force; perhaps it wouldn't work in foxhole combat or in the surface fleet. Nevertheless, he had what was needed to live in the Solomons aerie with his birds of prey.

As Guadalcanal became increasingly secure, Mitscher's living conditions changed. He now had a one-quarter Quonset, which he said he had "stolen," proudly calling it "my cottage." At dawn, he would often go out along the beach to shoot pigeons with General J. Lawton Collins, striving for a bag of four or five, and was elated to find the birds delicious, a welcome change from Spam.

He breakfasted at about seven. His cottage had the only piece of Crane plumbing on the island, and Mitscher was extremely proud of it. He was unselfish about its use but required a thorough cleaning since it served also as the watering trough for a doleful Alsatian puppy, Butch, a rather mild character belonging to Field Harris. Mitscher loved the dog, and Butch often slept in Mitscher's chair.

Flag officers and war correspondents traversing the Pacific theater often stopped on Guadalcanal for an overnight stay and would dine in the flag mess after a cocktail in the cottage. Mitscher was always amiable but was noticeably relieved to see them go, no matter how short their visit or how stimulating their conversation. He was afraid one of the Japanese night visitors might leave behind a distinguished corpse. Nimitz and Halsey insisted on after-dinner walks in the dark and Mitscher worried more about these strolls than he did about the dive-bombing Aichi 99's that rattled his dugout. The intense heat and humidity, which he never stood well, combined with the tension of the war of nerves, began sapping his strength. One visitor, Rear Admiral Putty Read, returned Stateside to report: "He doesn't look a day over eighty."

Just when it appeared that the sting had gone from the Japanese air attacks launched from Munda and Kahili, the enemy air commander in the Solomons decided on a sledge-hammer blow. There was a note of desperation in it. Just before noon on June 16, 120 Zeros and Aichi 99's took off for Guadalcanal.

Operations duty officer Charles Endweiss, a Marine major, notified Mitscher that a heavy raid, more than a hundred planes, was expected at 1430. Mitscher, seated in his chair in the operations hut, his feet propped on a desk, answered simply, "Thank you, Major." Endweiss hadn't known the enemy had that many aircraft left in the Solomons. He expected something more profound from the Admiral, but Mitscher had already returned to scanning the operational summaries that were in his lap. At about 1425, Endweiss said, "They should be here soon, Admiral."

"Thank you," Mitscher replied, with no apparent concern.

Then he got up slowly, put on his sun helmet, and said, "Let's go up to the top of the hill and watch the fun." Meanwhile, Henderson fighters had scrambled out to meet the strike. There was a large foxhole on the hill, but Mitscher remained in the open, his arms folded across his chest, watching the sky.

Action was joined. Lightnings downed the high-flying Zeros which provided cover for the Japanese bombers. Then Wildcats and Corsairs went to work on the Vals coming in to attack Henderson Field and shipping in Lunga Roads. The close, thick air was split with engine wails as dogfights whirled over the Slot, a narrow, navigable body of water separating the eastern and western Solomons, and Lunga Point. It was soon evident the Japanese pilots would be overwhelmingly defeated. Marine fighter planes bore the brunt of the attack. In his briefing report, one pilot, Lieutenant Kenneth T. Vial, USNR, said:

I caught up with a group of dive bombers that was attempting to rendezvous and made a pass at Tail-End Charley, and he burst into flames. Then I went after the next one and he caught fire and went into the water. I was about to close in on another when I saw an F4F with a Zero on his tail. I turned and got him with a full deflection shot. He exploded. By this time, planes were beginning to fall like flies.

Endweiss remembers that for the most part, Mitscher was silent. Then one of the Henderson pilots came by the hill and went into a slow roll—a victory roll—and Mitscher grinned. "That's about the end of it," he said, and walked leisurely to his cottage. It was the largest air battle of the Solomons war, also the largest kill. One hundred and seven enemy planes were downed. Mitscher's recognition of the day took the form of whisky by the case for the participating squadrons and an order to Read to see that the pilots were properly decorated.

Ever since he had been assigned to shore duty from the *Hornet*, Mitscher had been monitoring the carrier war. He read every summary he could find, pumped visitors for up-to-date information on the flattops. What were the new tactics? How were the American shipyards coming along with *Essex*-class hulls? What was new in carrier design? Often, he'd tell Harris or Ring or Read ideas which had occurred to him about carrier operation. His mind was at AIRSOLS, but his heart was really out across the water with the carriers.

Mitscher's flyers had softened up New Georgia, and now it was time for the fat amphibious ships to inch up to beach-heads. Small Marine landings took place on June 30, July 2, and July 3. Mitscher made a costly mistake during one of these landings. A flight of Bettys, covered by Zeros, attacked a group of amphibians ferrying Marines toward Rendova and caused heavy casualties—exactly ninety minutes after Mitscher had peremptorily recalled the AIRSOLS planes which had been protecting the troops, because "a storm was brewing." He had again acted out of concern for the pilots' welfare, but the amphibians were helpless during the short, intense raid. He took the entire blame, and hasty recall of aircraft covering invasion landings did not occur again during his tenure.

Shortly after this incident, Mitscher fell victim to the most vicious of the Solomon Islands raiders—the malaria mosquito. His health had been failing for some weeks and he was in no condition to ward off the fever. He ran a high temperature for two weeks. The command had been held by the Marines and the Navy; now it was time for the Army Air Forces to provide an AIRSOLS chieftain. Major General Nathan F. Twining, later Chief of Staff of the U.S. Air Force, was ordered to Henderson Field. Mitscher was informed he would be relieved late in July.

Meanwhile, on July 6, Mitscher received an urgent message calling for destruction of a Japanese position on Greenwich

Island which threatened invasion operations. The distance to the target was 700 miles. It was a volunteer mission, and Lieutenant Commander Bruce Avery Van Voorhis, who commanded Bombing Squadron 102, asked to go. Mitscher warned him that his chances of returning were very small because there could be no escort planes. Van Voorhis took off on the mission and did not return, but the Greenwich Island installation was destroyed. Fragments of the story, passed on by coast watchers and other observers, got back to Guadalcanal. Van Voorhis had fought a lone and relentless battle. Forced low by Zeros, he had executed six tree-level attacks to demolish the enemy radio station and other facilities. He had been caught in his own bomb blast.

"I want that man to get the Medal of Honor, and I won't be satisfied with less," Mitscher told Read. Van Voorhis did eventually receive the nation's top military decoration. In a way, it helped make up for continued denial of the medal to John Waldron's men.

Shortly thereafter, Mitscher turned over command to General Twining. The General stood by to read his orders; Mitscher, according to service protocol, had to publish his first. He was weak and ill. Several officers maintain that he suffered two separate heart attacks on Guadalcanal, but this cannot be substantiated. One story is that Mitscher ordered the medical officer not to report the attacks. However, it is known that he was suffering from a heart ailment prior to the fatal seizure in 1947.

When Mitscher finished reading the orders, he put down his papers and looked up and down the line. "I've had a lot of duty," Gus Read remembers him saying, "but I'm prouder of this organization than of any other. I thank you from the bottom of my heart for the teamwork you've shown. I can only remind you that things were once different here. I know that all of you men will give General Twining the same magnificent support you gave me. I'll take your leave now."

MITSCHER AND HARRIS SEND TO THE BEST AIR FORCE WE KNOW AND THE AIR FORCE BEST KNOWN TO THE JAPS X WE ARE SAD AT RELINQUISHING COMMAND OF THE TOUGHEST AND BEST BUNCH OF JAP KILLERS ON RECORD X BEST OF LUCK THE BEST OF LANDINGS AND THE BEST OF HUNTING X GOOD BYE GOOD LUCK AND GOD BLESS YOU

Mitscher had done his job, the hardest he had in the war. Many think this tour was even more difficult than Task Force 58. The air threat to the Solomons had been destroyed. His box score was 340 Japanese fighters and 132 Japanese bombers destroyed, 17 ships sunk, and 8 damaged. He'd spilled 2,083 tons of bombs on the enemy, but the single tally of which he was proudest was 131, representing that number of United States and New Zealand pilots who had been snatched from alien waters and beaches by his rescue planes.[1]

Mitscher left the next morning for Noumea. Later, as his plane banked into the landing pattern at Pearl Harbor, he looked out and saw seven aircraft carriers—more than he had seen in one spot in his life. They were forming up in preparation for strikes on the Gilberts. He made no comment, but it was evident that one of those 1917 dreams had materialized.

His stay at Pearl Harbor was merely a stop-over. In a letter to Frances Mitscher, Lieutenant Commander R. H. Weed, USNR, wrote: "He stopped in Pearl Harbor with Admiral Towers, and Admiral Towers, I guess, more or less pushed him to spend 20 minutes talking to about 5 of us younger and more junior officers. It must have been a dull occasion for Admiral Mitscher. But far more exciting for the young squirts he was talking to. I well remember thinking on that occasion he was just about through."

[1] Provided by Rear Admiral W. A. Read, USNR.

Eynon doctored him with quinine and atabrine throughout the rest of the flight homeward. He perked up as they neared San Diego. He knew Frances would be waiting for him. She had been waiting more than a year. As he stepped out of the plane, his eyes searching the ramp for Frances, Read and Eynon lingered behind, realizing the scene would be difficult for everyone gathered by the ladder. He put his arms around her and she broke into tears. The man she saw had hollow cheeks and dull, tired eyes. The skin on his face was pouched and a sickly yellow. He weighed 115 pounds. She had last seen him on Christmas Eve, 1941, several months before he took Doolittle on the Tokyo raid. She remembers vividly that she could not, for a moment, believe that a dirty little island had so ravaged her husband.

For a few minutes Mitscher talked to the admiral he was designated to relieve; then he drew Eynon and Read aside. "You know," he said, "that old —— wants me to relieve him tomorrow morning." Mitscher had hoped for two or three weeks of solid rest.

"Are you going to do it, Admiral?" Eynon asked worriedly.

"I guess so," Mitscher grunted.

And he did.

⚓ 24 ⚓

Fleet Air, West Coast

FLEET AIR, West Coast, was an administrative outfit with its headquarters at San Diego, and was chiefly concerned with reforming and retraining squadrons. Mitscher again showed little interest in the Navy's business transactions, viewing the duty as a recreation period, a breather from the Solomons. He kept away from his headquarters on North Island as much as possible. In fact, his chief of staff, Captain John Perry, had informal instructions from Pearl Harbor to "keep him in the open and get him back in shape as soon as possible." The San Diego command was running smoothly anyhow.

Mitscher's first project was an "inspection tour" of the Navy's Alaskan air outposts. Actually, his only interest in Alaska was the hunting and fishing. Later, he said, "When I made the Alaskan inspection, I inspected fishing streams, quite unofficially, against the day the war ends. While we were there, a senator from the Truman Committee heard we were on a little fishing trip and nosed over our way. I stuck a rod in his hand and took him to my best place. He whipped the stream for about ten minutes and caught himself a big silver salmon. Those Alaskan fish are politically astute."

Mitscher often talked about buying a home on Oregon's Rogue River. The Mitschers had lived in a series of hotel rooms, apartments, and rented houses, but had never had a place to call their own.

On returning to San Diego, he claimed Captain Perry for a duck-blind partner; they were off several times a week well before dawn, and often got their limit. One soggy morning while they were in a blind near the air station, cursing the flying boats which were conducting bounce drills—touching down on the water and roaring off again—they were spotted by one of the pilots. He decided to give two old duck hunters a thrill and dropped the PBY onto the water a few hundred feet off the blind, then thundered up again, spraying across the shelter at about eight or ten feet. Mitscher and Perry dove into the shallow, muddy water, but not before the Admiral sighted the number on the tail of the plane.

Soaked to his underwear and carrying his prize shotgun, now waterlogged, Mitscher returned straight to his office without pausing to change clothes. As he stepped through the door, past startled aides and sentries, he requested that the pilot of the plane report immediately.

Still in flying coveralls, the pilot was soon ushered in. After a long, silent stare at the unfortunate young man, the bedraggled two-star admiral arose majestically and said, "I want to shake hands with a damn fool."

Mitscher was always good company on a shoot but could also be disconcerting. In the late thirties, while on the *Wright*, he once went with George Henderson to Lake Otay, part of the public water system in southern California. He decided to row for a blind at the far end of the lake.

After a half hour of steady pulling, the husky Henderson began to feel the pace and suggested pausing for a while. Mitscher didn't answer and didn't miss a stroke. Henderson shrugged. Thirty minutes later, in front of the blind, Henderson noticed that Mitscher's hands were badly blistered. Mitscher shot the first duck about thirty yards from the blind. Worrying about the chafed hands, Henderson offered to retrieve it. "Wait a minute," Mitscher answered quickly. "I shot that duck and I'll get him." Then, to prove he was just as durable as George, he retrieved every other duck that afternoon, both Henderson's and his own. When they left the blind at sunset, Henderson said, "Captain, how about taking the stern seat and letting me row you back."

Again, Mitscher didn't answer, but wrapped a handkerchief around one swelling hand and grasped the oars. Henderson offered another handkerchief, and Mitscher accepted it reluctantly. He didn't stop once on the hour's pull back to the dock, although blood was showing through both handkerchiefs and Henderson knew he was in agony the entire distance.

When Mitscher's hunting and fishing companions got together to compare notes, someone was sure to describe an incident like this one. "For some odd reason, he wanted to do all the work," said Vice Admiral Pride, another of Mitscher's woods companions. In the woods or out, Mitscher would not knowingly let anyone do anything for him that he could do himself.

Both a fresh and salt water fisherman, he preferred the swift-moving streams. He fished Chesapeake Bay and some of the Maryland brooks when he had Washington duty and the Sierra Nevada streams and lakes when he was on the West Coast. He finally acquired a fine array of flies.

There had been a time, however, when he was strictly a worm man. In 1929, on a trip in the Sierras to an exclusive fishing camp, he pulled out a cane pole and a can of night crawlers. The rest of the party, uncasing their fancy rods and sets of flies, looked at him in pity.

"I must confess," he said blandly, "I'm a meat fisherman."

Sometimes he'd go on a talking jag about fishing, even introducing the subject without warning or cause. Often, he apparently just thought about it. One evening in the central Pacific, a few minutes before sunset, an aide saw him sitting in his chair on the bridge, smiling to himself with obvious satisfaction. They were less than twenty-four hours away from a heavy strike, and the aide supposed the Admiral was preoccupied with battle plans.

"What are you thinking about, Admiral?" he asked.

Mitscher turned and answered slowly, "I was just thinking that at home the trout season opens today."

PART THREE

⚓ ⚓
⚓

Fast-Carrier Task Force

CHAPTER

⚓ 25 ⚓

Command Organization

WHILE Mitscher was restlessly marking time at San Diego, Nimitz and Halsey conferred with King by dispatch to decide on a new commander for the fast-carrier spearhead of the Fifth Fleet. They agreed that Mitscher was the best prospect for the job. Although his performance at Guadalcanal was an important factor in his selection the most decisive consideration in their long-distance deliberation was his immediate availability. Blind fortune thus contributed to his obtaining the top naval-air combat job in the Pacific. It proved a most fortunate move for the Navy and for the total war effort.

He reported as Commander, Carrier Division Three. That command became Task Force 58/38 on January 6, 1944. Toward the end of his stay at San Diego, Mitscher had once again thought he was being shelved. Incredibly enough, this view was shared by other veteran naval aviators who were unaware of the informal instructions to Captain John Perry to get him back in shape. They pointed to the fact that not one of the Pensacola pioneers had reached the top echelon of combat command.

There was therefore rejoicing within the tight circle of old-time Navy pilots, and some understandable jealousy, when word circulated that Mitscher had been assigned to the newest, choicest of Pacific jobs. He received notice on December 23 and several days later flew to Pearl Harbor, establishing headquarters in the underground center on Ford Island. By January 10 he had placed his careful signature on the operation plan—labeled FLINTLOCK—and the big carriers made preparations to get underway.

The pioneer Task Force 58/38 was composed of new battleships, cruisers, and destroyers assembled around a core of big, fast aircraft carriers. In support were wide-bellied fleet oilers from the service force, ammunition ships, and refrigeration and dry-stores ships. Often there were more than a hundred ships, carrying a hundred thousand men. When the force was part of Admiral Raymond Spruance's Fifth Fleet, it bore the designation of 58; when it led Admiral William Halsey's Third Fleet, its designation was 38. Its composition remained much the same under either fleet commander.

Usually the task force included four task groups, each commanded by a rear admiral and centered around from two to four carriers. The new-style war did not disturb the traditions of the sea; the captain remained king on his individual ship. A task-group or task-force admiral was a guest on the flagship and had nothing to say about its internal operations. In the same way, each division of battleships and cruisers was led by its own admiral, and the destroyers were organized into squadrons, each with its own chief—usually a commodore.

At the top of the command pyramid of Task Force 58 was Admiral Mitscher, who deployed the task force as a whole, designating missions and setting forth policies to the task-group commanders. They in turn relayed orders to their subordinate commanders, including the ship captains, who gave orders to the air-group commanders, and so on down the chain of command.

Over Mitscher was the fleet commander—alternately Spruance and Halsey—who directed the entire fleet in accordance with the area strategy emanating from Nimitz's headquarters in Pearl Harbor. Operation of the fast-carrier task force itself was left to Mitscher. Spruance and Halsey rarely assumed tactical command. Both have said that Mitscher was supreme in that field; they could have added little or nothing.

Mitscher himself seldom interfered with his task-group commanders once he had told them what to do. He knew the capabilities of each. Occasionally his staff would suggest that he crack down on a task-group commander who was not performing according to standard operating procedures.

Mitscher would most often reply: "I tell them *what* I want done. Not *how!*"

Sometimes a task-group commander would be a hundred or more miles away, carrying out an independently assigned mission. Until battle was joined, radio silence was usually maintained to prevent enemy radio direction finders from locating them. Once battle began, radio silence was broken and Mitscher's busy flag bridge received necessary information from the widespread group commanders. Task groups operating in the same area as the force flagship transmitted information by short-range radio (TBS) or by visual signals. In addition, aircraft were employed for message drops.

The heart of Admiral Mitscher's command was a compact room in the flagship's island called Flag Plot. Packed with a staggering amount of tracking and communications equipment that hummed incessantly, Flag Plot had as its most prominent feature a huge chart table. Around the bulkheads were radar repeaters, showing the disposition of ships and aircraft, both friendly and enemy. There were large translucent ship- and aircraft-status boards to indicate, for example, the availability of aircraft, the type of bomb loads carried by the various planes in the force, and the times of launching of planes then in the air. Other status boards recorded information on every important phase of the operation. A quick glance by a trained eye would reveal both the current and the potential situation of the task force at any given moment. There were also repeater compasses, speed indicators, telephone systems, and various other communications circuits.

Also important in Flag Plot life was a brown leather couch —the transom—a long, comfortable seat which Mitscher occupied most of the time he was in the room. His tiny sea cabin was aft of Flag Plot.

From twelve to twenty people occupied Flag Plot, depending on the situation. He kept endeavoring to cut the number down, so that the area would be quieter. A staff duty officer, standing a watch of four hours, was always in charge; with him was an assistant. During daylight hours and far into the night, Mitscher and his chief of staff usually remained in Flag Plot or on the wing of the flag bridge, located just outside the door. The rest were communications people, plotters, "talkers," and the like. The flag bridge is generally tucked beneath the ship's bridge, which is the ship captain's headquarters.

But running a task force requires more than standing watch in Flag Plot. Information about attacks, the whereabouts of friendly planes, and the disposition of ships was tabulated in an often frenetic room called Combat Information Center (CIC). Here, aft of Flag Plot in the island (in later *Essex*-class carriers CIC was located in the gallery deck, suspended beneath the flight deck), officers attached to the staff kept pertinent data flowing up to Flag Plot and controlled the task group's combat air patrol (CAP) for defense against air attack. In another room, below Flag Plot level, Mitscher's intelligence officers scanned photographs, assessed damage, and pieced together information derived from interrogation of pilots. Flag communications personnel augmented those attached to the particular ship, handling traffic devoted to task-force rather than to ship operations. Still another staff unit, the flag administration office, prepared the directives and operations plans formulated in Flag Plot, and handled the business end of Mitscher's command.

According to those who were on his staff, Mitscher somehow seemed to know what was occurring at all those complex levels at all times. From his swivel chair on the wing of the flag bridge, or the transom in Flag Plot, he ran the task force with deceptive ease.

CHAPTER

⚓ 26 ⚓

The Invasion of the
Marshall Islands

THE Marshall Islands are two chains of once idyllic atolls, roughly 2,300 miles west of Honolulu, lying parallel to each other in a northwesterly and southeasterly direction. Ratak is the eastern chain; Ralik lies to the west. Until World War II, only those particularly interested in the area could have located Eniwetok or Kwajalein, member islands of Ralik. The Marshalls—target for Task Force 58—offered an operational base a thousand miles nearer the Japanese shore than any then in our possession, a springboard for the first real leap in central Pacific operations.

While countless mimeograph machines turned out operations plans, annexes, and appendixes, ships were loading and transports steamed steadily westward from the United States. Three of Mitscher's task groups were already gathered at Pearl Harbor. Another, commanded by Rear Admiral Frederick C. Sherman, was striking Kavieng, in the Bismarck Archipelago, northwest of the Solomons, but would rendezvous in time to join the strike against the Marshalls. The four task groups comprising the force numbered sixty-one ships, of which twelve were carriers. The cost of this force alone was equal to the annual budget of a half dozen prewar navies.

Mitscher's letters to Frances in the two weeks before sailing mentioned little but his concern over her being lonely now that he had gone again. She answered: "In your letter you seemed worried over having left me. Or rather in all your letters since you left. Please know, dear, that I feel only happiness for you, that you are doing what you have lived your life for."

Frances was right. In a sense, Mitscher was the complete air admiral. There were, of course, "aviation" admirals. Moffett was the first to wear wings. Men like Halsey, McCain, and Sherman, who had achieved wings comparatively late in life, were aviation admirals. In the same sense, Mitscher was termed a "pilot" and not a "flyer." Halsey and McCain were flyers. But to the combat pilot in his crowded cockpit, Mitscher was the complete air admiral—a man who had devoted all his life to flying and had finally made flag rank in his specialized profession. What made him complete, they maintained, was his role as a combat flag officer in the field. Towers and Bellinger were air admirals, certainly, but, through no fault of their own, they did not get into combat. To the pilots, Mitscher represented the ultimate of his profession. It was almost twenty-eight years since he had clipped on his wings at Pensacola; he had devoted more than a quarter of a century to a single purpose. Indeed, Mitscher was about to do what he had lived his life for.

On January 13, he was piped aboard the new U.S.S. *Yorktown*. He was holding a copy of *Send Me Another Coffin*, a detective novel, and the title was noticed as he stood exchanging greetings on the *Yorktown*'s quarterdeck. Somebody asked, "Are they going to need more coffins, Admiral?"

"I wouldn't be at all surprised," he said.

However, in the middle of January, 1944, the situation of the enemy in the Pacific did not seem desperate. Carrier tactics had been hit-and-run, consisting of surprise blows and quick retreats. The pilots were becoming accustomed to these aerial guerilla raids. The full power of the fast-carrier task force was yet to be developed. It was believed that Mitscher would be able to combine naval and air power in proper proportions for offensive action. But he was on trial as Commander, Task Force 58. A failure in the Marshalls, or elsewhere, would soon put him back on the beach. An admiral's head rolls more rapidly than an ensign's. The fact that he had the job was not important; what he did with it was very important.

The task groups at Pearl Harbor stood out to sea on January 16 and January 19. Task Group 58.1, the group in which Mitscher rode, was composed of the carriers *Yorktown, Enterprise,* and *Belleau Wood* and the battleships *Washington, Massachusetts,* and *Indiana.* It was commanded by Rear Admiral J. W. Reeves, Jr. Nine screening destroyers roamed the edges of the group. They steamed at 18 knots in precise formation, timing their western progress to arrive off the Marshalls on January 29.

Mitscher inherited his staff from the admiral he relieved, Charles Pownall, and was pleased to find Truman Joseph Hedding, a tall, easygoing aviator, formerly executive officer of the U.S.S. *Essex,* as chief of staff. He'd known Hedding when the latter had been a lieutenant, a quiet and efficient worker in the Bureau of Aeronautics in the middle thirties. The forty-four-year-old Naval Academy graduate from Colorado had done much of the planning for the carrier raids in late 1943, and pointed out some of the weaknesses of task-force operation to date. He had also readied the plans for FLINTLOCK.

En route to the launching area, the task groups topped off their fuel tanks and carried out frequent practice exercises,

Marc Andrew Mitscher, class of 1910, U.S. Naval Academy. A "wooden" student, he graduated near the bottom of his class. *Official U.S. Navy Photograph*

EARLY DAYS

Six years after graduation, his hair gone, but his wings achieved, Mitscher was flying from Pensacola Bay, Florida, in wood, wire, and canvas seaplanes with 100-horsepower pusher engines. *Official U.S. Navy Photograph*

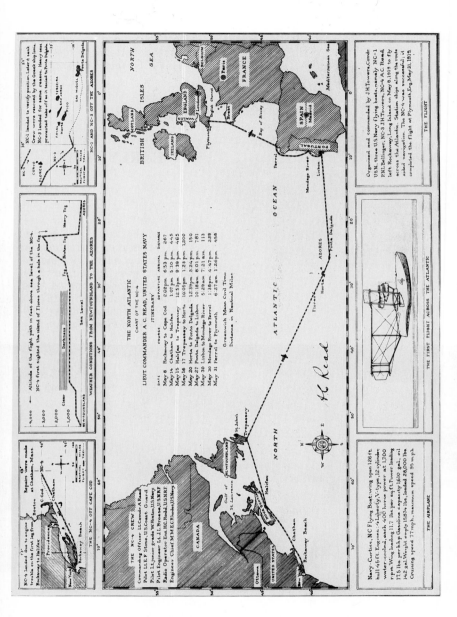

The flight of the "Nancys" in 1919. The chart was drawn by the then Lieutenant Commander A. C. Read, Mitscher's lifelong friend. It was the first flight over the Atlantic. Read commanded *NC-4.* Mitscher flew in *NC-1. Official U.S. Navy Photograph*

The *NC-1* leaving Trepassey Bay, Newfoundland, for the long jump to the Azores. Heavily laden, she behaved badly in the heavy chop. She finally became airborne after a long, wet run. *Official U.S. Navy Photograph*

Before the raid on Tokyo, Mitscher and Doolittle and the Army fliers who flew the famous mission—on the deck of the *Hornet* during the approach to Japan in April, 1942. *Official U.S. Navy Photograph*

COMMAND AT SEA

The takeoff. One of the Army B-25's taking off from Mitscher's *Hornet* in high wind and seas to raid Tokyo and crash in China. *Official U.S. Navy Photograph*

A carrier-plane photograph of a Japanese heavy cruiser after attack by Task Force 16 aircraft at the Battle of Midway.
Official U.S. Navy Photograph

Part of Mitscher's fast carrier task force. Two task groups only are visible, with both heavy and light carriers, battleships, cruisers, and destroyers. Task groups usually cruised about twenty miles apart. *Official U.S. Navy Photograph*

The enemy strikes. A Japanese torpedo plane, after failing in an attack on USS *Kitkun Bay* during the Marianas invasion. The torpedo wake can be seen crossing from right to left toward the carrier's stern. *Official U.S. Navy Photograph*

Under attack. The defensive nerve center of a carrier task group—the Combat Information Center of the flagship. Lieutenant Commander Francis Winston, U.S.N.R., giving directions to his intercept officer during an attack by enemy planes. He sits at the master plotting table of the inter-task-group radio and radar information center. All task-group airborne fighter planes assigned to protect the group are under his direct control. *Official U.S. Navy Photograph*

Carrier pilots. *Above,* after a raid. *Below,* the pilots with the "duty," relaxing in a carrier ready room, just under the flight deck and near their planes. *Official U.S. Navy Photograph*

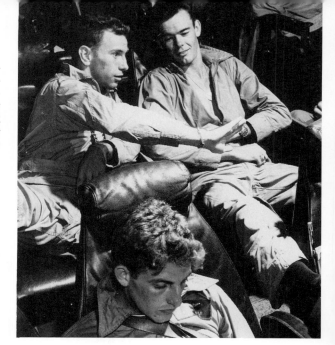

Mitscher on his perch on the *Lexington*'s flag bridge. With Mitscher is Vice Admiral J. S. McCain. Above him, on the ship's bridge, are Captain E. W. Litch and Commander J. M. Lane, captain and executive officer of the *Lexington.* Below Mitscher is the tally of Japanese planes shot down by the ship's Air Group 16. *Official U.S. Navy Photograph*

BALD EAGLE'S PERCH

Riding backwards, as always, Mitscher could watch flight operations from his perch on the flag bridge. Here he watches a takeoff, while another Grumman Hellcat is spotted to follow. *J. R. Eyerman, Life* magazine © Time Warner Inc.

The controversial brown shoes. Naval aviators took to brown shoes as a mark of differentiation from the surface men (black shoes). Mitscher's broke a tradition in Admiral's footwear. *By J. R. Eyerman, Life* magazine © Time Warner Inc.

Mitscher conferring with his staff on the flag bridge. His close friend, Luis de Florez—engineer, inventor, and innovator extraordinary—is at left. *J. R. Eyerman, Life* magazine © Time Warner Inc.

Mitscher receiving a verbal battle report from Commander Snowden just after the latter has landed from a combat flight. *J. R. Eyerman, Life* magazine © Time Warner Inc.

Mitscher and his chief-of-staff, Commodore Arleigh Burke. It took "31-Knot" Burke, a famous surface-navy man, a long time to win the Admiral's confidence. After that, Mitscher relied heavily on him until his death in 1947. They are shown here just after an important secret dispatch had arrived in flag plot and at the moment of actual command decision. *Official U.S. Navy Photograph*

The most formidable weapon in the fight across the Pacific, an *Essex*-class aircraft carrier. Capable of astonishing speed, they carried up to a hundred aircraft each. *Official U.S. Navy Photograph*

OPERATIONS

A destroyer taking on oil from an aircraft carrier while under way in heavy seas. *Official U.S. Navy Photograph*

Admiral Mitscher transferring by breeches buoy to his new flagship, the *Randolph*. He had had three flagships shot out from under him in the previous five days (*Enterprise, Franklin, Bunker Hill*—all damaged by suicide attacks). *Official U.S. Navy Photograph*

KAMIKAZE

Left, Japan's last, desperate, and brutally effective weapon—the *Kamikaze,* or "divine wind," suicide attack. This photograph was taken from the deck of the *Essex,* just before the plane, burning but still in control, crashed into her. *Below,* the *Essex* at the moment of impact. A flash fire has started at a forward gun mount. *Official U.S. Navy Photograph*

The *Bunker Hill* fighting a flight-deck fire after being hit by a suicide plane. *Official U.S. Navy Photograph*

HOME

In Pearl Harbor, on his way home late in 1944, Mitscher was presented with a second Navy Cross and the Legion of Merit by Admiral Nimitz before a multistarred audience of admirals and generals. *Official U.S. Navy Photograph*

Home, finally, in November, 1944, Mitscher was greeted in San Diego by his wife, Frances. *Official U.S. Navy Photograph*

Sea command in peacetime. Mitscher with Secretary of the Navy James Forrestal on the flag bridge of the new, large carrier, *Franklin D. Roosevelt*. *Official U.S. Navy Photograph*

This was Mitscher, the pilot of the *NC*-1, captain of the *Hornet* from which the Doolittle raid was launched, admiral of the air over the Solomons, developer of a new concept of naval war, and leader of the greatest naval striking force in history. *Oil portrait by Commander Albert K. Murray, USNR*

while Mitscher and his staff checked plans, studied weather reports, and prepared the force for action. Vice Admiral Raymond Spruance, the Fifth Fleet commander, was on board the *Indianapolis*. Although Spruance and Mitscher may have brushed sleeves at the Naval Academy—Spruance graduated in 1906, the year Mitscher bilged out—their paths had not crossed until the Battle of Midway. They were never shipmates.

In the days when Mitscher was snugging baling wire around airplane struts, Spruance's duties included gunnery, command at sea, engineering, and teaching at the Naval War College. Unquestionably, Spruance had one of the finest all-around naval minds of World War II; as his ability became apparent, in the years after he left Annapolis, he had continuously gained stature. Like Mitscher, Spruance worked at a stand-up desk; like Mitscher, he was reserved and taciturn. His nose was long and thin, slightly hooked; his appearance was commanding. He was a "walker," taking long, tigerish strides. Like Mitscher, he delegated authority easily.

But as the ships headed straight toward the Marshalls, Mitscher was wary of the shy, stern, Baltimore-born senior admiral. Computer-minded Raymond Spruance was a gunnery man and a surface sailor. Mitscher was afraid that a gunnery man might not fully appreciate the power ready within the fast carriers. He knew what he wanted to do, and his plans did not include fighting major offensive battles with the battleships' guns.

As Spruance and Mitscher began their sweep across the Pacific, there were several sharp disagreements over how best to use the task force. That was to be expected. Any commander worth his stars thinks for himself. It would be unhealthy for two senior commanders to have identical mental processes. Admiral Spruance, who later became our ambassador to the Philippines, has stated that he felt that Mitscher's proper function was primarily as a tactician, whereas he, as commander of the Fifth Fleet, had to be both strategist and tactician. At the same time, Spruance recognized that Mitscher was a master in handling carriers and their air groups.

Both were conservative in approach, with one important exception. Mitscher was never a conservative fighter. He was the eager fighter who had a Sunday punch in each hand and knew it, and was willing to take a blow to get in two. Spruance, the scientific boxer, wanted to make sure his opponent was worn down, and not faking, before closing for the kill.

Some of the members of Spruance's staff thought Mitscher was too often willing to take unnecessary risks, while the air-staff people considered the Spruance organization too cautious. Of course, Admiral Spruance, as the senior commander, always had the last word.

On the morning of January 29, D-Day minus two, Task Force 58 was in position to attack the initial targets.

Mitscher had deployed his task groups within a radius of 150 miles, so that the individual groups could be combined if an enemy surface unit should loom up. Such an engagement was pleasant to contemplate, but unlikely. At 0500, he had 700 aircraft, fully armed and fueled, ready to attack the Marshalls. Intelligence estimated that the defending Japanese had about 150 aircraft.

No signal from the *Yorktown*'s flag bridge told the task-group commanders to launch aircraft. The launching procedure had been worked out in minute detail beforehand. Wings were locked. Engines roared. One by one, the planes rose from the decks—fighters first, followed split seconds later by bombers and torpedo planes. Some Japanese battled briskly; some gave no battle at all. By noon, Mitscher had complete air control over the Marshalls. By the end of the day not an enemy plane remained operational east of Eniwetok.

Eniwetok, however, was still untouched, so on January 30,

Mitscher sent Rear Admiral Alfred E. Montgomery, in *Essex,* with Task Group 58.2 to attack the island that later became an atom-bomb proving ground. Meanwhile, he distributed his other groups around the islands to continue the destruction, which came to be called the "Mitscher shampoo." The surface ships then moved in close to hammer the Marshalls in what became known as the "Spruance haircut," a spectacular attack which left palm trees splintered like pinfeathers, shattered and smoking.

The Japanese lost an estimated 155 planes. Mitscher's losses were fifty-seven planes, thirty-one pilots and thirty-two crewmen, but the concentrated preinvasion slashing so reduced infantry casualties that the pattern of future Pacific invasions, and of naval air power usage, was established. Referring to this type of operation in his summary for the month of January, 1944, Admiral Nimitz said that it was "typical of what may be expected in the future."

Mitscher's operation plan for FLINTLOCK had assumed it would take at least two full days to wrest control of the air over the Marshalls from the Japanese. "As a matter of record," he said in his Action Report, "full and complete control was obtained in less than half a day." He thought this quick success was the result of striking all major air bases simultaneously, the use of dawn fighter strikes, and the effectiveness of incendiary bullets against planes parked on enemy air strips.

"Jap planes still burn very well," he concluded.

He began to express his ideas on ways and means to improve the Navy's air war, and asked for immediate training of special photographic units for carrier air groups. He believed, he said in the report, that future operations depended solely, for full effect, on prior photographic reports. He asked for development of a camera to take pictures of enemy installations or ships from a plane traveling 400 mph, flying at altitudes of less than a thousand feet.

He was also concerned about night training for the pilots. His type of operation called for predawn aircraft launches, and he feared the pilots would crack up after being launched because they couldn't see a horizon. His advice was to create an artificial horizon by having the screening destroyers, out ahead of the task force, turn on their truck lights, even though this meant the ships would be visible to submarines.

None of his hatred for the Japanese had rubbed off during the five-month lull at San Diego. Instead, it had grown more intense while he had time to reflect on the atrocities committed against American flyers.

"I hate those yellow —— worse than if I were a Marine," he once said. On such occasions his face assumed an expression that came to be known to his staff as the "Guadalcanal Smile."

CHAPTER

⚓ 27 ⚓

Truk

BRIEFING officers declared Truk should be pronounced "Trook, as in spook." Since World War I, Japan had administered the tiny atoll under the seemingly peaceful South Sea Prefectural Government. But military-intelligence personnel confessed they had only sketchy ideas of the actual armed strength of Dublon, the principal island, and of Eten, Moen, Uman, and Fefan. Truk was labeled a "major Japanese naval base," and various estimates put its air power at anywhere from a sensible 200 to a fantastic 1,000 aircraft.

Several Marine B-24's made a daring flight from the Solomons on February 3 to photograph Truk. But even the weather had succumbed to its spell. Clouds covered the atoll, except a few rifts, and one of these openings revealed the mast tops of more than twenty enemy warships. Experts studying the pictures became excited when they saw the outlines of a huge battleship. It resembled the *Yamato*, the world's largest battleship and a weapon of grave consequence.

Nimitz decided on immediate action. Meanwhile, Mitscher had steamed to Majuro (Arrowsmith) Island, in the Marshalls, one of the quick prizes of the campaign. Studded with palms, a former way-stop for the South Seas Trading Company schooners, it provided the task force with a convenient haven.

While planning for the raid on Truk progressed, Hedding and the other staff members were feeling out the new admiral, trying to anticipate his desires and form a pattern of operation that would please him. They soon learned not to show him fragments of ideas or plans. He wanted whatever was presented to be as polished as possible. When the plan had reached this near perfection, there was free discussion of it.

As at Guadalcanal, he would take an idea, alter it if need be, embellish it, or suggest a new approach. But he seldom destroyed the basic idea. They soon discovered the basis for his success in outwitting the enemy, which had been described as uncanny on Guadalcanal. It was principally a matter of imaginatively slipping into the boots of the opposing commander. Sometimes he would say to his staff: "Now, what would you be doing if you were that little saffron ——?"

Both Japanese and American carriers began using weather as an ally early in the war, and for the attack on Truk, Mitscher planned to hide under a front, then dart out to hammer the vaunted base. The front would probably limit the activity of enemy air search patrols. At this point, he reached deeper into his bag of fast-carrier tricks—a bag which he had been filling since the Battle of Midway. Use of an initial fighter sweep to destroy enemy air defenses before launching the slower bombers was common sense, but directing the pilots who flew the final strike at dusk to plant thousand-pound bombs on enemy runways, making overnight repair arduous, was unconventional. As he went along, he developed other bits of air-combat technique. For instance, he advised task-group commanders not to hit fuel dumps until the last strike of the day. Otherwise, so much smoke filled the air that targets couldn't be seen. These and similar recommendations seemed elementary, but taken all together they resulted in prosperous air tactics.

He decided to use three of the four task groups on the Truk raid. The fourth, under Rear Admiral S. P. Ginder, was needed to cover the invasion of Eniwetok. The Truk raid was diversionary, timed to coincide with the beach landings. If a Truk surface battle was forced, Spruance would have tactical command; if the fight was aerial, Mitscher would command the fleet.

The problem sounds exceedingly simple ten years afterward: You have a certain number of carriers and planes, steam to launching position, run up FOX flag (the signal indicating that a carrier was launching or landing aircraft), and the battle is joined. But to the men actually participating in the operation, the number of planes and carriers meant nothing against the doubt that came from a lack of information.

"They didn't tell us where we were going until we were well on the way," said Air Group Nine's new commander, Phil Torrey. "They announced our destination over the loudspeaker. It was Truk. My first instinct was to jump overboard." [1]

On this cruise, Mitscher had an opportunity to try close concentration of the task groups. Senior surface officers, fearing collision in maneuvering, had advised against it. But Mitscher told his staff emphatically that unless the captains could handle their vessels, they shouldn't be there.

Ships of the task groups remained in visual contact, and the launching point, 90 miles from Dublon Island, was reached at 0645, February 16. At 0650, seventy-two fighters streaked off the carrier decks, orbited for the join-up, and then headed for Truk. Bombing strikes were staggered over the two days of attack. The sleepy enemy lost fifty-six planes in a few hours and about seventy-two more were destroyed on the ground.

[1] Oliver O. Jensen, *Carrier War* (New York, Simon & Schuster, 1945).

The collection of ships at Truk—bait for the raid—was disappointing. The big one, thought to be the *Yamato*, had departed. At 1118, Spruance took tactical command to stop surface vessels fleeing the beleaguered isle.

Some aviators complained at not being chosen to sink the rest of the Truk fleet, but the surface-ship gunners deserved a chance too. Spruance swept the atoll counterclockwise with a surface element, catching a light training cruiser, a destroyer, and an armed trawler. Between air and surface attack, a total of thirty-seven ships, of which the largest were two cruisers, were left burning and sinking. Havoc had rained on the enemy's base.

Truk, with only the first day's strike over, was a graveyard. Mitscher chuckled over the preraid fears, hinting at his own misgivings. "All I knew about Truk was what I'd read in the *National Geographic.*" [2]

The *Essex*-class carrier *Intrepid* was hit by an aerial torpedo shortly after midnight and left the scene of action. Then Spruance pulled out of formation and headed toward Kwajalein, leaving Mitscher to proceed on still another raid. On completion of the Truk strike, Mitscher assigned Admiral Reeves, with the *Enterprise,* the cruiser *San Diego,* and six destroyers, to hit Jaluit, in the Marshalls, which had been bypassed in the previous raid. Then, with only two of his original four task groups, he steamed to an area about 1,200 miles east-southeast of the Marianas to reorganize and refuel.

[2] Probably the issue of June, 1942.

CHAPTER

⚓ 28 ⚓

Scouting the Marianas

NIMITZ's next assignment for Task Force 58 was a sneak raid on the Marianas which would both destroy planes, shipping, and base facilities and supply a fresh batch of aerial photographs which might reveal strengths and weaknesses to his Pearl Harbor planners, already forging a program to take Saipan, Tinian, and Rota, and retake Guam. Operation FORAGER was the program's code name. Mitscher's carrier strength consisted of three heavy carriers, *Essex, Yorktown,* and *Bunker Hill,* and three light carriers, *Monterey, Cowpens,* and *Belleau Wood.* His flagship was still the *Yorktown.*

Shortly before 1400 on February 21, with the task force penetrating deeper into Japanese-controlled waters than ever before, an enemy Betty roaming on search patrol happened on the two task groups. Fighters from the CAP were vectored after the twin-engined bomber but couldn't catch it. Unless the Japanese pilot was skylarking, Task Force 58 had been spotted. From the Marianas to Tokyo, the enemy would be alerted.

Captain Hedding was concerned, but Mitscher sat in his chair with his feet propped comfortably on the base of a gyro-

repeater compass and gave every appearance of not thinking about it. To Hedding there was something admirably but
also frustratingly complacent in the silence of the small figure
in the chair—especially since, as always, Mitscher rode facing aft.

However, he had said a few words on the subject earlier
in the day. When it was suggested that the enemy might spot
them, Mitscher, looking up over his glasses, had replied, "We
could always fight our way in. We could hide in the storms."

Yet as Mitscher sat staring moodily seaward, Hedding
almost felt that the new task-force chief did not fully realize
that no carrier task force ever had risked an all-out fight with
a land-based air force after discovery. And in the ready rooms,
between embroidery stitches and letters to home and fitful
naps, there was watchful waiting. The Admiral was still an
unknown quantity in carrier warfare, and the pilots were understandably careful in judging the man who was to send
them into battle.

Then a dispatch board was handed to Hedding, with a
message monitored from the enemy radio. The Japanese pilot
had seen Mitscher's caravan. Hedding passed the board to
Mitscher, who glanced at it and jotted his initials on it. Then
he grinned at his chief of staff, and instructed him to send this
signal:

WE HAVE BEEN SIGHTED BY THE ENEMY X WE WILL FIGHT OUR
WAY IN

It was Mitscher's first big command decision of the carrier
war, although few people who knew him really expected him
to do anything but fight his way in. The decision was char-
acteristic of his method throughout the rest of his service on
the flattops.

He predicted an attack shortly after sunset, and the ships
made ready. Because of the expected time of the attack, he
decided to let the antiaircraft gunners duel with the enemy

planes. Fighter defense would have been helpful, but the pilots were inexperienced in night operation.

At the turning of dusk, the twenty-nine warships steamed onward over the desolate waters of the west Pacific as gunners checked their magazines, limbered up their pieces, and plugged their ears with cotton. The bo'sun's mate sounded his pipe, and was answered by all the discordant sounds of a ship going to general quarters. Darkness came quickly. Mitscher stood on the wing of the flag bridge and 'talked with Elmont Waite, who was aboard to do an article for the *Saturday Evening Post*. "It's the first time we've done this, you know," Mitscher said rather proudly.

At 2100, with the sky flat black, the attack developed. Huddled down on the dark face of the ocean, tell-tale trails of phosphorus swirling astern, Mitscher's ships were not difficult to locate. The enemy pilots found them.

Eight bogeys rode in on Task Group 58.2, two of them aiming at the *Yorktown* and the *Essex*. Mitscher left his chair to lean against the bridge rail. Throughout the night, the enemy pressed the attack, concentrating mainly on the *Yorktown–Essex-Belleau Wood* task group. Steaming to the north, Admiral Frederick Sherman's group was hardly disturbed. After one long attack, Mitscher signaled to Sherman: BUT WHERE THE HELL WERE YOU.

Sherman came back: JAPS LIKE YOUR COMPANY BETTER THAN MINE.

The final phase of the enemy offensive took place from 0800 to 1000 on the morning of February 22; not a ship had been hit during the night, and Mitscher's planes were already airborne to retaliate for the loss of sleep. He signaled the task force: TODAY IS GEORGE WASHINGTONS BIRTHDAY X LETS CHOP DOWN A FEW NIP CHERRY TREES.

From 0800 until 1500, the planes of Task Force 58 whined over Guam, Saipan, Tinian, and Rota—bombing, strafing, photographing, and sinking ships. Smoke towered in the sky, and rubble and ruin were left behind. More than seventy enemy aircraft were destroyed on the ground and fifty-one in air combat. Mitscher had lost six planes, six pilots, and two aircrewmen. Some admirals, in making out their reports, would state: ". . . we lost *only* six planes and six pilots." But the loss of even one plane and one pilot disturbed Mitscher. He usually prefaced his casualty report by saying: "*Unfortunately*, we lost . . ."

Shortly after 1500 on February 22, he signaled to reverse course, and the task force started back to Majuro, while he questioned pilots of the *Yorktown* air group on the results of the strike. In the six weeks the task force had been under his command, a total of 5,456 sorties had been flown, two thousand tons of bombs dropped, and an estimated 484 aircraft destroyed, with thirty-two Japanese ships sunk and another eighteen damaged.

But of even greater significance as the ships steamed toward Majuro was Mitscher's victory in the ready rooms, in the wardrooms, and in the aircrewmen's mess, where men talked with their hands in airman's language. The commander of Task Force 58 had made the grade where it counted. Three separate fights—three wins. This was the prologue to a new type of naval-air warfare, utilizing many carriers, fast battleships, and a daring underlying concept. The immediate reason for the revolution in fast-carrier tactics, the change from hit-and-run to hit-and-stay, was easily recognized as the overwhelming increase in the number of fast combat ships since September, 1943. Perhaps even more important, however, was the fact that to this strength was joined a new spirit of persistence.

As Mitscher later told Captain Luis de Florez: "There are just so many Jap planes on any island. We'll go in and take it on the chin. We'll swap punches with them. I know I'll have losses, but I'm stronger than they are. If it takes two task forces, we'll get two task forces. I don't give a damn now if they do spot me. I can go anywhere and nobody can stop me. If I go in and destroy all their aircraft, their damned island is no good to them anyhow."

The role of aircraft carriers in the Pacific had changed almost overnight from sporadic raiding to steady offensive action.

While Task Force 58 freely roved the ocean, Admiral King was formulating a new policy. He decreed that all aviation task-force commanders would henceforth have surface chiefs of staff. King felt a nonaviator chief of staff would make possible better co-ordination with the screening ships and would balance thinking on air operations.

In due course, Mitscher received a message from the Bureau of Naval Personnel outlining the new policy. Hedding had already seen it and knew it meant his exodus as chief of staff. Mitscher brushed the paper aside in annoyance. "I'm not going to do it," he said. "It's my privilege to select my own chief of staff." Furthermore, it appeared to be direct Washington interference with the traditional prerogatives of sea commands.

"That's an order, Admiral," Hedding reminded him. "I don't see how you can do otherwise."

"If it's an order, Captain," Mitscher said sharply, "you select the man."

It was apparent to Hedding that Mitscher wanted no further discussion of King's new policy. The Bureau of Naval Personnel had suggested four possible candidates, all surface veterans. Hedding picked the last name on the list—Captain Arleigh Albert Burke, better known as 31-Knot Burke. Hedding drafted a dispatch to the Bureau of Naval Personnel, and unsuspecting 31-Knot Burke, directing his destroyer squadron around the Bismarck Archipelago, was in for the surprise of his life. The rough-and-tumble sailor was extremely fond of surface ships and gunnery, and not very fond of aircraft carriers.

CHAPTER
⚓ 29 ⚓

Arleigh Burke Arrives

MITSCHER had changed flagships. He was now aboard the U.S.S. *Lexington,* an *Essex*-class carrier, fresh out of a shipyard with a shiny welding job as the only sign of a December, 1943, torpedoing, and it was this 27,000 tonner that Captain Arleigh Albert Burke boarded at sea after much advance heralding. The stocky, sandy-haired, four-striper was already a naval celebrity in his own right. The dash and daring of the destroyer navy was personified by the forty-three-year-old Burke. A commissioned officer for twenty-one years, he had served in or commanded a half dozen ships. Burke was an expert in ordnance engineering, and not only knew how to shoot guns but understood the science of explosives. In 1943, after more than a year of badgering the Bureau of Naval Personnel to give him sea duty, he had gone to the Solomons to command a division of destroyers; then he was assigned a squadron of two divisions. The exploits of his "Little Beaver" squadron were numerous and spectacular. Burke seemed never to be making less than top speed, 30 knots or more, an astonishing pace for the little ships.

He was nicknamed "31-Knot" during the November, 1943,

clashes off Bougainville. "That bird has told us he could make *only* 30 knots," growled Captain H. R. Thurber, operations officer for Halsey's South Pacific command, when Burke reported he had built up to 31 knots as he careened after Japanese transports.[1] Another time, when Allied shipping blocked Burke from a covey of Japanese ships, the ubiquitous captain bawled: "Stand aside, I'm coming through at 31 knots." And come he did!

However, Mitscher was not outwardly impressed with Burke nor with his fresh string of surface triumphs the day they first met in late March, 1944. Burke had no special desire to be aboard the *Lexington*, and was not awed by the wizened man who had just been elevated to the rank of vice admiral. On the port wing of the *Lexington*'s bridge, Mitscher returned Burke's salute, and proffered his hand, asking if the captain's gear was aboard. Burke answered, "Yes, Admiral." Most of it was on his back.

"You live in my cabin," Mitscher said, meaning his gallery-deck space. Mitscher lived in his tiny sea cabin on the flag bridge. His in-port quarters, with a full bed instead of a bunk, and more luxurious than anything Burke had experienced, were vacant at the time.

Captain Burke knew practically nothing about the mazes of aircraft carriers but managed to find the Admiral's cabin; there he luxuriated in a shower, marveled at the finery, and decided that carriers were eminently more habitable than destroyers. Refreshed and ready for work, he reported back to the flag bridge, expecting Mitscher to brief him at length on the operations of a fast-carrier task force. Captain Hedding had been loaned to another staff temporarily, so he was not present to give Burke a fill-in.

Burke stood waiting on the bridge wing, a few feet away

[1] Walter Karig and others, *Battle Report*, Volume V (New York, Rinehart, 1949).

from the Admiral, rocking back and forth on his heels. But Mitscher remained silent, completely ignoring the presence of his new chief of staff. Somewhat chagrined, Burke finally walked away. He tried to learn what he could from other members of the staff, and to assimilate the rest by osmosis. It was not a happy situation, and Burke had been happy on the destroyers.

Captain Burke recalls that he would come out on the bridge wing two hours before dawn, hoping each day that the Admiral's ice would melt. He would greet Mitscher with all the pleasantness he could muster. Mitscher would do no more than grunt in return. Whether Mitscher thought he might cold-shoulder Burke into requesting another billet, thereby making it possible for him to retain Hedding, or whether he was just being unusually cantankerous, is anyone's guess. It is certain, however, that Mitscher did not want *any* surface officer for his chief of staff. Very probably, Burke was being punished for the policy Admiral King had instituted.

While this chill settled over the flag bridge, the task force proceeded on to the Carolines to strike at Palau, Yap, and Woleai. There were eleven carriers in three task groups, with the usual escorts. Admiral Spruance was in the battleship *New Jersey*, and Mitscher's flagship was in Ginder's group, 58.3, composed of the heavy carriers (CV) *Lexington* and *Yorktown*, and the light carriers (CVL) *Princeton* and *Langley*. Some elements sortied from Manus in the Admiralty Islands. Nimitz had assumed that the Japanese fleet element based in Palau—supposedly one to three battleships, four to six heavy cruisers, fifteen destroyers, and a few submarines—would withdraw from Palau rather than risk a brawl with carriers. The Japanese had an estimated 150 to 170 planes at Palau. There would be another air struggle, if anything.

When the destination was announced, the cooks and bakers, aviation mechanics and bo'suns, and gunners, and soda-fountain attendants, in the five or six labyrinthine decks below ran for their atlases and gasped. Palau was 1,200 miles west of Truk, 500 miles from powerful Japanese encampments in the Philippines. This would be the deepest penetration of the war. The operation was coded DESECRATE ONE.

By now, Mitscher knew that they could go anywhere whether or not they were discovered before attacking the enemy, and this confidence had filtered down to the puniest escort in Task Force 58. They were sighted by Japanese land-based aircraft on March 25, while proceeding south of Truk. On March 29, a few hours short of launching time, the United States submarine *Tunny* reported the hasty departure of the Japanese ship unit from Palau, as Nimitz had predicted.

During the day and on into the night of March 29, Japanese planes harassed the task force. Once, torpedo planes came boring in and no one on the bridge appeared to be doing anything about it. Mitscher seemed rather disinterested. Arleigh Burke grabbed the TBS and gave maneuvering orders to the fleet. Then, considerably worried, Burke went to Mitscher, expecting a severe dressing down for the precipitous action.

Mitscher swiveled around in his chair. "Well, it was about time, Captain Burke," he said. He had been waiting for days to see Burke exert his authority. After that, Burke reported, relations between them began to improve slowly—very, very slowly.

At 0630 on March 30, the three task groups were 90 miles south of Palau, and the attack was launched. According to Rear Admiral Montgomery, the raid on Palau was actually more daring and dangerous than the first strike on Truk, but Truk remained the pilots' symbol of a mission against overwhelming odds. Palau, even though it had some of the hypnotic quality of Truk, did not seem a discouragingly difficult undertaking. Dawn sweeps eliminated all the airborne Japanese even though Palau's defenses had been reinforced during the night.

Mitscher was forced to try a new approach in attacking Palau. Usually he was delighted to experiment with something novel, but not this time. Nimitz had ordered trial use of carrier-based aircraft to mine Palau; bottling up the harbor was one of the prime objectives of the raid. Mitscher's was a typical pilot's reaction to such a directive. His feelings were shared by pilots in the *Lexington*, the *Hornet* and the *Bunker Hill*. Low-level aerial mining through heavy ack-ack is not exactly a safe pastime. But the mission was successful, despite his fears. It was the first carrier-plane mining mission of the war.

At Palau, twenty-six out of forty-four pilots were snatched from probable death by cruiser float planes, submarines, and destroyers. However, this wasn't enough for Mitscher—although the percentage figure was the highest of the carrier war to date—and he told his staff not to feel satisfied until they could show him a seventy-five per cent or better rescue figure. On April 1, he ordered the task force to return to Majuro.

At Majuro, Truman Hedding returned to the flagship and renewed acquaintance with Arleigh Burke. It was not a joyous tale Burke had to tell. He did not like being just an observer, and Mitscher's sphinxlike attitude had not thawed appreciably. Captain Burke was not in the least ashamed of being a surface professional, and never would be. "I'm not going to put up with this too much longer," he warned.

"It's a job of great importance," replied Hedding. "In fact, it's one of the best jobs in the Pacific. He's hard to understand at first, but he's a great man."

Hedding then pointed out that when Mitscher got over being miffed at having a surface chief of staff, all would be well. Captain Burke, a very patient man, sucked on his pipe and answered slowly, agreeing to endure the frost a while longer.

Despite the treatment he accorded Captain Burke, Mitscher was really welding together the fast-carrier fighting force by his skill in human relations. Unlike Admiral Spruance, who certainly appreciated people but apparently found it difficult to show his appreciation, Mitscher knew a hundred different ways to say "thanks," and used them all.

When *Lexington*'s commanding officer, Captain Felix Stump, who is now Commander in Chief, Pacific, was relieved to assume promotion to rear admiral, he was replaced by a younger man, Captain Ernest Litch. Litch had been ashore since the beginning of the war. This was his first combat tour. Under these circumstances following in the path of the veteran Stump was bad enough; it was decidedly worse to take command on the task-force flagship, and Litch was extremely nervous. But at the end of the first day's operations, Mitscher called up to him, "Best day's combat operations I've ever seen." The fact that such a tribute would not normally be expected from such a retiring, taciturn personality made it even more effective. There was not the slightest doubt as to his sincerity. When the occasion arose, boot ensigns and orderlies were praised, as well as four-stripers.

Once, in Majuro, Henry Mustin, Jr., son of the late old-time aviator, came over from the *Cowpens* on an errand of mercy.

"Hi, Uncle Pete," said Mustin.

Mitscher coughed politely, and Mustin said quickly, "Admiral, sir," as the commander grinned. Henry explained his mission. The mother of a pilot on the *Cowpens* was dying of cancer. The *Cowpens* air group was trying to get him back to the States in time.

"Is he much good?" Mitscher asked.

"Well, no, he's clumsy on landing."

"We go in tomorrow and I need every pilot. I hate to take anybody out this late."

"He's really not a very good pilot, Admiral," Mustin insisted.

"We'll see what we can do."

That evening, the *Cowpens* pilot departed for Chicago, and he arrived there before his mother died. Another time, after

Guam was secured, Mitscher sent his two Chamorro mess boys, without their asking, on leave to see how their families were getting along.

In the military, this is called "looking out for the troops." It is easy for an infantry company commander or a destroyer skipper to show interest in personal welfare, but conveying this feeling to a hundred thousand men in a task force is almost a job for an advertising agency. But men have to be "looked out for" or they won't fight efficiently. Mitscher was criticized for coddling by some officers, who operated on the premise that anything approaching sympathy was dangerous to discipline. But he didn't coddle. He merely weighed advantages and disadvantages. Once, a senior admiral's staff prepared court-martial proceedings against a task-force air squadron commander for an alleged shoreside escapade. The man was a demon pilot. Mitscher's staff informed him of the situation.

"That fellow's pretty lively," he observed. "We should have been taking better care of him." The court-martial never materialized.

He quite sensibly paid most attention to the pilots. His efforts at air-sea rescue, which he made certain were known to the pilots, probably had more effect on morale than any other single measure. He watched carefully for signs of combat fatigue. The pilots, because of the great personal effort they expended, felt fatigue sooner than most of the others. He talked to them at every opportunity, seeing them not in large groups, but one or two at a time. He was certainly interested in what the pilots had to say, but one of his main reasons for summoning them was to check on their physical condition. Mitscher did little talking himself during these post-strike interviews. It was just as well.

"My ears were usually ringing from riding in the aircraft and he talked so low I couldn't hear him," said one pilot.

Mitscher had begun to hand-pick his staff, which numbered

140 officers and men, as reliefs were needed for members who were due for a rest. He had requested that Gus Widhelm be sent out as his operations officer. He hadn't seen him since leaving the *Hornet* after the Battle of Midway.

Meantime, Widhelm had become one of the most successful plane fighters in the South Pacific. He was quite happy as commander of Fighter Squadron 75, and hated to leave it, pinning his ribbons and wings on upside down at the squadron's farewell for him. He was still wearing that sign of mourning when he reported to Mitscher's bridge. The Admiral spotted the distress signal, greeted Gus warmly, and admonished, "It isn't going to be that bad."

Then another perennial reached Task Force 58. Captain Luis de Florez flew out to join the task force and check on pilot training. De Florez was probably doing more to accelerate the flow of pilots to the fleet than any other man in the Navy. His synthetic training devices were performing miracles, and he had stayed around Washington long enough to see his 1940 request for ten thousand engineers almost realized.

De Florez was soon up to his tricks, frequently providing Mitscher with what de Florez considered "comic relief" but were actually often valuable and invariably ingenious innovations. At times, it was sorely needed. In the Navy today, there is a carrier maneuver known as "Operation Pinwheel." It was later a point of emphasis in James Michener's novel on the Korean war, *The Bridges at Toko-Ri*. Pinwheel was born on Mitscher's flagship. De Florez said he could move the *Lexington* with aircraft engines alone.

Gus Widhelm piped up, "Impossible!"

Mitscher listened attentively while the two men argued. Then Widhelm bet de Florez a hundred dollars it couldn't be done. De Florez, however, had worked it out on paper and knew that it could.

"Go ahead and try it," said Mitscher. De Florez arranged

the planes herringbone style and had the air mechanics turn up the engines. There was no movement at first; then slowly the big *Lexington* began to stir; finally, it moved steadily ahead.

"Gus, you'd better stick to killing Japs," said Mitscher, as Widhelm paid de Florez his hundred dollars. Operation Pinwheel, although it pains the aircraft mechanics, has since been used many times to shunt carriers when tugs weren't available, or to maneuver them in tight spots.

Meanwhile, the climate on the flag bridge was warming up a bit. Mitscher was showing signs of respect toward 31-Knot Burke. Now and then, with restraint, he would apply humor to Burke's situation. A destroyer came alongside the *Lexington* and the Admiral, without smiling, said to his Marine orderly, "Secure Captain Burke until that destroyer casts off."

Burke was with the task force to stay; soon there would be peace between them.

CHAPTER

⚓ 30 ⚓

"Bald Eagle"

GIVEN his successes, Mitscher, with his wizened face, his long-billed cap, and his chair on the bridge, could not help attracting attention. William McGaffin, of the Chicago *Daily News*, was down on the *Lexington*'s flight deck one day and overheard several plane handlers: "The Old Man sits up there all day, riding backwards. The bow could drop off this ship and he wouldn't look around." Mitscher helped the mystery along sometimes, claiming he had looked ahead for so many years that it was time to reverse his position and see where he'd been. Actually, he rode facing aft to keep the wind out of his face.

Although several stories were attached to it at one time or another, the long-billed cap had no other purpose than to keep the sun out of his eyes; indeed, in 1946 the Navy adopted the cap style, so it could be worn officially as a part of the working uniform. When Mitscher went ashore, however, he doffed the famed headpiece, most often wearing an overseas cap instead. He never wore his fancy gold-braided dress hat at sea. He had several of the long-billed caps during the war, and they are now museum items. Once, he was given a new one and tried it out for several hours. Then his staff saw him duck into his sea cabin and come out with the older, more familiar cap.

If he boarded a flagship which did not happen to have a swivel-topped chair, elevated for easy view, and placed at the precise spot he preferred, a metalsmith would be assigned to construct one. His chair on the *Lexington* stood almost four feet high. Its fixed legs supported a swivel seat, and it had a footrest about twelve inches off the deck. Mitscher rested his feet alternately on the footrest and on the base of the nearby repeater compass. The chair was leather-cushioned but had a canvas slipcover over it most of the time to protect it from the weather.

When he emerged from his sea cabin in the morning for the day's work, the twin pockets of his shirt bulged with all the paraphernalia he would need. He kept his wallet, cigarettes, matches, glasses—practically everything but a handkerchief— in his shirt pockets. The shirts were always fresh and crisp and the creases in his khaki pants were knifelike.

Although the stewards did most of the major repair work on his clothing, he sometimes sewed on his own buttons. Frances had given him a sewing kit and he was moderately good with a needle and thread. The only ornamentation he wore was his wings, and he was never without them.

He smoked, on the average, about a pack and a half of cigarettes each day. But when there was heavy action, he'd puff through two packs. He could light his cigarette with a single match, even in high wind. He seldom missed, and took pleasure in showing landsmen exactly how the hand should be cupped to do the trick.

Mitscher was not a walker, at least not in the traditional bridge-pacing sense. Once he was asked why not, and replied that he was never good at dramatics. He seemed to stay physically fit without a great deal of walking. At the day's end, he would get into his bunk and read for about an hour. He once said he was tempted to bring the cop-and-robber stories out on the wing of the bridge to while away dull moments, which were few. However, he felt this wouldn't set a good example for the junior officers.

Even when the ship was at anchor, Mitscher seldom left flag country and consequently was not seen to any great extent by members of the flagship crew. He would not do anything that bordered on invasion of privacy. His flag country was private; so were the living and berthing spaces of the crew. For the same reason, he did not inject himself into gatherings aboard ship unless official duties required it. He would attend an infrequent movie, but his staff members cannot remember seeing him at divine services.

Mitscher was not a churchgoer, but neither was he an agnostic. A Mason, he respected the church and believed in God, although he seldom joined in formal worship. He had read Lloyd C. Douglas's *Magnificent Obsession* several times and often told Frances how much he believed in the idea of the book. He felt that giving to others was the basis of true religion, but that the giving should remain a secret.

Numerous popular magazine articles and newspaper stories published during World War II referred to Mitscher as "saltily profane." However, his profanity, wrote William McGaffin, "was so soft and unemphatic that it sounded like prayer." In times of excessive stress, he was addicted to saying, "Goddammitohell." Generally, his expletives were mild.

In the middle of the war he looked much the same as he had in prewar days. His eyes had always impressed those around him; it was Rear Admiral William Read who said, "He was one of the few men I've known who could give an order with a glance."

Mitscher's code name was now Bald Eagle, and it suited him perfectly.

CHAPTER

⚓ 31 ⚓

Hollandia and Truk Again

IT WAS time to be moving. The Army was ready for the invasion of Hollandia, in Dutch New Guinea, and the conference boats had completed their trips back and forth across Majuro harbor. The task force steamed out to sea. Mitscher was taking three carrier groups to Hollandia. The battleship force was under Vice Admiral Willis A. Lee, Jr., as usual. There were six battleships. More and more, this looked like the ideal combination: fast carriers and a liberal number of fast battleships, cruisers, and destroyers. Back in 1943, Spruance had added the fast battleships for the Gilbert Islands operations, and their heavy firepower and huge concentrations of antiaircraft guns were invaluable.

In rough, abrupt "Ching" Lee, the Fifth Fleet possessed one of the most able but least recognized talents of World War II. "Putting Ching Lee and Pete Mitscher together was the smartest thing the Navy ever did. You had the best surface tactics and the best air tactics the world has ever known," Admiral Halsey once remarked.

MacArthur's main landings were to take place at Tanahmerah Bay, but the task force was appointed to bang away at targets more than a hundred miles on either side, to neutralize enemy air power. As the carriers neared Dutch New Guinea, General Kenney's Fifth Army air force paid an advance visit. Pickings were therefore bound to be slimmer than usual for the Navy pilots.

Throughout April 21, strikes were launched at various fields on Hollandia. On April 22 and 23, Mitscher's fellow Oklahoman, Cherokee-blooded Rear Admiral Jocko Clark hit Wakde, while other groups hovered around to provide close support, a Navy specialty. The Army landings went off smoothly.

The Japanese fleet declined action, although for a while Mitscher thought there would be a battle. An Army search plane reported a large enemy fleet of combatant ships in the area near Halmahera. If this report was true, Mitscher's force would be in for a hard fight, and the landing would be in danger. However, Navy search planes, sent to verify and amplify the sighting, discovered that the target was a group of small craft about the size of junks.

Mitscher spent much time studying the maneuvers of the foot soldiers. To the casual observer, it sometimes appeared that he was fighting a land battle instead of operating ships. However, close co-ordination was necessary to avoid bombing friendly troops, as happened occasionally despite precautions. Besides, Mitscher was an informal student of soldiering and plotted the movements of the infantrymen for his own personal knowledge. He had the full Army plans for Hollandia, but they were so voluminous he couldn't unravel them after the initial landings had taken place. The operation was made especially complex by the division of command responsibility. He regularly sent planes over the area to bring back late information and check on the beach situation.

The day before an Army-Navy conference on how best to complete the campaign, Mitscher ordered Burke to personally reconnoiter the lines. When Burke, riding as a passenger in a torpedo plane, was airborne, Mitscher addressed his officers on

the TBS, outlining Burke's mission and saying that more details about the operations of the campaign would be available
when he returned. Then he added, "Of course, if he gets back."

When Burke bounced down on the *Lexington* again, with
the starboard wing of the plane full of holes and one aileron
gone, and reported his findings, Mitscher solemnly announced
the progress ashore to his commanders, then signed off with,
"Thirty-one-Knot Burke also reports he thinks the airplane is
here to stay." He still could not resist a dig at his surface-ship
chief of staff.

At the joint conference, several Army officers were amazed
to find that the Admiral knew more about the shore situation
than they did. Burke had come back to the flagship with detailed sketches of the Army positions. One result of the Hollandia operation, where the Army had no real knowledge of
carrier capabilities and limitations and the Navy had little say
in the conduct of land warfare, was a plea from Mitscher to
Nimitz (through his Action Report to Spruance) for a method
of obtaining more co-operation.

With Hollandia going well, General MacArthur's press officers sent out a story on the invasion, leaving no doubts as to the
hero of the day. Mitscher didn't care a whit about the inflated
press release but became angry when he saw that the story had
been paraphrased from a dispatch sent in the top general-
admiral code, and therefore compromised a communications
code and possibly made all previous communications in that
code available to the enemy, who it was assumed, monitored
every Task Force 58 transmission.

Mitscher had already shown dislike for the man with the
corncob pipe. The irritation was intensified at Hollandia, the
first occasion on which Mitscher worked directly with the
MacArthur organization. Nevertheless, during this period he
continued to be meticulous in delivering everything the carriers had to offer. He never pulled away from the landing

beaches until Burke had reported, after a last visit ashore, that Task Force 58 could be of no further use.

While the Hollandia episode of Task Force 58 is rather dull compared to previous and subsequent events, Mitscher did add a few more footnotes to the fast-carrier textbook. Other pilots had advocated the use of carrier-based fighter-bombers, but there had always been some objection. A fighter sacrifices speed when bomb racks are hooked on to it. However, Mitscher had a number fitted up for Hollandia, and they were successfully used until the end of the war, greatly increasing bomb tonnages delivered on target. Also, Hollandia saw the debut of extensive night-fighter operations by the fast carriers. Mitscher used the new night fighters for after-dark combat-air-patrol and heckling missions which kept the enemy up all night.

As Mitscher discussed the return to Majuro for replenishment of supplies, his staff saw that the course line, already laid out on the charts, would bring them invitingly close to Truk again. Burke knew what Mitscher was thinking: Plenty of bombs were left in the carriers. Hollandia had been relatively inexpensive.

"Let's hit Truk again," Mitscher said.

It threw the staff into a turmoil. They dragged out large-scale charts of Truk and began working. On April 26 the carriers were refueled in an area roughly 200 miles west of the Admiralties, escaping two submarine attacks that day without damage. On April 28, Mitscher signaled the task force: THE NEXT OPERATION IS OVER PET HATE X PLASTER IT WITH EVERY-THING YOU HAVE INCLUDING EMPTY BEER BOTTLES IF YOU HAVE ANY X WE HAVEN'T.

At 0650 on April 29, the Japanese sighted Mitscher and his ships and prepared a warm reception. At about 0800, an estimated twenty to forty-five enemy planes penetrated the American fighter defense and headed for the carriers, going after the

Yorktown and the *Monterey* first. But after some ticklish moments, the majority of the attackers were knocked down. Then an enemy submarine attacked. It was sunk by a destroyer, with a little assistance from the *Monterey*.

As action mounted, the *Lexington*'s bull horn bleated. Two Judys (single-engined Japanese dive bombers) had selected the flagship. The rows of gassed and armed bombers and torpedo planes on the carrier made her a potential pyre. One of the Judys was hit and plummeted into the sea less than a hundred feet off the deck; the other dropped a bomb. Fortunately, it missed; it was a shoddy performance by the enemy.

"Why the hell don't they use their machine guns," yelled de Florez.

"Shut up, Luis," Mitscher called over. "They might hear you!"

The surviving Judy fled for Truk with a bevy of Task Force 58 fighters buzzing behind.

Over "Pet Hate," the pilots found enemy aircraft tough and aggressive and antiaircraft fire heavy and extremely accurate—almost three times as intense as it had been during Mitscher's first call at Truk back in February. But by 1000—the time at which he usually sipped his morning cup of tea—mastery of the Truk sky was assured. Task Force 58 continued to batter the island the remainder of April 29 and most of April 30. While hitting Truk, he also ordered an attack on Satawan, in the Nomoi group, with both bombs and cruiser fire. On May 1, Ponape was hit. Then the ships headed for Majuro.

When offensive operations were secured, he signaled the force:

THIS TIME OUR WAY HAS BEEN LONG AND OUR DUTIES TIRESOME. THE LONGED FOR ENGAGEMENT WITH THE ENEMY FLEET FORCES WAS NOT ACCOMPLISHED DUE TO THEIR TIMIDITY X WE CANNOT GUARANTEE A FIGHT EVERY TIME WE GO TO SEA BUT WE

CAN ASSURE OURSELVES AND OUR PEOPLE AT HOME THAT WE
WILL BE IN THERE HITTING WHEN THE TIME DOES COME X

A Japanese pilot shot down near the task force was retrieved
and brought over to the *Lexington* by a destroyer. Captain de
Florez listened for a while to the attempts made by the inter-
preter to question the prisoner, and then returned to the bridge
to brief Mitscher.

"What did he say?" Mitscher asked.

"He's a sad man, Admiral," de Florez replied thoughtfully.
"He said he was disgraced and could never go home again. He
said he'd have to live in America all his life."

Mitscher had no sympathy and said so profanely.

Another time, when a destroyer picked up several prisoners,
its skipper proudly announced his feat. Mitscher signaled back:
"Why?"

May was a month of little action but much planning.
Mitscher sent Task Group 58.6, composed of the *Essex*, the
Wasp and the *San Jacinto*, with five cruisers and twelve destroyers, to hit Wake and Marcus, while he stayed on at Majuro
for final conferences on the invasion of the Marianas.

Although the force needed a rest, and did have some leisure
during May, Mitscher was busy. During these planning periods, when the immediate battle was over, he always seemed
very tired. The constant offensive, and the ever-present tension, which he camouflaged skillfully, were extracting energy
faster than he could replace it. His periods of silence grew
longer, and he tended to avoid contact with everyone but
his immediate staff. He would talk to de Florez and a few of
the newsmen, but de Florez distinctly felt that Mitscher wanted
to shut out the regular-line professionals during these periods,
to divorce himself for a few moments from the present and all
its symbols.

CHAPTER

⚓ 32 ⚓

Softening the Marianas

MITSCHER believed, as did Halsey, that the application of a light touch to otherwise grim operations plans issued to the task groups helped relieve prebattle tension. Once, he okayed a battle-plan cover consisting of a drawing of a pin-up girl asking the force, "How do you like this form?" For operations against the Marianas, basic tactical concepts were outlined under plans GUS, JOHNNY, and JEEPERS. Such frivolous titles were not in keeping with the dignified instructions of the War College. However, the moments in naval air-war history about to unfold must forever be irreverently remembered as stemming from GUS, JOHNNY, and JEEPERS.

Plan GUS was named, of course, for swashbuckling Gus Widhelm of Mitscher's staff; Plan JOHNNY was named for Lieutenant Commander John Myers, Widhelm's assistant in planning; and JEEPERS was derived from the favorite expression of Lieutenant Commander Burris D. Wood, Jr., the staff gunnery officer. These three officers functioned as Mitscher's planning group on the working level.

They set about, with Burke and Hedding as senior advisors, to implement the Task Force 58 major objectives assigned by

Admiral Spruance: Prevent enemy air interference with the capture of Saipan, protect the troops, destroy enemy aircraft with strikes three days prior to invasion, destroy enemy defenses in the Marianas, and neutralize Iwo Jima and Chichi Jima. It was a big order. Then were held sessions with Mitscher presiding, with task-group staffs and task-group admirals shuttling to and fro across Majuro's placid waters.

They first made a change in the assigned objectives, advancing the fighter strike from June 12 to June 11. This change in date, Mitscher reasoned, would enable him to surprise the Japanese even though they would certainly have observed his force approaching. For all of his previous strikes had been at dawn. The enemy therefore doubtless thought Task Force 58 was strictly a sun-up hitter. So he rescheduled the first strike for the late afternoon, planning to destroy enemy aircraft while they roosted on Saipan, Guam, Tinian, and Rota, waiting to come out at nightfall and hit his carriers. This was plan JOHNNY.

Plan GUS was the use of destroyers both as rescue vessels and as fighter-director ships. It was the first time a destroyer scouting line, twenty miles ahead of the task force and available to direct the CAP against enemy air raids, had been contemplated. Plan JEEPERS was the early-morning strike on D-Day minus three, the one originally envisioned by Admiral Spruance.

The Marianas form part of the almost continuous chain of islands stretching nearly 1,350 miles due south of Tokyo. The Japanese had used them as stepping stones to revitalize their defensive war, and they were a definite barrier to further American offensive action in the western Pacific. Saipan, for instance, was 1,000 miles from our advance base position in Eniwetok, 3,000 miles from Pearl Harbor. Saipan was selected as the first invasion target; Guam and Tinian would follow.

It was known that the Japanese had been strengthening the

Marianas and that there was heavy enemy fleet activity in the Tawitawi–Davao Gulf area. But the Imperial fleet had avoided battle for a long time, and there was nothing positive to indicate it would fight now. However, Mitscher suspected that Admiral Soemu Toyoda, latest in the line of Japanese commanders in chief, might be lured into action. He prescribed tentative measures to deal with the enemy fleet if it did appear, but did not alert the task force.

Saipan, the principal Japanese base in the Marianas, is a raised coral formation with a volcanic core, and is topped by arable land. Mount Tapotchau was identified a major landmark for pilots during their interminable briefings. By now, there was a sculptor aboard to make bas-relief miniatures of the targets. On these miniatures could be made out Mitscher's first concern —Saipan's three airfields.

When Task Force 58 sortied from Majuro on June 6, 1944, it consisted of ninety-three ships, of which fifteen were carriers. Mitscher took a generally northwesterly course, with the task groups keeping station twelve to fifteen miles from each other. On June 7 and 8, training exercises were held, and all but the heavy ships refueled on June 9. The staff worked on the plans until almost the eve of the initial attack, readying them for delivery by destroyer to all ships. Then Burke stepped out on the bridge, holding the completed, corrected document, and handed it to the Admiral. He handed it right back without a glance.

"Don't you even want to look at it?" Captain Burke asked, stunned. They'd been slaving and worrying over the plans for weeks.

Mitscher studied Burke for a minute, then grinned. "No, Captain Burke, I'm just going to sit here and watch it all unfold." He knew all of the essential parts of the plan. Besides, he felt anything else of importance would have to be decided on the spot. When Burke left the bridge wing, Mitscher was contentedly eating ice cream from a large china bowl.

Before the loudspeakers blared noontime "chow down" on June 11, Jocko Clark's Task Group 58.1 set out over the oily calm sea and steamed for Guam, where he struck Agana Field. At 1300, fighters from 58.2, 58.3, and 58.4 went aloft to carry out plan JOHNNY over Saipan, Tinian, and Rota. As the aircraft came home late that evening, after the final strike, Mitscher estimated that 150 enemy aircraft had been destroyed. The Japanese, once again, had been caught with their planes down. The pilots were disappointed at the low score, but plan JOHNNY had achieved its purpose.

Then, for three days Task Force 58 bombed, strafed, and bombarded the Marianas, while invasion ships moved slowly toward the islands. On June 14, the task groups of admirals Harrill and Clark ranged toward Iwo Jima and Chichi Jima, while underwater demolition teams probed Saipan beaches and mine sweepers cleared the seas off the island.

On this cruise there were some new faces around flag country. One was Captain Gus Read, who was the new administrative officer for the staff. In addition to his regular duties he had one unique job—that of awarding decorations, almost on the spot. Previously this had taken weeks and months, with the papers flowing from Mitscher up through senior commands and to Washington. The rapidity with which outstanding action could now be formally recognized further contributed to the high morale of the task force.

By this time, Mitscher's waking hours were well covered, in picture and prose, by newsmen traveling with the carrier caravan. Photographer J. R. Eyerman, of *Life*, had been aboard several months; Elmont Waite of the *Saturday Evening Post* was still there, and Noel Busch had joined to report for the

Luce publications. One day a message came from *Time* magazine, inquiring whether or not Admiral Mitscher would make a suitable candidate for its front cover. He saw the message first. "Definitely not," he told Eyerman, "I'm not going to appear with all those international crooks." *Time* had been running portraits of Hitler and other Axis partners.

Meanwhile, one relatively nearby international troublemaker was preparing to fight. Admiral Toyoda had already decided to make a stand in the Marianas. The United States submarine *Redfin* reported enemy fleet movements on June 13, sighting a force estimated at six carriers, four battleships, eight cruisers, and six destroyers. They were proceeding north into the Sulu Sea.

On June 15, coast watchers reported the progress of a "large carrier and battleship force" toward San Bernardino Strait (separating Luzon and Samar in the Philippines). On the same day, the submarine *Flying Fish* verified the movement through the strait and the submarine *Sea Horse* reported a group 200 miles east of Surigao Strait, which is between Leyte and Mindanao. Evidently two enemy forces were proceeding toward the Marianas.

Mitscher was jubilant, and began working over the charts, plotting each report, although Gus Widhelm had already done so. Search planes were readied. Mitscher had been hoping for this encounter since Midway. The reports of two enemy forces on the prowl also made it necessary to reconsider the invasion plans. Specifically, Spruance had to decide whether to cancel the invasion of Guam, scheduled for June 18.

Mitscher prepared to recall the two task groups under Clark and Harrill from their strike on Chichi Jima and Iwo Jima. Clark wanted to steam southwestward and try to swing in behind the Japanese fleet, but the proposal was rejected. After the war, however, Mitscher told him that such an attempt should have been made. It might have developed into a pincers movement, although the odds would have been against it.

United States submarines slithered through the night and watched by day. Mitscher extended his air search to the limit, using flying boats to cover great distances. Meanwhile, Marines were flowing ashore at Saipan, but the opposition was stiffer than expected.

By the evening of June 15, the Navy was in a rather precarious spot in the Marianas. The largest amphibious operation of the Pacific war was grinding ahead and could not be halted. The enemy fleet was on the offensive, and the striking power of Task Force 58 was tied to the protection of that amphibious force.

If the Japanese admirals pressed on, their situation would continue to improve. The wind was favoring Jisaburo Ozawa, the admiral in tactical command. He could launch from his carriers while headed toward the Marianas, hit Task Force 58 while still at one-way flight range, then land the aircraft on Guam, Tinian and Rota, refuel, rearm, and hit the American fleet again, finally landing back on the carriers. Also, island-based enemy air power had recently been strengthened. Once Task Force 58 was scattered, the destruction of Vice Admiral Richmond Kelly Turner's amphibians would be relatively easy. That was the plan. The Japanese held the tactical advantage, momentarily.

As dusk spread across the southern Marianas, enemy island-based aircraft took off from Guam and headed for the task force, which steamed slowly west of Saipan. Every radar in groups 58.2 and 58.3 tracked them carefully. Soon, the enemy fighters and torpedo planes were visible even without radar.

Admiral Reeves's fighter director vectored his *San Jacinto* CAP to meet them. The dogfight meant sudden death for seven covering Zekes—the name given the modified Zeros—but eight to ten torpedo planes, low on the water, below radar horizon until the last minute, and hidden by the increasing darkness, broke through the defense and attacked. They headed directly for *Lexington* and *Enterprise*, straight into a fusillade of ack-ack. Mitscher remained in his chair on the bridge as the TBS reported their advance. They appeared to be the new type of torpedo planes which air intelligence had already labeled "Franceses." They were twin-engined and fast.

Admiral Reeves hoisted an emergency turn signal, and the task group wheeled. Eyerman, the *Life* photographer, got his camera ready; famed fighter pilot Jimmy Thach, who was aboard as a "makee learn" and would eventually become an operations officer on Admiral McCain's staff, joined others in seeking protected spots from which they could view the attack. Burke was at his battle station on the starboard wing; Hedding, who had remained as deputy chief of staff, hovered nearby. Almost every man wore a helmet, but Mitscher wouldn't be separated from his cap.

On they came. Their torpedoes dropped and plunged into the water. Captain Ernest Litch, in a superb piece of ship handling, swung the *Lexington* between the wakes of the hot running missiles. Two streaked down the starboard side, close aboard, in fact so close that Arleigh Burke had to lean out over the side to see them. Three skimmed by on the port side. By now, the attacking planes were aflame. Their doomed pilots, having delivered their torpedoes, drove head-on for the *Lexington*. Two of them roared down the starboard side—one coming in over the bow, about twenty feet off the flight deck. They were huge, self-propelled torches. The Frances angling toward the flight deck seemed certain to hit. Flame licked across its fuselage, with heat so intense that it reportedly singed the hair on several men in exposed positions on *Lexington*'s bridge. Somehow, it missed the ship, and Mitscher, still calmly seated, turned to watch it roll into the ocean in the wake of the *Lexington*.

Antiaircraft fire had been so furious that two men were killed and fifty wounded from ricochetting bullets. Poor Eyerman had become so excited he didn't pull the trigger on his camera, thereby missing what might have been one of the most spectacular shots of the war.

Mitscher remarked, "Fine thing, they send a Frances after me."

This whirlwind flurry caused no damage, except for the flak, but it did add to the tension building in Task Force 58. It was now common knowledge that the enemy fleet was steaming for Saipan. Mitscher believed Task Force 58 could attack the enemy force if it approached directly from the west or southwest, and that the Japanese could do nothing to seriously interrupt the Saipan landings if action was joined far away from the invasion beach. There was no valid reason not to steam Task Force 58 toward the Japanese fleet so long as the American forces remained intact. The other carrier admirals agreed with Mitscher. Naval airmen, by and large, they had been deprived of the chance to pursue the remnants of the Japanese fleet at Midway, and wanted to close with the enemy and get it over with.

Admiral Reeves signaled Mitscher, suggesting Task Force 58 get moving. But Mitscher, agreeing but also understanding the nature of the problem facing his superiors and sensing their decision, replied:

YOUR SUGGESTIONS ARE GOOD BUT IRRITATING X I HAVE NO INTENTION OF PASSING THEM HIGHER UP X THEY CERTAINLY KNOW THE SITUATION BETTER THAN WE DO X OUR PRIMARY MISSION IS TO STAY HERE TO AWAIT W DAY [Guam invasion] AND ASSIST THE GROUND FORCES X SUBMARINE HAZARDS MUST BE ACCEPTED X I HOPE IN YOUR MESSAGE YOU ARE NOT RECOMMENDING ABANDONMENT OF OUR PRIMARY OBJECTIVE

Actually, according to Reeves, his message was meant primarily for the eyes of Admiral Spruance, to emphasize to him the carrier men's belief that the best way to protect Saipan from the onrushing enemy was to hit him far to the westward, keeping enemy planes out of easy range of Saipan.

On the morning of June 16, Mitscher flew ashore to Aslito Field [1] to confer with Admiral Spruance and Vice Admiral Richmond Kelly Turner, who commanded the forces at the beach-head. Mitscher could not hide his delight at being able to get up in a plane. He was dressed in a flight suit and a Mae West, and grinned widely as he got into the plane.

As Lieutenant Commander Ralph Weymouth's plane powered swiftly down the deck, Mitscher turned his face up toward the flag bridge and gestured. It appeared to some that he was thumbing his nose. It was one of the few carrier flights he made during the war, and he enjoyed every minute of it. Four fighters flew cover; Weymouth was carrying valuable cargo. The staff sent out a mock dispatch, announcing to the task force: "A strike against targets of opportunity on Saipan. Strike leader, Vice Admiral Marc A. Mitscher."

It read on: "Arming: one 10,000 pound operations plan—with permanent delay fusing."

[1] Renamed Isely Field, after Commander Robert Isely, killed over Saipan.

CHAPTER

⚓ 33 ⚓

The Japanese Fleet Comes Out

AT THE conference, held in the U.S.S. *Rocky Mount*, Turner's flagship, it was decided to postpone indefinitely the invasion of Guam, also to release an element of combatant ships from the beach-head area to augment Task Force 58. Then Mitscher went back to the beach and reboarded the torpedo plane at Aslito Field.

Later, messages flowed back and forth between Spruance, Mitscher, and Turner, intensifying the feeling in the *Lexington*'s flag country that Admiral Spruance did not contemplate an immediate attack on the Japanese fleet. But on the afternoon of June 17, Spruance signaled Mitscher and Lee:

OUR AIR WILL FIRST KNOCK OUT ENEMY CARRIERS THEN WILL ATTACK ENEMY BATTLESHIPS AND CRUISERS TO SLOW OR DISABLE THEM X BATTLE LINE WILL DESTROY ENEMY FLEET IF ENEMY ELECTS TO FIGHT OR BY SINKING SLOWED OR CRIPPLED SHIPS IF ENEMY RETREATS X ACTION AGAINST THE ENEMY WILL BE PUSHED VIGOROUSLY BY ALL HANDS TO ENSURE COMPLETE DE-STRUCTION OF HIS FLEET X DESTROYERS RUNNING SHORT OF FUEL MAY BE RETURNED TO SAIPAN IF NECESSARY FOR REFUELING

Following receipt of this message, Mitscher signaled Spruance, asking whether or not he—Mitscher—was still in tactical command. Mitscher wanted to be very clear on that point. Spruance replied that he was, advising Mitscher and Lee to proceed at their discretion, selecting the dispositions and movements best calculated to meet the enemy under advantageous conditions. Meanwhile, Clark and Harrill were steaming at top speed for the task force. Their work in the Bonin and Volcano islands would later pay off. En route to the rendezvous, they were sending out searches north and west.

Just before 0400 on June 18, Mitscher was awakened by Burke, who brought him a dispatch from the submarine *Cavalla*, reporting that the Japanese fleet was still steaming eastward, traveling at an estimated 19 knots. Mitscher joined Burke and Hedding in Flag Plot. Quick figuring indicated the enemy would be 660 miles from Saipan at dawn. This was the news Mitscher had been waiting for. In the soft, soothing light of Flag Plot, the three men worked for a few minutes, projecting the enemy's probable route.

Mitscher felt he could reach the enemy by late afternoon if he steamed directly for him. With luck, there might be enough light remaining for one attack. The plan was dependent, of course, on whether or not Ozawa maintained his course and speed.

Spruance and Lee also received the *Cavalla* report but their reaction was not the same.

Mitscher signaled Lee: DO YOU SEEK NIGHT ENGAGEMENT X IT MAY BE WE CAN MAKE AIR CONTACT LATE THIS AFTERNOON X AND ATTACK TONIGHT X OTHERWISE WE SHOULD RETIRE EASTWARD TONIGHT X

Lee replied: DO NOT X REPEAT NOT X BELIEVE WE SHOULD SEEK NIGHT ENGAGEMENT

Lee further stated that possible advantages of radar were more than offset by night communication problems and lack of night training. Both Spruance and Lee were just as interested as Mitscher in sending the enemy fleet to the bottom. The difference was in method. Mitscher believed he had the power to do the job. He wanted to go in and fight.

At 1030 on June 18, Clark and Harrill hove into view with Task Groups 58.1 and 58.4, adding seven more carriers to the task force. In all, Mitscher had about nine hundred planes, in addition to the heavy surface forces. Just before the join-up, Spruance had again reaffirmed his desire to keep the task force around Saipan, a decision which was not greeted with joy on the carrier bridges.

Rear Admiral Gerald Bogan's jeep carriers, along with old battleships and cruisers, were at the beaches and could fight off a considerable attack if an enemy force outflanked Mitscher as he went after the main body of Admiral Ozawa's fleet. Mitscher remained silent, but it was evident he was angry. Other members of the staff paced the wings of the bridge and swallowed their disappointment in Flag Plot. The scene was being repeated on virtually all the other carrier bridges.

By noon of June 18, Mitscher had made his disposition for battle, deploying task groups 58.1, 58.3, and 58.2, in that order, on a north-to-south line, about twelve to fifteen miles apart. Lee, with the surface heavies—the battle line—detached from their carrier groups for separate operation, took up station twelve to fifteen miles westward of the central part of the carrier line, and Harrill's task group 58.4 was stationed to the north of Lee. In publishing final instructions in case of action that night, Mitscher ordered the task force to recover all planes prior to dusk and then head into the setting sun.

As night came on, air mechanics worked over engines, and ordnancemen readied bombs and ammunition. At 2030, Mitscher set the task force on an easterly course, away from the enemy fleet, in accordance with the instructions of Admiral Spruance. Two hours later, however, Nimitz sent a message saying that HF/DF (Huff-Duff), the radio direction-finding and monitoring stations spotted in the Pacific, had intercepted a dispatch from Admiral Ozawa to his land-based air forces on Guam. Plotting the sender's position located the approaching Japanese fleet roughly 355 miles west-southwest of Task Force 58.

Once again, the staff set to work with rules and dividers. The report was consistent with the previous submarine sightings. As far as Mitscher was concerned, it was more than time to change course and steam out to meet Ozawa. If the task force had to continue retiring eastward, the distance from the Japanese would remain the same all night—355 miles.

The Marianas wind, blowing from the east in June, was the key. It is interesting to note that in 1944, while scientists were involved in the problems of the atom, the breeze was of almost as much importance to naval operations as it had been in the days of John Paul Jones. The wind enabled the Japanese to launch aircraft as they steamed uninterruptedly eastward. On the other hand, the carriers of Task Force 58 had to reverse course each time they launched or landed their planes. It was difficult to gain much westage in the periods of the day when flight operations were underway.

For this reason Mitscher wanted to close with Ozawa at night, so that the distance between them, when the time came to attack, would be short enough to insure the pilots a round trip back to the American carriers. He took into account the possibility of a slugging match, but felt he could win. Furthermore, if the enemy ships were disabled and tried to withdraw, the tables would be reversed. They would then be able to launch aircraft only by turning back toward Mitscher, and would be at his mercy.

Calculating rapidly, Mitscher estimated he could get Task Force 58 within 200 miles of Ozawa by 0500 on June 19, enabling dawn strikes with Hellcats and Avengers. "It might be a hell of a battle for a while, but I think we can win it," he said to Burke.

Then he ordered Reeves to launch a night search and an attack strike at 0200. Following that, he told Burke: "Inform Admiral Spruance we propose to come to a westerly course in order to commence treatment of the enemy at 0500."

When the contents of this "commence treatment" message got down to the pilots of Air Group 16—those still awake—there was unbridled joy. "We came ten feet off the deck," said Group Commander Ernest Snowden.

Burke picked up the TBS microphone and his clear voice traveled the radio waves over to the *Indianapolis* Flag Plot, where Spruance and his staff listened to the message from Mitscher.

As usual, it went: "Blue Jacket, Blue Jacket, this is Bald Eagle; this is Bald Eagle."

Back came the go-ahead from Blue Jacket.

"Blue Jacket," said Burke, "we propose to come to a westerly course at 0130 in order to commence a treatment of the enemy at 0500. Advise. Over."

Blue Jacket acknowledged the message, and Mitscher began the wait. It was believed that the Commander, Fifth Fleet, would approve the proposal. But the minutes began to tick off insidiously. Mitscher sat on the edge of the transom awaiting the reply. Every key member of the staff was now awake and on the bridge. Whatever Spruance's decision, much work would have to be done.

They waited an agonizing hour. At midnight, there had still been no call from the Fifth Fleet Staff. Except for the low humming of communications equipment, Flag Plot was almost silent.

At 0038, the words "Bald Eagle—Bald Eagle, this is Blue Jacket," began to drone tinnily out of the TBS speaker. The reply was heartbreaking: "The change proposed in your message does not seem desirable." Admiral Spruance feared an "end run by other carrier groups."

That was the end of Mitscher's plan to attack. There would be no strike against the Japanese fleet that night. Admiral Spruance had received an information copy of a message from Pearl Harbor to the submarine *Stingray* mentioning that one of the *Stingray*'s messages had been unreadable. Spruance, knowing the *Stingray* was near the enemy fleet, thought the garbled message might have been a position report. The issue was confused. With tremendous responsibility in his hands, he decided to play it safe.

Mitscher walked silently out of Flag Plot to his sea cabin, while the staff spent the rest of the short night laboring on plans for the morrow. Mitscher accepted the decision as final, and made no attempt to change the attitude on the *Indianapolis*.

"We knew we were going to have hell slugged out of us in the morning and we were making sure we were ready for it. We knew we couldn't reach them. We knew they could reach us. And we were preparing plans, throwing most of them in the waste basket, to get set as early as possible for an air attack which was bound to develop," said Burke.[1]

"Every one of the pilots felt depressed when we heard we couldn't go," said Snowden.

Mitscher returned to Flag Plot later. He had not slept. The bleary-eyed staff members were trying to pull all the multiple odd details together. Those aboard the *Lexington* that night say one could almost feel the movements of the enemy as he armed his planes and sped toward the American task force.

As dawn approached, Mitscher worked on his plans. Among his main problems were how far they could steam toward the Marianas on an easterly course and still launch aircraft against

[1] Commodore A. A. Burke, USN, narrative (transcript of voice recording) on the Battle of the Philippine Sea, August 20, 1945.

Ozawa; and how to time the attack so that the decks would be clear of bombers and torpedo planes when it was necessary to rearm and launch the fighters to knock down Ozawa's attacking aircraft. The predawn search planes from Task Force 58 were already airborne, gliding through the fresh morning in hopes of ferreting out advance elements of the approaching fleet.

A message came from Admiral Spruance: "If searches do not flush targets, suggest neutralizing airfields on Guam and Rota."

Having spent bombs extravagantly since June 11, Mitscher felt that his supply was too low and the remainder should be saved until the situation resolved itself. He informed Spruance he could not launch the proposed strikes.

As dawn spread across the ocean, the Task Force 58 search planes were silent. They had seen nothing.

But not a man in any ship expected to do anything but fight, for the presence of the Imperial fleet was as certain as the sun's rise.

CHAPTER

⚓ 34 ⚓

First Battle of the Philippine Sea (1)

A TINY thunderhead of battle had appeared from the direction of Guam at 0530. Two or three bogeys had been spotted on the radar screens, and fighters from the *Monterey* had darted after them. The squawk box connecting Flag Plot to the Combat Information Center reported the results: "Tally-hoed two Judys; splash one."

Not enough to cause even momentary interruption, the sprinkle of action was duly transcribed by a yeoman who sat at a desk in Flag Plot. There was nothing to indicate this was really the beginning of such a robust day as June 19, 1944—the day of the "Marianas Turkey Shoot."

Mitscher had breakfasted in his sea cabin about 0630, after strolling out on the wing of the bridge to look at the disposition of the force. His staff insists his conversation that morning, if recorded, would not have filled a medium-sized memorandum blank. In spite of certain knowledge that enemy planes would soon arrive, he acted as though Task Force 58 were on routine practice maneuvers off the Virginia capes.

At 0714 *Belleau Wood* fighters patrolling over Guam radioed that many bogeys were taking off, and asked for help. Mitscher nodded, and Hellcats were launched from a half dozen carriers. In the brief battle that ensued, the pattern of the day was set: Thirty Navy fighter planes knocked down thirty-five enemy aircraft. Mitscher's loss was one Hellcat.

Then, at 0950 radar screens from one end of the sprawling task force to the other picked up large bogey targets. The battle was on. Mitscher said to Burke: "Get those fighters back from Guam." Burke relayed the orders and the Guam battlers rolled over and headed for the task force. At 1004, the *Lexington*'s bugler hurried through his general-quarters call, competing with the bong-bong-bong of the warning bell. Sailors throughout the big ship raced through passageways as watertight doors banged shut behind them—some to the flight deck, some to damage-control stations, others flopping into gun tubs topside. The air officer's voice was strident and urgent. To this clamor was added the coughing, sputtering, then roaring, of engines. Color flashed as busy figures scurried among the aircraft on deck—plane handlers in blue shirts and blue helmets; plane directors in yellow shirts and helmets; hookmen in green; chockmen in purple; firefighters in red, accompanied by two Frankensteinian apparitions in asbestos suits. In the ready rooms, pilots sat up to watch the ticker tape as it fed information to the screens in front of them. Some pilots had already gone up on deck to man their planes. On every carrier in the task force, the same carefully controlled frenzy was being repeated.

Mitscher sat in his swivel chair viewing the action on the flight deck below. J. R. Eyerman, the *Life* photographer, stopped on his way to his battle station to take a quick picture of the man in the chair.

Scarcely raising his voice, Mitscher asked, "Are you excited?"

Eyerman's pulse was pounding. He ventured a meek, "I guess so."

Mitscher turned, his eyes dancing, and in a firm, measured voice said, "Well, *I'm* excited." But when Eyerman developed his negatives, he found he hadn't captured Mitscher's suppressed excitement at all.

The planes were away as fast as they could be launched. Mitscher gave orders to the task force to send all bombers and torpedo planes to the east to orbit, thus making room for the fighters to land, refuel, rearm, and take off again. Meanwhile, fighters were being vectored out from all the carriers by their CIC fighter directors.

An alert sailor on the *Yorktown* transcribed the patter of his ship's fighter-director officer:

1015: Large bogey at 265–105 miles on course 090 at estimated angels 24 [24,000 feet].
1017: Scramble all ready rooms. Disengaged side to the east.
1025: Coal 1, 2, 3, and 4 have been launched and instructed to go to angels 25. [Coal 1, 2, 3, and 4 were divisions of *Yorktown* fighters already in the air.]
1026: Bogey now at 260–95 miles.
1037: Friendly planes have tally-hoed bogey at angels 15 to 25. [*Essex* Hellcats, led by Commander David McCampbell of Air Group Fifteen, had made the first interception of the oncoming Japanese planes.]

The fight raged from 90 miles out on in close to the fleet, with Japanese planes "falling like leaves," as Commander McCampbell reported it. A few Japanese bombers, though, came relentlessly on and scored a minor hit on the *South Dakota*, and one made a suicide attack on the *Indiana*. The sky action held the attention of Mitscher and the task-group commanders, but could not entirely divert them from the knowledge that the bogeys were from enemy aircraft carriers that were enjoying complete immunity.

At 1103, Reeves said he wanted a search and attack group

from his task group, already airborne, to go out 250 miles in an effort to find the Imperial carriers. Mitscher signaled back enthusiastically: APPROVED X APPROVED X WISH WE COULD GO WITH YOU.

But Reeves, because of jamming caused by the huge number of aircraft airborne and using radio, could not get his message through to the bombers and torpedo planes that awaited instruction while orbiting to the east. And shortly thereafter Mitscher recalled them. "Tell 'em to drop their bombs on Guam and Rota on the way back," he said to Burke. This would pit the air strips and make it more difficult for the bogeys to shuttle between the islands and their carriers.

At 1109, a new crop of bogeys—estimated at sixty-five planes—skimmed into the radar screens. CIC located them at high altitude; range, 130 miles. The fighter director, doing one of the finest jobs of the war, vectored out enough strength to decimate them. The pilots landing on the *Lexington* and other carriers to regas and rearm were in high spirits.

Down in Fighting Sixteen ready room, one sweaty pilot yelled, "Hell, this is like an old time turkey shoot." His chief, Lieutenant Commander Paul Buie, overheard the remark, and the phrase "Marianas Turkey Shoot" was born.

From 1130 to 1430, sporadic raids were met. Claims of kills were approaching the fantastic even when allowance was made for exaggeration. Throughout, Mitscher stayed on the wing of the bridge, while Burke, Hedding, or Widhelm periodically emerged from Flag Plot to pass information to him, get a decision, or obtain his initials on a nonroutine dispatch. Lieutenant Commander Joseph Eggert, USNR, the staff fighter-director officer, co-ordinated the immensely complicated air defense perfectly.

Four Judys attacked *Lexington, Enterprise,* and *Princeton,* and were loudly contested by every trainable gun in the task group. Two torpedoes splashed into the water, bubbling toward the *Lexington*, but missed the flagship by a wide margin.

By 1430, the heaviest enemy strikes were over and Mitscher began requesting the task-group commanders to report the results. As the replies flowed in over the TBS and by blinker, the slaughter didn't seem possible. Ozawa had fed planes in recklessly from both carriers and island bases. The early-after-noon score indicated more than three hundred Japanese planes destroyed, an air victory beyond all expectations.[1]

But Mitscher received the reports with little comment. He was more concerned, and had been all morning, with the groups of enemy carriers somewhere to the west. No amount of destruction of planes could entirely make up for the fact that the enemy fleet had escaped damage. Not one task-force plane had come within sight of the Japanese formation.

At 1500, Spruance, realizing that the enemy force had lost its weapon of attack, signaled what amounted to a release. At that moment, Mitscher could look southeast and see smoking Guam, barely fifteen or twenty miles off the *Lexington*'s beam. The miles between his carriers and Ozawa's carriers had been opening all day. The situation had not changed appreciably since dawn. Mitscher was between the enemy land bases and the Japanese carriers down-wind from him.

He detached Harrill's group, which was low on fuel, and prepared to steam for the enemy with the remaining groups. Permission to put the task force on a westerly heading did not arouse much elation on the *Lexington*'s flag bridge, however. Most of the staff thought the best opportunity for sinking the Japanese fleet had been missed in two days of east-and-west shuttling.

Sporadic raids were still occurring and destruction of Japa-nese planes continued. Individual totals were staggering. Com-

[1] An estimated 346 were lost on June 19 according to Samuel E. Morison's *History of U. S. Naval Operations in World War II*, Volume VIII (Boston, Atlantic–Little, Brown & Company, 1953).

mander McCampbell's VF-15, from *Essex*, accounted for seventy enemy planes, for example. On *Lexington* Lieutenant (j.g.) Alexander Vraciu, USNR, took the LSO's cut, bounced to the deck, and beamed as he crawled out of the Hellcat's cockpit. He held up six fingers and Mitscher waved from the bridge. Vraciu was an ace of the carrier war. Six "turkeys" had fallen under his guns in less than eighteen minutes. His total score was now eighteen Japanese planes.

Mitscher left the flag bridge and made his way down to the flight deck to congratulate young Vraciu personally. He shook his hand, then moved out of the way as photographers focused their cameras from every angle. Then he said, with evident embarrassment, "I'd like to pose with him. Not for publication. To keep for myself."

At 1630, Admiral Spruance signaled: DESIRE TO ATTACK ENEMY TOMORROW IF WE KNOW HIS POSITION WITH SUFFICIENT ACCURACY X.

But as the sun set over the Marianas, Mitscher and his staff were not optimistic about finding the enemy. Until 1900, occasional bogeys roamed into the formation, but they were either chased away or splashed. The Admiral came off the wing and sat down on the transom to look at the night orders Burke had prepared. Then he briefly discussed what might be done the next day. He decided not to launch searches that night because of the distance involved.

Finally Mitscher stood up and stretched. "You know," he said, "tomorrow I'm going to get a haircut. Personally, I hate barbers. I hate them like hell. But all the same, tomorrow I'm going to get a haircut." Then he parted the blackout curtains and disappeared toward his sea cabin.

CHAPTER

⚓ 35 ⚓

First Battle of the Philippine Sea (2)

JUST after breakfast the next morning, Commander Ernest Snowden went up to the flag bridge and offered to lead a group of Hellcats in a search for the enemy.

"They're a long way off," Mitscher said.

"I'll use volunteers," Snowden replied. Then he briefly outlined a plan to load the Hellcats with five-hundred-pound bombs, with delayed-action fuses.

Mitscher seemed receptive. He said, "You'd better take a bomber with you." Some of the bombers had radar sets in them. Mitscher was concerned about navigation on the long flight.

Finally, he said, "I've got a search out that should be back about eleven hundred. If I don't get anything, I'll send you out."

Snowden, who was General "Hap" Arnold's son-in-law, went down to the fighter ready room and chalked twelve numbers on the bulletin board, with his own name beside the first. Then he turned to the pilots: "Gentlemen, this is strictly volunteer. Chances are less than fifty-fifty you'll get back. I need eleven people. My name is on the top of the list." Snowden left the ready room, and when he came back about a half hour later, all the numbers had names beside them.

The early-morning search group was recovered shortly after 1100, having found nothing. Snowden ran up to the bridge, and the Admiral nodded his okay. Then, as Snowden walked toward the ladder, Mitscher called after him: "I want you to go back and tell those boys that if you make contact and anybody gets shot down, I'll come and pick them up even if I have to steam the whole damn fleet up after them."

Snowden's long-range search group was launched at 1200. They went out 475 nautical miles—on the longest search of the war up to that time—and then Snowden turned them back toward the task force. There was not a sign of the Japanese fleet. At 1512, during the three-hour return leg, Snowden heard an *Enterprise* plane radio a contact to the task force.

Back on the *Lexington*, Mitscher slid down from his chair and followed Burke into Flag Plot. Seconds later, Burke was on the TBS: "Indications are our birds have sighted something big."

Mitscher waited for verification, along with information about distance, course, and speed. It came finally. The enemy was about 275 miles away. At the same time—1548—Burke was back on the TBS:

Have received following. Enemy fleet sighted 15–02 N, 135–25 E, speed 20 knots. Course, 270. Reception was poor. Anybody heard different transmission check position, course and speed. Anybody heard different transmission contact Commander, Task Force 58.

Gus Widhelm was exuberant. He had wagered two air-group commanders a thousand dollars the Japanese fleet would be sighted.

If Mitscher launched a strike now, it would be late afternoon before the planes could reach the enemy and completely dark by the time they could get home. He could count on heavy losses. Operating at such extreme range, many planes would run out of gas as they searched in the dark for their carriers, and would be forced into the sea. Each second of indecision, however, brought nightfall closer and reduced the chances of success.

Mitscher conferred with Burke and the other senior staff members, but Burke felt the Admiral had already made up his mind. Then Mitscher gave the order to launch planes. The ticker tapes in the ready rooms recorded the range and bearing —all the information the pilots needed—and the squawk box ordered: "Pilots, man your planes." At 1553, Mitscher informed Spruance he intended to launch everything he had. His Action Report said later:

> The decision to launch strikes was based on so damaging and slowing enemy carriers and her ships that our battle line could close during the night and at daylight sink all the ships that our battle line could reach. It was believed that this was the last time that the Japanese could be brought to grips and their enemy fleet destroyed once and for all. Taking advantage of this opportunity was going to cost us a great deal in planes and pilots because we were launching at maximum range of our aircraft at such time as it would be necessary to recover them after dark. It was realized also that this single shot venture for planes which were sent out in the afternoon would probably be not all operational for a morning strike. Consequently, Fifth Fleet was informed that the carriers were firing their bolt.

By 1630, the first deckloads were away—eighty-five fighters, seventy-seven dive bombers, and fifty-four torpedo planes. As they dropped out of sight, a second message came in from searchers, locating the enemy fleet sixty miles farther away. It was a stunning blow. At best, the original position gave the pilots an even chance in returning to the task force. The new position would strain the last ounce of fuel, and make night landings inevitable. If Mitscher didn't recall the planes, the casualty list was sure to be heavy.

After rechecking the charts, Mitscher decided not to recall them. However, he did tell Burke to cancel the second deckload and inform Admiral Spruance that the rest of the planes would be held until morning.

Mitscher's decision to launch planes that afternoon has received much attention, but his decision not to recall the first deckload of pilots was far more difficult. It hung over him until midnight.

A few minutes before sunset, Task Force 58 pilots found small Japanese units and then finally reached the wildly maneuvering enemy carriers. Ozawa had lost most of his fighters in the previous day's shooting, but launched what he had as the American dive bombers and torpedo planes attacked. Although the attacks were not co-ordinated, there was little interference. In the shadows, it was difficult to see how much damage was being done, although the inter-plane radios chattered enthusiastically. Actually, only one carrier, the *Hitaka*, was sunk. Two had been previously downed by submarines, and in addition, two oilers had been sunk.

Then the planes started home, but not in usual formation. They flew independently, or flocked together in any order for company. Mitscher had been out on the bridge wing since he launched them and ate his dinner from a tray. Every minute or so, he'd look at the sun's position, and check the big, luminous-dialed watch on his left wrist. At the turn of dusk, the loudspeaker in Flag Plot announced: "Attacks completed. Two CV sunk." Ralph Weymouth, a bit optimistic, had sent the message as the planes flew toward the force, now shadowy in the twilight.

Mitscher changed the axis of the fleet and spread the task groups to a distance of fifteen miles apart. By then, the pilots were within 70 miles. They had picked up homing signals and were visible on the task-force radar screens. But it was very late. Fuel tanks were almost dry. Mitscher informed Spruance of several course changes he planned to make after recovering the pilots who managed to reach the task-force disposition. He told Spruance he intended to steam the task force in a direction that would enable recovery of the pilots who had gone down in the ocean, and he also urgently requested Dumbo planes to join the search for pilots. Mitscher was facing the worst disaster in naval-aviation history.

He added speed until the carriers were surging along at 22 knots. By 2030, planes were sighted, scattered without pattern in the western sky. To the south were rays of lightning, and some pilots headed toward the false beacon. At 2045, a few aircraft began to orbit in confusion, their red and green lights flashing.

Mitscher knew their fuel supply was almost exhausted. They had to be brought in. Now the sky was filling up over the task groups. The pilots knew the task force was down there—they could even see the wakes of the ships—but there was no way to distinguish the carriers.

Ernest Snowden ran up to Gus Widhelm: "We gotta give these guys some light."

Admiral Mitscher slipped down from his swivel chair and walked into Flag Plot, sitting down at the very end of the transom. He lit a cigarette and looked up at Captain Burke.

"Turn on the lights," he said.

Task Force 58 suddenly leaped from the darkness, temptingly visible to any nearby submarines.

Searchlight beams climbed straight into the sky; others pointed toward the carrier decks. Glow lights outlined the decks; truck lights flashed on mastheads in the outer screen. Cruisers threw up a procession of star shells, flooding the ocean with light.

Said one carrier pilot, Lieutenant Commander Robert A. Winston, USNR: "The effect on the pilots left behind was magnetic. They stood open mouthed for the sheer audacity of asking the Japs to come and get us. Then a spontaneous cheer went up. To hell with the Japs around us. Our pilots were not to be expendable."

Then the planes started coming in. They were trying to locate their home ships. Mitscher said, "Tell 'em to land on any carrier."

Some made landing approaches on cruisers and battleships. More ran out of gas and made controlled water landings. Some glided right into the paths of destroyer searchlight beams. The destroyers were working overtime. Through the din could be heard the mournful beeping of the whistles on pilots' life-jackets. Men adrift!

Six planes settled safely on the *Lexington* but the seventh refused a wave-off. He was high, but cut his engines and landed, bouncing over the barrier and plowing into a row of parked planes on the bow, sparks and flame lighting up the deck. A rear-seat gunner in one of the planes that had just landed was killed by the propeller; another body was pulled from the wreckage.

Mitscher sent for the pilot, who was unhurt. A raw bundle of nerves and fear, he approached the man seated on the flag-bridge wing.

"Do I understand you refused a wave-off?" Mitscher asked.

"Yes, Admiral," the pilot answered, "my hydraulics were shot away. I didn't have enough gas to go around again."

Mitscher looked at him for a long time. Then he said, very gently, "Son, you always could have gone into the drink."

In ten minutes, an incredibly short time to clear up the strewn wreckage, Flight Deck Chief Prather had the *Lexington* ready to operate again, and the planes began landing. On *Cabot*, *Yorktown*, and *Bunker Hill*, and all the other carriers, the tumultuous drama was being repeated. Several carriers had so many planes on the flight deck that airborne craft couldn't be landed. Their captains ordered planes pushed over the side.

Although he had set a precedent for these rescue procedures in the Battle of Midway, Mitscher's decision to light up the fleet in the Marianas stands in naval-aviation history with the surface Navy's "Damn the torpedoes! Go ahead!" That night, Mitscher endeared himself to every man who wore gold wings, and won the admiration of all sailors. When the account of what had happened reached the press, Mitscher acquired new and greater stature. In stories about the Admiral words like "compassion" and "humanitarian" began to accompany appraisals of his fighting ability.

Two hundred and sixteen planes had been launched. By 2230, when the last of the surviving aircraft landed and Mitscher once again turned the task force after the enemy, only a hundred of the planes that had taken part in the strike were left. It was impossible rapidly to count the survivors and tally the missing. By early morning, it was estimated that eighty planes had gone down in the sea or been destroyed in landing accidents. Twenty were estimated to be combat losses. Rescues continued throughout the night and into the next day. By dusk of June 21, all but sixteen pilots and twenty-two crewmen had been rescued.

Meanwhile, at 0450, on June 21, Mitscher informed Spruance he did not think it would be possible to close the enemy at a speed greater than 15 knots. Fuel shortage would not permit them to move faster, and the recovery of the pilots had taken the force a good 60 miles farther away from Ozawa's battered remnants.

During the morning, Mitscher reorganized Task Force 58, sending a carrier group with the battle-line forces chasing the fleeing enemy. As the day wore on and other searches were futilely launched, it became increasingly evident that the Japanese would probably get away. Admiral Spruance canceled the search at 1920 that night.

But there was gloom on the flag bridge of the *Lexington*. Mitscher had gambled at the last moment. He had won, but his winnings were small compared to what they might have been. A considerable portion of the Japanese fleet had escaped. He summed up the battle in his Action Report: "The enemy had escaped. He had been badly hurt by one aggressive carrier strike at the one time he was within range. His fleet was not sunk."

So ended the Battle of the Philippine Sea in flag country of the U.S.S. *Lexington*, June 21, 1944.

CHAPTER

⚓ 36 ⚓

The Controversial Decision

THE Battle of the Philippine Sea will be refought by naval students, both professional and parlor, for many years. Hindsight indicates that Admiral Spruance made a mistake—just as hindsight also would put Army and Navy interceptor planes into the air at dawn on Pearl Harbor day. Naval aviators and surface men have generally differed in their evaluation of Spruance's decision, with most naval aviators insisting that Spruance should have let Mitscher go after Ozawa earlier, and the surface officers maintaining that he was right to concentrate on his basic mission of protecting and securing Saipan.

Fleet Admiral King said, "In his plans for what developed into the battle of the Philippine Sea, Spruance was rightly guided by this basic obligation." [1]

The noted naval historian Samuel Eliot Morison (Rear Admiral, USNR) supports the Commander, Fifth Fleet, in his *History of U. S. Naval Operations in World War II*.[2] In the same volume, Admiral Spruance himself is quoted:

[1] Ernest J. King and Walter Muir Whitehill, *Fleet Admiral King* (New York, W. W. Norton & Company, 1952).
[2] Volume VIII—New Guinea and the Marianas (Boston, Atlantic–Little, Brown & Company, 1953).

As a matter of tactics I think that going after the Japanese and knocking their carriers out would have been much better and more satisfactory than waiting for them to attack us; but we were at the start of a very important and large amphibious operation and we could not afford to gamble and place it in jeopardy. The way Togo waited at Tsushima has always been in my mind. We had somewhat the same basic situation, only it was modified by the long range striking power of the carriers.

A work by the Navy's own Aviation History Unit agreed that Admiral Spruance displayed "proper hesitation to leave the amphibious operations at Saipan uncovered," but also said succinctly, "The campaign in the Marianas was saved, but the Japanese fleet escaped with its major strength, to fight again." [3]

Less diplomatic was Admiral Frederick C. Sherman, himself a participant in many Pacific battles, who wrote, in his *Combat Command:* [4]

He [Spruance] directed Mitscher to head east during the night and concluded his message with, "Beware of an end run." It indicated that Spruance was still thinking in terms of a surface action. He did not grasp the tremendous power of our air weapons or their ability to strike in any direction to the limit of their fuel. There were no end runs in aerial warfare.

From Pearl Harbor came the thoughts of Admiral Nimitz, and his staff, who wrote in the CINCPAC (Commander in Chief, Pacific) summary for June 1944:

There may be disappointment to some in the fact that in addition to the successful accomplishment of our purpose—the occupation of the Southern Marianas—there was not also a decisive "fleet action," in which we would naturally hope to have been victorious, and to have thereby shortened the war materially.

It may be argued that the Japanese never had any intention of evading Task Force 58 with part or all of their forces, and making their major air attack against our shipping at Saipan. From this

[3] Aviation History Unit OP-519B, DCNO (Air), *The Navy's Air War*, edited by A. R. Buchanan (New York, Harper and Brothers, 1946).
[4] New York, Dutton, 1950.

premise it can be proved that our main body of carriers and gunnery ships could have pushed to the westward without concern for
the expeditionary forces, and that had it done so, a decisive fleet
air action could have been fought, the Jap fleet destroyed, and the
ending of the war hastened.

There is no restriction on surmising how a hand might have been
played and how much could have been won had the cards fallen
differently from the way they did.

Nimitz, too, felt that Admiral Spruance had played his hand
properly. Of course, the whole Marianas affair was to be soon
overshadowed by a materially most costly error in the Battle
for Leyte Gulf. Soon, word was passed from Pearl Harbor
advising that discussion of the views of naval airmen and surface
men be ended. In effect: Shut up, and get on with the fighting.

CHAPTER

⚓ 37 ⚓

Leader of Pilots

AFTER Saipan fell on July 9, Premier Tojo's cabinet teetered for a few days, then collapsed. Tinian was attacked next, with air strikes, then shore bombardment, and finally the beach invasions. Then Guam, in the same way, was restored to United States control. It was almost a case of choosing the next objective, setting up a timetable, and initiating action behind the attacks of Task Force 58.

The remainder of July was busy in the Marianas, and the force also raided the Western Carolines. In early August, Mitscher hit Iwo Jima and the Bonins, including Chichi Jima, Haha Jima, and Muko Jima—islands which always seemed to invigorate Admiral Clark's Cherokee fighting blood. Then the ships departed for Eniwetok to rest, take on supplies, and plan for operations against the Philippines.

For almost seven months, Mitscher had been waging air warfare of unparalleled ferocity. Yet his own pilot losses were unbelievably low. His method of running the carriers was well established, and through no effort of his own, well publicized. He once wrote a memorandum to the newsmen: "There are more interesting things to write about aboard an aircraft carrier than an admiral." He shunned public-information officers and would not have them on his staff.

Yet his presence among the more than a thousand airmen of Task Force 58 was living and vibrant. He needed no public-information men. Mitscher understood the professional language of the finished pilot and was sympathetic to the neophyte. It is doubtful that any World War II commander, whether air admiral or air general, on the Allied side or in an enemy camp, had quite the same sense of kinship with his pilots, or managed to communicate it so well. As a leader of pilots, he was second to none.

Mitscher believed that harsh discipline ruined more men than it made. He had not forgotten the Naval Academy and its 1904 sundowners. He said that pilots could not be handled with inflexible discipline because they were a different breed, a new breed; the flying temperament could not be turned off or on with rules. Yet he demanded rigid "air discipline" and would break a man who violated it.

You can train a combat pilot for $50,000. But never, ever tell a pilot that. We can't buy pilots with money. The way we run the Navy we spend millions of dollars designing and building a big carrier. We put 3,000 men aboard and a big screen of ships around her and then send her 7,000 miles from home. Then we launch planes. The whole striking force of this carrier, all we spent in preparation and operation up to this point, finally is spearheaded by a hundred young pilots. Each of these boys is captain of his own ship. What he thinks, his confidence in what he is doing, how hard he presses home the attack is exactly how effective we are. Such pilots are not cheap.[1]

Carrier planes have always pressed in closer for attack than their land-based counterparts. Even in primary training, Navy pilots are urged to fly tight and close. Later their formations are so compact that the planes appear to be glued together.

[1] Statement by Mitscher quoted in the unpublished manuscript by J. R. Eyerman.

The effective use of airpower in connection with sea power requires this. But to get the pilots to press in close under combat conditions is another thing:

We don't hypnotize them. These kids aren't crazy. They know we don't want them to commit suicide. He, himself, has to feel he has a chance of getting out or he won't bore in. These kids aren't Japs.[2]

Mitscher understood his pilots as human beings, and as individual war machines, and of course, he understood the tactics they would have to employ once they were airborne:

We have one-bomb planes. If you want to kill a man with one bullet, you put the gun in his belly and pull the trigger. To get into the Jap's belly, we send in a perfectly coordinated, perfectly timed attack, heavy strafing, then bombs and torpedoes, all in a few seconds. We do a great deal of damage and our losses are very light.[3]

Finally, Mitscher understood the importance of the rescue factor, which would balance the scale weighted on the other side by fear. He felt that the prestrike attitude of any pilot was governed solely by the percentage chance of his being rescued. If the pilot thought rescue was relatively certain, he could take off in the proper frame of mind. Mitscher reasoned that few, if any, pilots thought they would be killed by antiaircraft fire or in dogfights, but that many of them were concerned about being adrift on a life raft.

On the second day of the two-day strike at the Bonins in early August, one of the fighter pilots bailed out of a burning plane over Chichi Jima harbor. A wingman dropped him a raft, but he was stuck in the harbor under heavy automatic crossfire from the beaches. The Japanese guns prevented the usual procedure of sending a cruiser float plane to make the pick-up. The whole task force was scheduled to pull out within the hour

2 *Ibid.*
3 *Ibid.*

and tension mounted in Flag Plot. Mitscher sat silently on the transom. No one wanted to say it aloud, but a decision had to be made to leave the pilot or to risk a great deal to save one man's life. As the moment for leaving approached, Captain Burke broke the silence.

"Well, what about it, Admiral?"

Mitscher looked up, fully realizing what every man in Flag Plot had been thinking. He said quietly, without the slightest profane effect, "Jesus Christ, I can't leave that fellow in there. It'll be dark in an hour. Keep the fighters circling until dark, then get a submarine to come in close to the reef and send their rubber boat in after him."

In war at sea, where there is not as much to talk about as one would imagine, such deeds easily lead to hero worship. All the while, Mitscher himself had what amounted to hero worship for the pilots:

We got the best Goddamned men in the world. People talk about deterioration of the race. They don't know what they're talking about. Why, with their eyes wide open and their chins up, these kids go into places their pioneer grandparents would be too dumb to be scared of. They have nothing but guts. I tell you, training and selection have given us the best Navy and Marine Corps in the world.[4]

After each strike, when the leader customarily trotted up to Flag Plot to give a first-hand account of the results, Mitscher would seat the pilot, lean far back on the transom, and order coffee. Next he would push his spectacles down on his nose so he could look directly at the pilot—and then he would listen. If the pilot was out of breath from running up the ladders, he would wait, giving him a chance to collect his thoughts. At the end of the visit, Mitscher would ask for recommendations as to the need for further strikes and the choice of targets. These interviews were not limited to strike leaders. Many times, en-

[4] *Ibid.*

signs would come up. The ability to listen to ensigns is possessed by very few good admirals, and by no bad ones.

To many of the pilots, he was a sort of beloved older school-
teacher—glasses on his nose, his manner gentle—with the knack
of painlessly drawing every ounce of information out of his
students. They deeply admired his quick approach to decision
and action. Captain Hugh Winters, USN, later said of him:

> He never quibbled. . . . When two alternates were close
> enough to be argued about, he chose one and by quick and ex-
> cellent execution, never failed his major missions. He proved to us
> that a second best choice, done on time or ahead of time, invari-
> ably paid off, whereas dilly-dallying around, waiting to pick the
> perfect course of action, can fail to pay off or even cause the major
> missions to be aborted. We also learned from him that few things
> go according to plan, and that they often go differently, and bet-
> ter, in combat.

On August 10, Admiral Nimitz arrived in the Marshalls for
final conferences prior to the Philippines campaign. He had
a Gold Star with him, in lieu of a third Distinguished Service
Medal, to present to Mitscher. Nimitz stood up to read the
citation, but prefaced it by saying: "Ninety-one years ago,
a Naval officer opened up the ports of Japan and now another
officer is doing his damndest to close them."

Mitscher was adding another medal or star to his growing
expanse of ribbons with almost every raid, but he thrust all
of them into his foot locker to await his eventual return to
the United States.

Another event in late August was the departure from the
fighting area of Admiral Spruance. His command was taken
over by Admiral Halsey, and "Task Force 58" immediately
became a paper fleet, while the ships and most of the same personnel stayed on under the Halsey banner as Task Force 38.
In the same way, what had formerly been the Fifth Fleet was
now designated as the Third Fleet. For a while, even the Japa-

nese were fooled, and assumed that two giants were operating in the Pacific.

Another new arrival was Vice Admiral John Sidney McCain, a volatile little man from Mississippi. McCain had been selected as eventual commander of the fast carriers but Mitscher wanted to remain until the Philippines show was completed. Meanwhile, McCain took over Clark's task group for the experience.

Back in Washington, gossip in Bureau of Aeronautics corridors had Mitscher on the way out. Said *Newsweek* magazine:

. . . naval airmen heard a rumor about Marc Mitscher that had them quietly simmering. Wizened, solemn little Admiral Mitscher, who had been a naval airman since 1916, who commanded the carrier *Hornet*, "Shangri-La" of the Tokyo raid, who commanded the carrier task forces which spectacularly raided Truk, Guam, Palau, is due—said the rumor—to be yanked out of the Pacific.

A new kind of chair warming job—said rumor—is being prepared for him.

But it was only rumor, for King, Nimitz, Halsey, and Spruance agreed that it would be much better to keep Mitscher in combat, for the good of all.

CHAPTER

⚓ 38 ⚓

Next Stop Manila

MANY people have confused Admiral Mitscher and Admiral McCain. They resembled each other in build and shared a slight facial similarity. Both were unorthodox in habit and tactics. Mitscher's trademarks, of course, were the long-billed cap and the backward-riding chair, while McCain sported an astonishing squashy green cap on which was laced his regulation hat frame with the gold-braided brim. Halsey affectionately said it was the most disreputable officer's hat he'd ever seen. But Mitscher and McCain were far from twins.

While Mitscher surveyed the world from his icebox, Vice Admiral McCain, trailing the ashes from his hand-rolled cigarettes all over the flag bridge, was everywhere at once. His boiling point was low. Physically, he appeared as gentle as Mitscher, but when McCain exploded, his staff scattered. McCain had not entered aviation until the 1930's but nonetheless had acquired a broad understanding of air warfare.

McCain had been commanding a desk—first as Chief of the Bureau of Aeronautics, then as Deputy Chief of Naval Operations for Air—for two years, vainly attempting to get out to the Pacific. In fact, he'd flown to Majuro during one of Mitsch-

er's rest and replenishment periods to persuade the Admiral
to relinquish Task Force 58. Mitscher knew McCain was coming aboard, and probably realized the intent of his mission.
He did not personally meet the distinguished visitor at the
after brow, although such courtesy is usually extended to a
brother admiral, especially one who is senior. Instead, he stayed
in his cabin.

McCain went to Mitscher's quarters and the door was closed.
About an hour later, he left the *Lexington*, his face grim. "Pete
thought he still had plenty of work to do," McCain told his
son, Captain John Sidney McCain, Jr., a submarine officer, but
unfortunately he would say no more about that high-command
session. Admiral McCain was also understandably chagrined
when Mitscher did not soon follow Spruance back to Pearl
Harbor.

The Western Carolines, especially Palau, had been worked
over repeatedly since late spring. It was time for invasion. The
Third Fleet loaded up with bombs and fuel and prepared to
duplicate what had been done at Saipan. The fast carriers, now
Task Force 38, still led the fleet, and the task force had grown
more powerful with each passing week.

Vice Admiral McCain commanded Task Group 38.1, with
Wasp, Hornet, Cowpens, and *Monterey;* Rear Admiral Gerald
Bogan, one of Mitscher's favorite fighters, led 38.2, with
Bunker Hill, Intrepid, Cabot, and *Independence;* Rear Admiral Sherman had *Essex, Enterprise, Langley,* and *Princeton*
in 38.3, and Rear Admiral Ralph E. Davison commanded 38.4,
with *Lexington,* still Mitscher's flagship, *Franklin, Belleau
Wood,* and *San Jacinto.* Once again, Lee commanded the battle
line.

First, Mitscher sent 38.4 out of Eniwetok on August 28 to
attack the Bonins, directing the other task groups to sail the
next day for Palau to start the preinvasion treatment, which

was concentrated mainly on Peleliu, the first objective for the Marines. Then the carriers steamed on to old Navy territory —the Philippines—with the aim of neutralizing the enemy air forces based there. Mindanao and Luzon were hit hard. Opposition was weak, and targets, to Mitscher's surprise, were relatively few.

When Halsey received Mitscher's report of weak opposition in the Philippines, he recommended to Admiral Nimitz that the date for the invasion of Leyte be advanced from December to October. Meanwhile, the amphibious forces were nearing Peleliu. At 0745, on September 11, Admiral Halsey, Rear Admiral Robert B. Carney, and several other Third Fleet staff members came alongside the *Lexington* in the destroyer *Hunt*. Mitscher went down to meet them.

Command protocol demanded that Mitscher visit Halsey aboard his flagship, the *New Jersey*, but the ebullient four-star admiral wanted to visit the new carriers. "If I remember correctly," said Halsey, "the chair that swung me aboard Pete's flagship was equipped with an ash tray and surrey top." [1]

It was the heaviest collection of gold braid the *Lexington* had ever entertained. They conferred in Mitscher's mess on plans for striking the Philippines, mainly the central portion. Targets to the south had been so disappointing that both Halsey and Mitscher felt any great effort there would be wasted. One outcome of the session was an order to Commander James Flatley, who had relieved Gus Widhelm as operations officer, to begin work on plans to raid Manila and Luzon.

Fortunately, the weather was fine for carrier operations. There were big, heavy, gray-black clouds, and the sea was steady and smooth. The sun-filled days in the Marshalls and Marianas had been pleasant, but the threatening skies of the

[1] William F. Halsey and Joseph Bryan III, *Admiral Halsey's Story* (New York, Whittlesey House, 1947).

Philippines were safer for carrier warfare. Mitscher was a rather good weatherman, but relied more on "sniffing the breeze" than on scientific instruments.

His staff weatherman, named Vonk, was probably the most positive aerographer in the task force. Vonk would give the Admiral a weather plot and Mitscher would invariably mention late information he had obtained from another source.

"Admiral," Vonk would say respectfully, "are you going to believe those bastards or are you going to believe me?"

Each time the Admiral would then smile thinly but not commit himself. However, he usually followed Vonk's advice, which was usually right. "Vonk," he said admiringly, "has a feeling for sea-going air."

On September 12, Leyte, Cebu, and the Negros were hit. Task Force 38 pilots had a field day, surprising the Japanese on their air strips, and attacking shipping. Over 1,200 strikes were launched. The next day, Mitscher duplicated the attack. At nightfall, Burke informed Admiral Halsey that Leyte was wide open. A rescued pilot had come back with information that enemy troops there were sparse and ill-equipped. This report added substance to Halsey's previous request to advance the invasion schedule. By the end of the third day, Task Force 38 aircraft had destroyed 173 Japanese planes in combat and 305 on the ground. Fifty-nine ships were declared sunk and fifty-eight probably sunk. Placed against the United States loss of but eight aircraft in combat and one operationally, the results were more than satisfactory.

On September 16, General MacArthur informed Nimitz that the results of Mitscher's carrier strikes had placed the enemy in such a precarious position that he was confident a simultaneous Luzon-Leyte assault could be successfully launched. Already in high gear, the war in the Pacific clicked into overdrive. Meeting in Ottawa, the Combined Chiefs of Staff made the final decision. Meanwhile, covered by dark clouds and tropical rains, with a frothy, running sea this time, Mitscher slipped silently toward the eastern coast of Luzon. The charts in Flag Plot plainly showed the next stopping place to be Manila— and six months before they'd been worried by thoughts of Truk.

On the morning of September 21, he was about 40 miles off the eastern shore of Luzon. The planes and pilots were ready, but the weather was not. Burke and Flatley stepped out on the wing occasionally to search for a break in the thick, low-lying clouds around them. One of the big status boards indicated a ceiling of from 300 to 1,000 feet, and the weather prophets predicted that the situation was the same for many miles inland. It seemed certain that Mitscher would not launch the planes until the weather cleared.

After perhaps an hour, however, the Flag Plot squawk box reported a bogey on the radar at about 60 miles, in the direction of Luzon. Mitscher stepped into Flag Plot. "Let's get them off the decks," he murmured.

Flatley, a veteran pilot with a veteran pilot's respect for the weather, expressed his worry, but Mitscher replied, "If the Japs can fly in this, so can we."

Mitscher's decision paid off handsomely. Five or ten minutes west of the task force, the strike planes ran into weather described as CAVU—ceiling and visibility unlimited. Mitscher had had a hunch that the area of rain and mist was localized. Within the next eight hours, a thousand planes struck targets on Luzon, with fighter sweeps against Clark and Nichols fields in Manila.

The night was spent peacefully but vigilantly off Luzon, and early-morning strikes took the air at 0615 on September 22. At noon, Mitscher ordered Burke to call a halt. Halsey was informed that aircraft were being recalled and further strikes canceled, and that the force would retire to the southeast to refuel. On the next day, Burke visited the *New Jersey* to discuss the possibility of attacking Okinawa, Formosa, and the Japanese home islands with Carney and the Third Fleet staffers. Meanwhile, the task force was underway on another dash, proceeding at high speed toward San Bernadino Strait.

At dawn on September 24, 1944, fighters and bombers flew over land to hit the Japanese shipping beyond, in Coron bay, in the Calamanian group, also raiding the Visayas—Cebu, Negros, Masbate, and Panay.

Burke, Read, Flatley—all the staff members—knew that this pace, day in, day out, was taking its toll. Once again, Mitscher's periods of silence were lengthening. He didn't hop energetically off the chair as he had done in the Marshalls and Carolines, but rose rather gingerly. Often, Burke looked toward Task Group 38.1, where Admiral McCain, in that fantastic squash cap, was capably running his end of the show. McCain's learning period was certainly over. In another month, Mitscher would *have* to go home. But the staff knew he wouldn't leave until the Philippines had been successfully invaded.

In these waning days of September, Mitscher began talking about an idea he'd had for some months, an idea for an aircraft carrier larger than anything the Navy had ever designed. A carrier without a conventional island structure to interfere with flight operations, it would be capable of operating heavy planes with large bomb loads.

The strikes at the Philippines had clearly indicated the need for such a ship. With heavier bomb loads, there would be less shuttling back and forth to the carriers, less fuel consumed, less wear and tear on the pilots. Mitscher talked about such a carrier with his staff and said he planned to campaign for one when he returned to Washington. The U.S.S. *Forrestal* was conceived off the Philippines in September, 1944.

CHAPTER

⚓ 39 ⚓

Leyte Gulf (1)

THE stormy month of October, 1944, was ushered in by a typhoon which formed north of Yap, in the Carolines, and moved slowly northwest of Okinawa, Mitscher's next target. He swung in behind the storm to avoid detection. The carriers and screening ships plunged and rolled as the typhoon, designated "Task Force Zero," a friend of the fast carriers, kicked up gale winds and long, white-flecked swells for two hundred miles around.

On October 6, at the point of rendezvous, Mitscher was still in tactical command, and he led the task groups toward Okinawa, arriving on the morning of October 10. The squalls and turbulence of Task Force Zero had served him well—he had sneaked in. There was little opposition and the task-group commanders went to work on airfields in northern Okinawa. At sunset, he withdrew southward.

Mitscher hoped that the Japanese would think he had decided to attack Luzon again. They were not fooled, however, and when he reached Formosa at dawn of October 12, the enemy was waiting. Okinawa had been rather lazily defended, but at Formosa between October 12 and October 16, Task Force 38 was under almost continuous attack from land-based aircraft. With the probable exception of the Marianas Turkey Shoot, it was the heaviest action yet encountered by the task force, and it was considerably more effective than the June offensive. On October 13, Mitscher's forces were fighting for their lives. At dusk the cruiser *Canberra*, riding in 38.1, was torpedoed. After daybreak on the 14th, the enemy swirled out again, and before the day was over, the carrier *Hancock* had been damaged, the cruiser *Reno* hit by what apparently was a suicide plane, and the cruiser *Houston* torpedoed. The enemy pilots were aggressive and determined.

Not since Midway and the Solomons had the Navy been mauled this way in the Pacific. The sudden, furious opposition caused consternation on the *Lexington*'s flag bridge and over in Halsey country. Mitscher and Halsey conferred by TBS. Either the cruisers had to be abandoned and sunk, or they had to be towed to safety, and the fleet withdrawn. The latter course was quickly chosen. But the Japanese were rejoicing, boasting that the American fleet was routed and much of it sunk. Their news report was as follows:

October 17 (Domei)—The name of Vice Admiral Mitscher . . . together with the name Saipan, is indelibly stamped in the hearts of us, the one hundred million people of Japan, as a name to be remembered for vengeance. He was one of the planners of the Doolittle raid . . . participated in the Battle of Midway . . . was made air force commander in the Solomons. His ability was recognized [and] he became commander of the jewel of the Pacific fleet, the 58th Task Force, and invaded Saipan. The pitiful end of [the 58th Task Force] . . . must have been vividly witnessed by him from his watery grave.

The radioman who monitored this broadcast, based on copy from the Japanese news-gathering association, commented: "It's a socko finish for the scenario, boys, but its going to leave you in a tight spot when you have to write the sequel."

On October 16, a search plane reported units of the Japanese fleet on the move. It was late afternoon, and for a few tense moments, the pilots thought they'd be off on another "lights on" attack. But Mitscher evaluated the reports, sounded out the staff members, and decided the movement was merely a feint— a guess which turned out to be correct. He kept his armor-piercing bombs for another day. The landings in the water on June 20 were still fresh in his memory. But it was now evident that the enemy was considering another fleet engagement. Radio Tokyo was ecstatic over the Formosa "defeat" of the American Navy, and Halsey surmised that Admiral Toyoda might well believe his own propaganda. Thereupon, Halsey ordered Mitscher to depart eastward with groups 38.2 and 38.3 to act as a surprise committee should the enemy steam out from behind the Philippines.

Halsey felt tethered, as Mitscher had felt in the Marianas, by CINCPAC's orders to cover MacArthur's Leyte landings, scheduled for October 20. He informed Nimitz that he wanted to operate in the China Sea also, instead of limiting his activity to the general landing area, but CINCPAC would not alter his primary mission.

The command setup was complicated, inviting confusion. Halsey was responsible directly to Nimitz, while Vice Admiral Thomas C. Kinkaid, Commander, Seventh Fleet—six pre-war battleships, eleven cruisers, eighteen escort carriers, and destroyers and frigates—was under General MacArthur. Hence, there were two major naval commands operating in almost the same territory, with Halsey's chain of command extending to Pearl Harbor, and MacArthur's to the Joint Chiefs of Staff in Washington.

On October 22, enemy oilers were sighted on the move. Submarine reports of sightings, attacks, and sinkings flowed in. On the 23rd, Admiral Kinkaid informed Halsey he believed Japanese surface forces would operate against Allied expeditionary forces at Leyte. Halsey agreed.

Meanwhile, Mitscher, with three carrier task groups, 38.2, 38.3, and 38.4, in an area roughly 260 miles northeast of Samar, was disturbed by these developments. The carriers needed re-arming—except, fortunately, for torpedoes and armor-piercing bombs, the ordnance needed for a fleet engagement—and the pilots needed a few days of complete rest after the tiring operations against Okinawa, Luzon, and Formosa. McCain, with the most powerful of all the task groups, had been ordered to Ulithi to refuel and rearm. The task force was not in prime condition.

At dawn on October 24, while carrier search planes fanned out in the Philippines from the southern tip of Mindanao north to Cape Engaño, Halsey was well aware of the existence of a Japanese fleet element moving through the Sibuyan Sea on a course which would bring it into the Pacific through the San Bernardino Strait. Ever since a few minutes after midnight, this element had been under more or less constant observation by both submarines and aircraft. It was plain that this force, later designated the Japanese Central Force, intended to come out and attack the American invasion ships. Vice Admiral Takeo Kurita was in command. Two of his cruisers were already on the bottom as the result of attacks by *Darter* and *Dace*, submarines.

So began the prelude to the Battle for Leyte Gulf (still occasionally called the Second Battle of the Philippine Sea). A sprawling, immensely complicated fight, stretching along six hundred miles of Philippine island coastline, it became the greatest naval engagement in history. Of necessity, it must be viewed mainly from Mitscher's flag bridge.

Between 0800 and 0900 that morning, the battle broke out from the Sulu Sea north to Mindoro. The position of the Central Force in the Sibuyan Sea, charging determinedly for San Bernardino Strait, had been definitely established; then an *Enterprise* search plane located another Japanese force to the south. Flatley immediately labeled this group the Southern Force.

The report of this contact reached Mitscher before instructions to the task-group commanders for hitting the Central Force—including what appeared to be most certainly the *Musashi* and the *Yamato*—could be fully transmitted. The *Musashi* was the *Yamato*'s sister ship, and like her carried eighteen-inch guns.

Already, Rear Admirals Ralph Davison and Gerald Bogan were launching aircraft; Sherman was attempting to launch planes from 38.3 and at the same time ward off an attack that had broken through the defending American fighters. *Lexington*, *Essex*, *Langley*, and *Princeton* were being harassed simultaneously. CIC on the *Lexington* reported forty enemy aircraft coming in, with a second group behind them. Sherman immediately canceled strikes from 38.3 to concentrate on defense.

Mitscher left Flag Plot—where Burke and Flatley were working out plans to repel the Central Force—for the vantage of the wing. He wanted to know whether the attacking planes were carrier-based or land-based. If they were carrier-based, it meant the Japanese had still another group of ships underway, perhaps to the north.

At 0939, while he was still on the wing, a Judy dived out of a low cloud, dodged through an umbrella of antiaircraft fire, and dropped a bomb near the after elevator on the *Princeton*. Six torpedo planes, with full gas tanks, exploded on her hangar deck. Later, a plane pulled up from its dive and flashed across the *Lexington*, its machine guns spitting a stream of bullets.

Mitscher leaped from his chair and dashed into Flag Plot. "What kind of deal was that?" he asked. "That fellow was actually firing at us!"

Captain Read said, "That's the first time I've seen you jump up like that."

Mitscher studied the *Princeton* through his binoculars. He couldn't see much, but early reports did not indicate a catastrophe. Other ships with far worse wounds had survived. Mitscher didn't seem particularly alarmed by her condition. Meanwhile, CIC reported that the attacking Japanese planes were of a carrier type, but presumably were flying off Luzon strips.

Earlier, Halsey had received an urgent top-secret dispatch on the same subject. If the planes were indeed carrier-based, were not operating from land strips, it was essential to locate the enemy's carriers. Halsey suggested intensifying the searches to the north, the most logical location for them. Mitscher had already told Burke to set up thorough searches northward, and at 1155, Sherman was ordered to send out planes for the same purpose.

After a few delays by incoming raids, the hunt began. Attacks on the task group continued until early afternoon. *Essex* air-group commander David McCampbell shot down nine Zekes in frantic dogfighting that day, a record for one sortie. Just after 1300, a Judy dove on the *Lexington* and dropped a bomb that exploded about fifty feet off the starboard side, fanning some breeze through flag country.

Reports from the first strikes against the Japanese Central Force were filtering in. Apparently the enemy had taken a fierce beating already, and Sherman's planes were on their way to deliver another blow. Mitscher sent a message to Halsey at 1608, saying cautiously that the enemy fleet—Central Force —was milling around in several groups, with two cruisers and one battleship, presumably the *Musashi*, badly damaged.

Some ten miles from the *Lexington*, throughout the morning and into the early afternoon, a fight to save the *Princeton* had been waged. At 1400, it appeared she would survive, and Mitscher began to think about the problem of escorting her back to safety. But at 1523, an explosion blew off her stern, the force of it riddling the cruiser *Birmingham*, which was standing nearby and making ready a tow. Casualties on the *Birmingham* were great—229 dead and 400 more injured.

Mitscher watched through his binoculars. "There was a steely glint in his eyes," according to Read. In all the months of the war, he had never lost a ship. There was still a very slight chance the hull could be saved, and he put off the decision for more than an hour. But at 1640, Burke ran out of Flag Plot with a message that would not allow further discussion nor wasted time. A *Lexington* search plane had located the Japanese carriers to the north. Three of them had been sighted, along with three or four cruisers and several destroyers. Flatley penciled in the reported position and labeled this group the Northern Force.

Mitscher said, "Tell Sherman to sink the *Princeton*." He could not afford such a liability while pursuing the Japanese carriers. At dusk, the destroyer *Irwin* and the cruiser *Reno* steamed in for the killing by torpedo.

"Tell Halsey we've sunk the *Princeton*," he said to Burke later, when the big ship was reported to be careening. Burke then signaled Sherman to take the task group north and rendezvous with Bogan's 38.2. Planes from the Sibuyan Sea strike were still returning, and darkness would be over the task force in less than two hours. Mitscher decided against trying to hit the carriers to the north in the remaining daylight. He never overcame his dislike of night flight operations.

CHAPTER

⚓ 40 ⚓

Leyte Gulf (2)

FLAG PLOT was straining under the load of contact reports and reports of damage to the Japanese Central Force. Mitscher, Burke, and Flatley had interviewed many of the *Lexington* pilots in an effort to evaluate accurately the damage sustained by the enemy. The accounts conflicted.

Mitscher told Burke to draw up plans for hitting the enemy carriers that night with a surface force made up of battle-ships and cruisers detached from the task groups; then Task Force 38 aircraft could take over at dawn to finish the remaining ships. The measure was discussed in detail, but he decided not to offer it to Admiral Halsey because he thought it might upset some of Halsey's plans. Looking back, some of his staff members now feel he definitely should have offered it.

At 2024, Admiral Halsey sent a dispatch to Admiral Kinkaid, who was preparing for night action against the Southern Force, saying that he was "proceeding north with three groups" to attack the enemy carrier forces. The same message was also directed to all task-group commanders of the Third and Seventh Fleets. It reached the *Lexington* at 2029. Halsey also sent another message, saying the battle line would form, and

Kinkaid interpreted this to mean that the fast battleships were being left behind to cover San Bernardino Strait.

At this point, Admiral Mitscher felt he had been relieved of tactical command of Task Force 38. While Halsey had not formally taken tactical command, his order, in the light of naval command structure, could not be construed otherwise. Definitely, it was felt, Admiral Halsey was going to determine the tactics of this particular fight. Admiral Mitscher retired for the night, saying, "Admiral Halsey is in command now." There could not be two tactical commanders. It was apparent that Mitscher was not happy over the situation.

Just before Mitscher left Flag Plot to go to his sea cabin, Captain Burke said, "We'd better see where that fleet is." He was referring to the Japanese Central Force.

"Yes," Mitscher replied, eying Burke steadily.

They'd been worrying about it since early afternoon because of the contradictions among the various reports of damage done to the Japanese heavies. Admiral Halsey had made his decision to send Task Force 38 northward mainly because he felt the Central Force was too badly damaged to bother the Seventh Fleet, and that the oncoming Northern Force, the still intact Japanese carriers, constituted the greatest threat to the Leyte beach-head and shipping.

But Admiral Kinkaid, busy with the Japanese Southern Force down at Surigao Strait, did not understand that Halsey had pulled all the carrier and fast-battleship strength away from the San Bernardino area. He assumed that the fast battleships had been detached when the rest of the force moved northward and thought that he had their protection.

About 2045, a search plane from the light carrier *Independence* reported the enemy Central Force still very much afloat and still moving toward San Bernardino. Halsey's staff was alarmed. The pilots had previously reported the Central Force to be routed, and Admiral Halsey had based his decision on those reports.

Burke and Flatley studied the search-plane contact report. Burke decided not to awaken Mitscher until a clarifying report came through. At about 2305, a dispatch board was handed to Burke. There was little doubt that the Central Force was driving on in a northwesterly direction at 12 knots, heading for San Bernardino Strait. Admiral Kurita's mission was to destroy the invading ships, and he had the guns to do it.

Meanwhile, Mitscher slept soundly. Flatley drew a large X on San Bernardino Strait on the chart and went off to awaken the Admiral. Both Burke and Flatley thought the fast battleships should be immediately detached from the Task Force and hurried back to the soft middle of the Philippines.

"Admiral, we'd better tell Halsey to turn around," Commander Flatley said.

Mitscher was on one elbow. His eyes widened as Flatley explained the *Independence* search-plane report. "Does Admiral Halsey have that report?" he asked.

"Yes, he does," replied Flatley.

"If he wants my advice he'll ask for it," said Admiral Mitscher softly. Then he rolled over and went back to sleep.

Meanwhile, the three carrier task groups had joined together and were steaming at 25 knots. The last search report, made on the afternoon of October 24, indicated that if the Japanese carriers of the Northern Force held their southerly course, the two forces would practically collide about daybreak. With Task Force 38 going north at 25 knots, and the Japanese coming south at the same rate, closing speed was 50 knots. Halsey slowed the Task Force to 16 knots. Then he returned tactical command to Admiral Mitscher, who went back to 20 knots, hoping to close the enemy task force shortly after daylight if he could.

Halsey had ordered an air search launched from the *Inde-*

pendence as soon as possible. Mitscher recommended that there be no night search, as it might warn the Japanese and cause them to change course.

"Have you any information that we don't have?" Halsey asked.

Mitscher replied that he did not.

"Launch the search," said Halsey.

At 0205 the search plane reported Admiral Ozawa's force to be about 80 miles north of Task Force 38. Mitscher had come out of his sea cabin and now stood in Flag Plot, wearing a light robe and the long billed-cap. He studied the chart and the contact reports, and then recommended to Halsey that they change course from northeast to due north and form Task Force 34 (the battle-line surface ships). Halsey concurred, and at 0255 Mitscher signaled Admiral Lee to dispose his battleships ten miles ahead of the fast carriers. Every man in Flag Plot fervently hoped that Lee would get his surface ships into action before dawn, join the battle, and get it over with. Mitscher guessed that action might begin at 0430.[1]

Meanwhile, Halsey had received word that Rear Admiral Jesse Oldendorf, in tactical command down at Surigao Strait, was engaging the Japanese Southern Force. Halsey ordered the advance of Task Force 38 slowed down. Also, Ozawa had dropped the advancing speed of his decoy carriers, *Zuikaku*, *Chitose*, *Chiyoda*, and *Zuiho*, and the odd battleship-carriers, *Ise* and *Hyuga*.

At about 0410, Kinkaid sent a message to Halsey asking if Lee's fast battleships were still guarding San Bernardino Strait. But the message was not received in the *New Jersey* for more than two hours. The answer was a surprised negative.

As dawn approached, with still no work for Lee's battle line to do, the carriers prepared to launch aircraft. Mitscher

[1] Commodore A. A. Burke, USN, narrative (transcript of voice recording) on the Battle for Leyte Gulf, August 20, 1945.

had ordered a daybreak launch. CAP cleared off the deck; then, with the faintest paling of the sky to accompany them, the searchers took off. After that, strike divisions headed toward the northeast to await contact flashes from the search party. Mitscher was still uneasy about San Bernardino, still uncertain about the claims made by the search planes of the day before.

At 0735, the Japanese force was reported 140 miles north-east of the task force. Obviously, they had turned north during the night at high speed. The airborne planes headed for them. Carriers were launching more planes. Lee's fast battle-ships sprinted for the fight. The battle plan to rid the seas of the enemy carriers was working to perfection. The scene, off Cape Engaño, seemed set for a final crushing blow.

But at 0822 came a message that was astounding, if not terrifying. The thin-skinned American escort carriers off Samar were being attacked by the enemy Central Force. Returned from the "dead," Kurita had paraded through San Bernardino Strait and was about to obliterate the jeep carriers, then bombard the transports of Kinkaid's invasion fleet. For more than an hour, Kinkaid sent pleas for help. What had been sheer exultation on Halsey's bridge at 0800 was now despair.

Meanwhile, Mitscher was directing the strikes against the carrier force. There was little fighter opposition—only a few planes guarded the carriers and they were dispersed hurriedly. Ozawa had fulfilled his end of the plan; he had lured Halsey north.

At 1030, Mitscher signaled Halsey that the enemy carrier force was seriously damaged and partly sunk. The planes shuttled back and forth. Commander Hugh Winters, the *Lexington*'s air-group commander, who had replaced Ernest Snowden back in August, was co-ordinating one strike, and saw two Japanese carriers sinking. Every few minutes he would report their progress. Mitscher was calm and patient but the Japanese ships seemed to take forever to sink under. Then, at last, the *Zuiho* and the *Zuikaku* rolled over and went under. Later, the *Chitose* also sank.

Down off Samar Island, the Japanese Central Force punched away at the lightly armed jeep carriers. Halsey, meanwhile, had detached himself from the main body of Task Force 38, pulled along the fast-battleship strength, and was speeding southward to their rescue; Admiral McCain, recalled from his refueling and replenishment journey, was launching strikes against Kurita's forces.

As the smoke cleared away, and before Kurita amazingly disengaged after delivering both a gunnery and aircraft attack, the escort carriers *Gambier Bay* and *St. Lo* had been sunk; the destroyers *Johnston, Hoel,* and *Roberts* were also under, after one of the most gallant, self-sacrificing attacks of any war. Ten other ships had been damaged. Had Kurita continued the attack—he was winning when he stopped—he might have doubled the score.

Admiral Halsey's decision to go after the bait Toyoda had placed to the north, pulling all the fast battleships with him, had been costly. The Japanese carrier strength, however, had been wiped out, and Japanese sea power was totally smashed by dusk of October 25.

Admiral Halsey had this to say: "I wish that Spruance had been with Mitscher at Leyte Gulf and I had been with Mitscher in the Battle of the Philippine Sea." [2] In Halsey's opinion, it may be concluded, Admiral Spruance would not have gone north. More interesting to contemplate, however, is the possibility that the Battle for Leyte Gulf might never have been fought if Halsey had been in the Marianas in June, for it is highly probable he would have sent Mitscher westward in pursuit of the Japanese fleet right then and there. Again, in the

---

[2] Statement to the author, April 9, 1953. This thesis has been entered elsewhere. See, for instance, *The Forrestal Diaries*, edited by Walter Millis with the collaboration of E. S. Duffield (New York, Viking Press, 1951), p. 20.

words of Admiral Nimitz, "Hindsight is notably cleverer than foresight."

The activity off Cape Engaño changed from an air war to a surface fight at 1753, when Mitscher ordered Cruiser Division Thirteen to pursue crippled enemy ships. He was still chasing the Japanese by air, but that old Mitscher bugaboo—night—was closing in over the Philippines. At 2200, Mitscher led the forces southward, leaving the rest of the mop-up to submarines. In the Battle off Cape Engaño, the third part of the Battle for Leyte Gulf, four carriers, the light cruiser *Tama*, and two destroyers were demolished. In addition, the battleship *Musashi* was stricken from the Navy's wanted list. Her destruction was confirmed, although it was not certain that aircraft had nailed her. Only the *Yamato* remained a serious threat. For all practical purposes, the Japanese had no fleet.

After refueling, Mitscher took groups 38.2 and 38.3 southward to rejoin Halsey and continue hitting shore targets. On October 29—the day the *Intrepid* was hit by a Kamikaze and became the first of many fast carriers to be struck by a suicider—Mitscher departed for Ulithi, which had replaced Eniwetok as the operating home of the task force. He reached that island on October 30, and the reins of Task Force 38 were transferred to Admiral McCain.

Naturally, everyone was dragging a bit. The weariness went far beyond the top officers in flag country. During the September–October period, the task force had flown off 17,285 combat sorties. Losses in pilots and aircraft were higher, comparatively, than during the preceding months; Japanese losses, in the same period, were in the thousands.

In his Action Report, the Admiral said:

It is one very nice thing to have the ships, but it is also a very serious responsibility to keep these same ships ready for battle; their crews enthusiastic and ready to fight. Attention is invited to the fact that the ships of TF 58/38 have been under constant pressure in the tropics for over ten months. Probably ten thousand men have never put a foot on shore during this period. No other force in the world has been subjected to such a period of constant operation without rest or rehabilitation. The spirit of these ships is commendable. However, the reactions of their crews are slowed down. The result is that they are not completely effective against attack.

Mitscher was speaking for himself as well as the "crews" of the task force. However, his own long stint with the Task Force was of his own choosing. He had spent most of the short trip back to Ulithi, on his sea-cabin bunk, and Burke had given orders not to disturb him. When the *Lexington* had anchored at Ulithi, Admiral Halsey offered his seaplane to fly Mitscher back to Pearl Harbor.

During the late afternoon of October 31, word circulated about the *Lexington* that Mitscher would leave early the next morning. It was about 0400 when Mitscher made his way down through the dimly lit hangar deck. Near the after brow stood more than a hundred people. Almost all of Air Group Nineteen had assembled there. Most of them hadn't had a full night's sleep in weeks. Hugh Winters had set his alarm for 0330, and then awakened the pilots—by their own request. They waited quietly, some in uniform, others in the background clad in pajamas and bathrobes.

Mitscher glanced up and saw them. "What the devil are all these people doing here?" he asked Burke. "I don't know, Admiral," said Burke.

Hugh Winters answered. "Well, Admiral, they just wanted to be here when you left."

The Admiral ducked away quickly. After he got down to his barge, chugging at the end of the gangway, they saw him take out a handkerchief.

CHAPTER

⚓ 41 ⚓

Return to Pearl Harbor

PRACTICALLY the entire staff returned to Pearl Harbor with Mitscher. Most of them then went on to the United States for several weeks' leave, but Mitscher stayed in Pearl Harbor for a few days to discuss the war with Nimitz and Spruance. It was customary for returning flag officers to be invited to the morning conferences held by Admiral Nimitz.

Commodore Burke—he had received a promotion to flag rank in October—and Commander Flatley went with Mitscher to the conference. Burke and Flatley did not expect him to speak extravagantly about the historic battle. However, they were not prepared for Mitscher's summary, lasting less than three minutes. Neither were some of the other admirals seated around Chester Nimitz's long table. The Battle for Leyte Gulf was a fitting subject for a three-hour lecture.

Outside the conference room, Flatley said, "Admiral, you didn't tell them very much."

"They're all after my job," he joked. "If I told them everything I knew they'd be as smart as I am." Of course, Nimitz and his staff already had the complete report.

Flatley remained in Pearl Harbor to work with Admiral

Spruance's staff on plans for Fifth Fleet action in early 1945, while Burke and Read accompanied Mitscher home. Already basic plans for securing the rest of the Pacific had been formulated. Mitscher's timetable called for him to relieve McCain in late January, when Spruance would take over again from Halsey.

Frances was waiting for the Admiral in San Diego, and they retreated down to Coronado. Between the visits of friends and telephone calls from reporters, there was little rest or privacy. During the last week of November, he left for Washington on several important errands. One was the procurement of a staff surgeon to advise him on the physical condition of the pilots and to help him make certain that the carriers got enough medical supplies. He selected Captain Ray Hege, a veteran flight surgeon. He also wanted to get the Marine flyers aboard the fast carriers, and to discuss the big-carrier idea with some of the air admirals, and he accomplished both of these purposes during his trip.

Marine aviation was running out of work. There was nothing like the Solomons left to keep the hard-flying Marines in practice, and they were now relegated mainly to patrol tasks, although MacArthur had a Marine air group in the Philippines. Mitscher had never understood why the Marines couldn't operate from the big carriers. Furthermore, he had a selfish motive. He wanted all the Corsairs he could get, and practically all of these tough, fast-climbing fighters, which had been introduced to the war in the Solomons, were Marine property. The way to get them was to annex the Marine Corps fighting squadrons. That was fine with the Leathernecks.

"He put the Marines on fast carriers in one day," said General Field Harris.[1]

On November 29, Mitscher was in the Navy Department

[1] Robert Sherrod, *History of Marine Corps Aviation* (Washington, Combat Forces Press, 1952).

building for a press conference—the weekly gathering at which Secretary Forrestal presided. "Gentlemen, I think you are familiar with the face of this gentleman here," he said. Someone of the press answered, "He hasn't got that cap."

"I tried to make him wear it but he demurred," the Secretary of the Navy answered.

Then Forrestal asked Mitscher to proceed. He arose. "I want to stand up because I speak very low, in the first place, and in the second place, I have brought a California cold with me."

The press asked what he thought of Japanese leadership.

"Well—you know, I don't care very much for them. No, I wouldn't call them skilled at all. In fact, I think they're just a vicious brute and they resort to type. That is, they are just a savage who is a shrewd fighter, but you educate him and in order to fight, he will revert back to native instincts. That's the man I met in the field. Now I'll admit they may have some pretty good officers in Japan but they haven't trotted them out yet."

Before leaving for Pearl Harbor again in early January, he held another press conference in San Diego. This time, he was a bit more caustic in his utter contempt for the Japanese. "They are the poorest specimen of man on earth today, and I've had the opportunity to compare them with the so-called head-hunters of the Solomons," he said.

He needed the cold, unrelenting, almost unreasoning hatred of the enemy. A staff member once said, "Admiral, you can't hate them that much!" Mitscher wheeled on the man and stared at him with monumental scorn, then walked away.

December was happily spent around Coronado with Frances. Fan mail was stacked in one room. He had brought back a few trophies and hoped to put them in a special den after the war. They caught up a bit on social life, but Frances dodged many invitations in order to let him sit in an easy chair and enjoy his late-afternoon old-fashioneds. He was home.

Meanwhile, back in Pearl Harbor, Flatley was deep into the operations plans for strikes against Tokyo and the Japanese mainland. Burke, Gus Read, Frank Dingfelder, who was communications officer, Robert North, who was gunnery officer, Arthur Malsin, Robert Cheston, and Byron "Whizzer" White, the All-American football player of the late thirties, Mitscher's intelligence officers, and Flag Secretary Charles Steele, soon returned.

They were working night and day, but the plans were not materializing. Burke recognized the problem. The underground command post was depressing, and thoughts of the wives and children they had left just at the start of the Christmas season were no help. He announced New Year's Eve as the deadline, but the order was halfhearted and lacked the ring of authority. The deadline approached, and Flatley shook his head.

"Aw, hell," said Burke, "go on out and have fun tonight. Then finish them up."

The staff brought in a thundering 1945, shook off thundering headaches, and within a few days, in time for the Admiral's inspection, presented a masterpiece. Mitscher then settled down in his headquarters on Ford Island and set to work on plans to reactivate Task Force 58. He conferred many times with Spruance and Nimitz and also found leisure to pitch horseshoes every evening.

Lieutenant Commander Max Miller, USNR, author of *I Cover the Waterfront*, then serving as a public-information officer, had in tow a man the Navy and Marine Corps had captured from the Army. His name was Ernest Pyle. Since Pyle was going out with the task force, he was introduced to Mitscher on Ford Island. Within a few minutes after his arrival, they were pitching horseshoes, something Ernie hadn't done since leaving Indiana and enjoyed very much. They pitched until dusk.

"The Admiral seemed pensive and his thoughts far away as he flung the heavy shoes toward the peg," Pyle wrote in *Last Chapter*,[2] which was published after his death. The coming operations could have been on Ernie's mind, too, since he had never been beyond Honolulu and definitely hated the sea. He usually got dreadfully seasick as soon as the lines were slipped off the piers.

In outlining his plans to Pyle, Mitscher said: "I've told you, and having told you, the one thing I'll forbid you to do is take a flight on one of the raids. The reason for this is that if you do have to bail out and are captured, the enemy, as we understand it, has a peculiar medicine or whatever it is called, for getting information out of you, regardless of how determined you are not to give in."

Ernie said he understood. Later that night, as Miller and Pyle rode away from Ford Island in the shuttle boat, Ernie turned to Max and said, "I've been with the Army so long in Europe that I didn't think the Navy had such human people.

"From now on," said Pyle, "Mitscher is one of my gods."

Whenever Mitscher got back from the Stateside leaves—back to the war—he apparently thought of little besides Frances. Evidently he was even more lonely during these periods of waiting at Pearl Harbor than he was when his ships were at sea. He talked of her reverently.

On January 13, he wrote:

In about another week I expect to be heading southwest and I believe this will be my last tour. Unless the war lasts forever. The Philippine show seems to be going along all right so far according to the papers, but we will have to stick around until MacArthur is well dug in.

Have just finished a book sent me by the publishers, "Pacific Victory, 1945" by Joseph Driscoll, a reporter who was down at Guadalcanal. He is optimistic regarding the Pacific victory, but

[2] New York, Holt, 1946.

he gives me a good write-up but not so good about others. Do not remember him particularly.

As the New Year starts, my dear, my first thought goes back some thirty years ago to January 16, 1913, when I married you. In all my thirty-two years of married life I have considered myself the most fortunate man in the world to have been married to you. You were the best the U. S. had to offer and I was the lucky man. It is the one event of my life that I have been truly grateful for, the one accomplishment that makes life worthwhile to me.

Frances would read his letters, have a small cry, say a little prayer, and then scan newspapers and magazines and monitor the San Diego radio station for each evening's news broadcast. His letters did not mention action, the possibility of action, or what was occurring in the task force. But on most days she read or heard something about him.

Mitscher's fame as a fighter was spreading; fan mail stuffed their box at Coronado, and more arrived at staff headquarters. It came from the United States, from Canada, and from Europe. He got a letter once from Poona City, India, from Dattatraya Vasudeo Gokhole: "Most Noble Admiral M. A. Mitscher, we drink to the health of you, most Noble Mr. Mitscher, His Excellency, Mr. Roosevelt, and His Majesty."

He couldn't understand it. As he studied a batch of fan letters, he rubbed his hand across his head, and said, in sincere bewilderment, "Why, I don't believe I know these people."

January was coming to an end, and Halsey was winding up five months of hitting the Philippines and raiding in the South China Sea. Mitscher flew from Pearl Harbor to Ulithi and relieved McCain on January 30. Task Force 38 was placed on paper again, and Mitscher's flag broke to renew the same organization as Task Force 58. The titles were still confusing. Task Force 58/38, First Carrier Task Force, Second Carrier Task Force, Fast Carrier Task Force—physically, all were the same outfit. Under any name, the force was equally destructive.

Halsey's five months of operations, much of the time in bad weather, had slowed the task force to a crawl. Ships needed repairs; men needed repairs. Instead of immediately rushing into action, Spruance and Mitscher decided on a rest and recreation period. The sands of unforgettable Mogmog, a lovely islet in the Ulithi group, were occupied daily by thousands of sailors, and cases of beer were stacked twenty feet high. The recuperation period was interspersed with training and conferences; but there was emphasis on recreation.

All the while, however, the staff worked on preparations first to hit the Japanese mainland in conjunction with the invasion of Iwo Jima, and then to attack Okinawa, next on the invasion list. Top-level conferences were held almost daily. Major General Curtis LeMay, commanding the Army Air Force 21st Bombers, flew in for talks on co-ordination of the B-29's with the task force. There was an influx of newsmen who sensed a canter to the barn.

CHAPTER

⚓ 42 ⚓

The End of the Japanese Fleet

ON FEBRUARY 10, the task force left Ulithi, with Mitscher in the U.S.S. *Bunker Hill*. Nimitz had decided to send Task Force 58 against Tokyo, hoping to divert attention from the invasion of Iwo Jima. The force had waited many weeks for this decision. It was symbolic of the extraordinary advance of naval aviation in two years. As the ships proceeded toward the launching point, Mitscher sent a message over to the ship in which Ernie Pyle was riding: "How is Ernie getting along? Does he wish he was back in a fox hole?"

"We messaged back that I was happy, hadn't been seasick yet and hoped that all my future fox holes could be as plush as this one," Pyle reported in *Last Chapter*. A few weeks after this exchange of pleasantries, Ernie Pyle, the GI's darling, was dead from a sniper's bullet on Ie Shima.

Mitscher's radio call name was now Mohawk, and the task force was on the warpath again. Some called the islands ahead "Indian Country." The pilots knew Mitscher would take them in close. They expected to be brought about 150 miles from the coast before taking off for Tokyo. But on the gray, unpleasant morning of February 16, they discovered Mitscher had steamed to an area about 60 miles off the coast. That day, Tokyo was hit for the first time by genuine carrier aircraft. On the next day, with continued rain, high winds, and even light snow, planes from the task groups launched again for the Imperial City. Then Mitscher doubled back to Iwo Jima to offer direct air support for the invasion.

Since the Philippines campaign, the Divine Wind—which first blew for the Japanese in the thirteenth century, chasing away a Mongol fleet and which now took the form of suicide-plane attacks—had been soughing with spectacular success. In fact, details of its full effect were kept top secret. Both Pearl Harbor and Washington were alarmed. The Kamikaze had replaced the submarine as the enemy's greatest threat to our fleet. During the five days the task force lay off Iwo Jima, suicide aircraft attacked each nightfall, usually approaching the Task Force undetected. They came in singly, often following friendly planes, or flew low with a land background to avoid radar detection. On February 21, the *Saratoga* was hit by four Kamikazes and two bombs. The *Saratoga* was rugged. She survived and proceeded toward Pearl Harbor under her own power. However, the attack was a frightening preview of events to come.

Mitscher again hit Tokyo on February 25, successfully coordinating his raids with those of General LeMay's B-29's. Then he sent two task groups to Okinawa to test enemy air defenses there and take photographs.

Operations plans emphasized that heavy Kamikaze attacks were probable, and before the task force got underway from Ulithi on March 14, much gunnery practice was ordered. Mitscher's flagship, the *Bunker Hill*, moved out to the gunnery range during this period for a day's workout. It wasn't a danger area, so Mitscher went down to the gallery-deck flag mess to eat with his staff instead of having his meals in his sea cabin.

During lunch of this day the *Bunker Hill*'s gun chief, Lieutenant Commander James Shaw, leveled his five-inch guns
across the flight deck and opened up on an aerial target. Each
explosion slapped across the deck. Flag mess shook. Dishes
went up into the air, and the table and deck were covered with
chipped crockery. Mitscher himself jumped up, startled by
the sudden havoc. Somebody said, "For Christ's sake, can't
they wait until we have lunch?"

"I don't give a damn what they do," said Mitscher, "so long
as they learn how to shoot."

Obviously they did, for later in his Action Report, he commented on the effect of ship's gunfire on one day's crop of
Kamikazes: "The shooting was excellent—particularly impressive was the quick firing and opening of fire and the rapid
training and firing of *Bunker Hill*'s five-inch turrets."

He then headed for Okinawa. The landings were scheduled
for April 1. Mitscher had four task groups, with such familiar
commanders as Admirals Clark, Sherman, and Davison still
around. Newcomers to Mitscher's task-group command were
Rear Admirals Arthur W. Radford and Matthias B. Gardner,
although Radford previously had been in the Gilberts. The
task force was now so large that it included not only day carriers but night carriers, which provided night fighter support
and CAP. In all, there were sixteen fast carriers available to
him. In addition, operating in the general area and sometimes
under Mitscher's command, was a newly constituted force of
British ships centered on four carriers.

In an effort to eliminate one source of enemy planes, almost
certain to include Kamikazes, Mitscher decided to strike at
Kyushu and the islands of the Inland Sea area. By dusk of
March 17, he was a fighter-plane flight away from his targets,
but he did not launch them until dawn of March 18. During the
day, the *Yamato* was spotted alongside a pier at Kobe in the
Inland Sea. He directed his staff to keep a special watch on the

big battleship. In the Kyushu and Inland Sea raid, forty-five enemy airfields were attacked and the Japanese lost more than four hundred planes in the two-day strike. All the attacks were made from low levels; Mitscher was still not convinced by the Army's claims for high-altitude bombing. The Japanese suicide corps had not lost its zest, however; the *Yorktown* and the *Enterprise* took hits, and the *Intrepid* was shaken by a near miss.

Two task groups concentrated on the remains of the enemy fleet at Kure, while a third pounded the Kure Naval Air Depot. Shortly after the strikes were launched, bogeys came out after Davison's group, stationed about 20 miles north of the force's central disposition, which was about 50 miles from the Japanese coast. The U.S.S. *Franklin* had not launched all her planes, and many were on deck when she was hit by a well-aimed five-hundred pounder. In a few moments, there was a holocaust. From the *Bunker Hill*'s flag bridge, to the south, six tremendous explosions could be seen. The *Wasp* was also hit, but not seriously. Almost simultaneously, the entire task force was threatened.

Admiral Davison, unable to operate his task group from the flaming *Franklin*, was taken off by destroyer and reported to Mitscher that he believed the *Franklin* would have to be abandoned. But the *Franklin*'s captain didn't agree with his task-group commander. His TBS was still functioning, and Captain Leslie Gehres addressed Mitscher over it: "This is the commanding officer of the *Franklin*. You save us from the Japs and we'll save this ship."

At that moment, Mitscher was watching the black coils of smoke on the horizon, and had no idea of the real condition of the *Franklin*. But he had faith in Gehres. "You tell him we'll save him," Mitscher said to Burke; then he gave orders for the task force to retire, covering the *Franklin* and the *Wasp*. The *Enterprise* was hit again the next day, this time by ack-

ack from a friendly ship, and the destroyer *Halsey Powell* took aboard a Kamikaze. The operation was only a few days old and already five of the ships had been damaged.

Thus began the Okinawa operation, lasting from mid-March until mid-June, one of the wildest, bloodiest chapters in naval history. During the Okinawa campaign, Mitscher had his narrowest escapes from death and one of his greatest triumphs. The Okinawa air campaign, the longest sustained carrier operation of World War II, climaxed his fighting career. From the time *Yorktown, Enterprise,* and *Intrepid* were hit on March 18 until Mitscher gave up the command, elements of the task force were under almost continuous attack.

The capture of Okinawa, the central and largest island of the Ryukyu chain, which runs southwest from the Japanese home island of Kyushu to Formosa, was vital to American victory. It would provide a fleet anchorage, and airfields and staging bases for troops in the assault against Japan proper. The Imperial high command recognized Okinawa's importance and accordingly mobilized all its resources to save the island. Okinawa was defended with a fury equaled only by the defense of London. For reckless disregard of human life, Okinawa's defense by the Japanese is unparalleled in history. The charge at Balaclava was a paltry sacrificial offering in comparison with the Divine Wind of the suicide Kamikazes.

The task-force assignment was to support the landings of the Marines and the Tenth Army on Okinawa and adjacent islands. To carry out this assignment, Mitscher planned strikes against fields on Kyushu, and on the Amami and Minami Daito groups. In addition, the force was to give air support to the troops ashore. Every man on the staff knew that the task force was shackled to Okinawa. "There was nothing to do but take it—the suicide attack—and fight back like hell," Mitscher said later at a press conference.

The Kamikazes were bad enough, but on March 21, Admiral

Clark reported the Japanese had a new weapon. Two dozen fighters from his group were launched to intercept a flock of bogeys and shot down thirty-two Bettys and about half that number of single-engined planes. The twin-engined Bettys were slower than usual and somehow looked odd. Intelligence photos revealed a small plane or winged bomb carried under each fuselage. This was the first appearance of what Allied forces called the Baka bomb, "Baka" being the Japanese word for "fool." It was a "guided missile" employing a young suicide pilot instead of an electronic brain. Apparently the Imperial command was now committed to hara-kiri on a mass basis.

For nine days, beginning on March 23, Mitscher's planes attacked Okinawa and nearby islands in preparation for the April 1 landings. As a result of the heavy attacks on Kyushu, D-Day opposition by enemy aircraft was light. An air strip on Okinawa (Yontan Field) was captured in the early hours of the assault.

On April 3, Marine Major Herbert H. Long, one of Mitscher's Guadalcanal pilots, took off in a Corsair on a bombing and strafing mission over Okinawa. Soon he developed engine trouble, and he landed on Yontan—the first American pilot to do so. He decided to gather information on the ground fighting for Mitscher and talked to the Marines, dirty and chewed up from the sledge-hammer action. After fixing his plane, he returned to the *Bunker Hill*. Plane handlers saw mud on it, and not having touched land for almost a month, started heaving the mud around the flight deck. Mitscher saw the mud, too, and the bull horn said: "Request pilot of the plane that just landed report to the flag bridge."

Long rather proudly briefed Mitscher on events ashore in minute detail, thinking he was doing an excellent job. Arms folded across his chest, the Admiral nodded the while. When

Long finished, Mitscher said, "Now, Major, I'll tell *you* what is actually going on."

Then for ten minutes, Mitscher explained to Long the tactical situation ashore, what had happened to the soldiers up to that point, and the general course of ground fighting that probably would follow.

On April 6 an estimated four hundred Kamikazes visited Task Force 58, and an estimated 233 of them were splashed by fighters. Perhaps ninety more fell to ships' guns. On the same day the *Yamato* left Tokuyama, in the Inland Sea, bound for Okinawa on a suicide mission. Few of her crew, according to Japanese accounts, felt they would live past April 8, her estimated time of arrival off Okinawa. With the battleship was a cruiser and eight destroyers. A submarine reported them in Bungo Channel, between Kyushu and Shikoku.

Mitscher, without awaiting word from Spruance, ordered all task groups to concentrate northeast of Okinawa. Perhaps some of the old battleship-versus-aircraft debates were recalled during the moments he studied the charts with Burke and Flatley. Naval airmen thought they had sunk the *Musashi* in the Battle for Leyte Gulf, but there was also the possibility that submarines had actually put her down. The appearance of the *Yamato* provided a clean-cut chance to prove, if proof was needed, aircraft superiority.

Shortly after midnight on April 6, Spruance directed Mitscher to let the enemy task force come south, leaving it to the guns of Task Force 51, the old battleships, and of Task Force 54, the new ones. Also, Mitscher was to "concentrate the offensive effort of Task Force 58 in combat air patrols to meet enemy air attacks." But Mitscher had already made his plans to sink the enemy fleet with aircraft.

By the time the dispatch was logged in with communications and initialed all the way around, Mitscher was speeding north. Admiral Spruance had not actually countermanded Mitscher's order to the task force to concentrate to the northeast.[1] Unless Spruance explicitly forbade him to make the attack, Mitscher had no intention of letting battleship guns do a job that aircraft could do sooner. Mitscher kept his own counsel. He was doing a bit more than his orders required—perhaps enough more to sink an enemy fleet.

A few hours later, Spruance signaled Rear Admiral Morton L. Deyo, who commanded Task Force 51, to form his two battleship divisions, two cruiser divisions, and twenty destroyers for action. Mitscher saw a copy of the dispatch and dismissed it without comment. Throughout the night, ordnance men worked on the fast carriers, readying armor-piercing bombs and torpedoes.

At dawn, Mitscher's search planes fanned out over the sea east of Kyushu. The weather was squally. Meanwhile, both submarines and flying boats had been tracking the oncoming enemy force. Down in the ready rooms, the pilots were impatient. Word of the friendly rivalry with the battleship guns had reached them. The pilots had heard that Admiral Mitscher "planned to ram this one through."

"We knew we'd get it for him if he gave us the chance and we thought he would," said Major Long.

A few minutes after 0800 one of Admiral Clark's *Essex* search planes found the suicide fleet, steaming southward. The report was relayed back to the *Bunker Hill* by a series of communications linking planes, another Mitscher innovation for the task force, introduced because of the relatively short range of aircraft radios. It fanned out to all the task groups and to Admiral Spruance, who ordered Deyo to push his battleship fleet to the attack. At the same time, Mitscher had

[1] Action Report, Commander, First Carrier Task Force, June 18, 1945.

sent off a force of sixteen planes to cover and track the approaching enemy, but it would be more than an hour before they could make contact. Planes were manned, and as soon as the search aircraft disappeared, Mitscher gave orders to attack the Japanese fleet. It was now 1000. As the planes, from groups 58.1 and 58.2, orbited, joined up, and sped away, the Admiral watched in silence. A few minutes after they were out of sight, he turned to Burke.

"Inform Admiral Spruance that I propose to strike the *Yamato* sortie group at 1200 unless otherwise directed."

"But," said a British observer, "you have launched before you can possibly be sure of their location."

"We are taking a chance," explained Burke, "we are launching against the spot where we would be if we were the *Yamato*." [2]

Actually, with submarines, flying boats, and carrier-based aircraft on the *Yamato*'s trail, the chances of finding the enemy were good, even though the weather was thick. But if the planes could not find her, there wouldn't be enough red paint in the fleet to match the color of Mitscher's face. His launch order to destroy the enemy fleet by aircraft ran contrary to Spruance's desire to let the battleships slug it out in what would probably be the last opportunity for a big-ship gunnery fight, then and forever more.

From 1000 until noon, Mitscher's position there on the wing of the *Bunker Hill* bridge was thoroughly uncomfortable. As time stretched by, there was still no signal from Spruance countermanding Mitscher's orders. At last the planes were so close to the *Yamato* that recall would serve no purpose except to save a few dollars' worth of gas. The Avengers carried torpedoes; the dive bombers (Curtiss Helldivers) car-

[2] Walter Karig and others, *Battle Report*, Volume V (New York, Rinehart, 1949).

ried mixed loads of 1,000- and 250-pound bombs; each fighter had a 500-pound bomb as well as a long-range droppable gas tank. Estimated distance to the target was 240 miles.

Shortly after noon, planes from the Clark and Sherman task groups found the Japanese fleet and circled it for the kill. The weather was still bad, with clouds ranging from 1,500 to 3,000 feet, and intermittent rain. The low ceiling and large number of planes—nearly three hundred arrived simultaneously—made co-ordination impossible. Heavy ack-ack began bursting. Even the *Yamato*'s eighteen-inch guns were elevated to attempt blasting the Yankees from the sky.

The weather made it impossible to see results, and Japanese jamming made it impossible to hear over the voice radio. In the words of Lieutenant Thaddeus T. Coleman, it was the "most confusing sea-air battle of all time." He said:

Our training instructions, to dive steeply from 10,000 feet or higher, proved useless. Here the ceiling was only 3,000 feet with rain squalls all around. Bomber pilots pushed over in all sorts of crazy dives, fighter pilots used every maneuver in the book, torpedo pilots stuck their necks all the way out, dropped right down on the surface and delivered their parcels so near the ships that many of them missed the ships' superstructures by inches.[3]

However confused the Americans were, the Japanese were worse. A *Yamato* gunnery officer who survived told American interrogators that the combination of dive bombers and torpedo planes made it impossible to take evasive action. The first two waves, he said, left three bomb hits forward of the great turret on her stern, and three torpedo hits in the hull. In later attacks she was hit by at least seven more torpedoes, according to his account.

At any rate, when Admiral Radford's strike group, which was launched late, arrived, the *Yamato* was listing, and his planes struck her on the high side. She finally blew up and

[3] *Ibid.*

sank, joining the cruiser *Yahagi* and four destroyers on the bottom. Photographs were handed Mitscher showing the sinking while Admiral Deyo was just getting well into his northward charge with the old battleships. A short while later, after Mitscher had signaled that the enemy had been met and dealt with, Spruance countermanded the previous order sending the ships to destroy the Japanese fleet.

When Admiral Deyo got word of Mitscher's successful attack, he good-naturedly broadcast regrets that his force wouldn't have "Japanese scrambled eggs for breakfast." Mitscher's losses were four bombers, three torpedo planes, and three fighters. Personnel losses were held to four pilots and eight aircrewmen by virtue of quick rescue work.

Mitscher didn't say much, except to congratulate the pilots. But the greatest battleship in the world was marked only by an oil slick, and it was a tremendous personal victory for Mitscher.

CHAPTER
⚓ 43 ⚓

Bombed Out

AT THE end of each day canvas shrouds slipped into the waters off Okinawa. Death was in the air and on the face of the sea. The Divine Wind blew hot and steadily. In April, including both the task force and the invasion forces, 120 ships received minor damages, a hundred were damaged severely, and twenty-four were sunk.

Even before breakfast on April 11, all signs pointed to a busy day. Support missions over Okinawa were abandoned and Mitscher ordered all torpedo planes and bombers to be emptied of ammunition and fuel. Twenty-four fighters orbited over each task group. Twenty-five miles to the northeast, a division of destroyers steamed slowly on picket duty, their weary radar operators scanning the scopes for a glimpse of the Kamikazes. These were the radar pickets. Five were sunk in April, fifty-seven damaged. A hundred miles to the north, Mitscher had stationed another group of twenty-four fighters, staggered at different heights in hopes of intercepting the maniacal onslaught. Antiaircraft guns were fully manned. Facials of antiflash ointment were applied; antiflash hoods and gloves were adjusted. Attack was certain.

Before the mess cooks could clear away the breakfast garbage, the attack began. The Kamikazes hid in a low cloud cover at 4,000 feet, then came in singly from the massed clouds or dove out of the dazzling sun when it burst through. Sometimes they bombed; sometimes they smashed directly into the decks. Ships spiraled across the water, maneuvering like rabbits under a hunter's gun, pouring a stream of ack-ack upward while running.

The *Missouri* and the *Essex* were hit but not put out of action for long. The *Enterprise* was almost hit by four of the Kamikazes, the destroyer *Kidd* was put out of action, and three others were damaged. The destroyers moved out for Ulithi in a limping formation, with the *Enterprise* supplying air cover. That night the attack resumed. The next day, the radar pickets were selected as targets by the Kamikazes.

So went the month of April. Mitscher often scanned his status boards and cursed the position he was in. Afterward, in July, 1946, Mitscher testified before the Senate Naval Affairs Committee:

The sea and air battles off Okinawa could have been shortened considerably if the Army had established airfields and put them into operation as rapidly as the Seabees had done in other places. The Army could not. As a result the Navy supported the landing force long after the Army should have been able to supply its own air cover. The Navy suffered losses and damage to which it should never have been subjected.

On April 14, the gallant radar pickets were hit again, and the destroyer *Sigsbee* left the force. On the 16th, the carrier *Intrepid* took a Kamikaze on the flight deck and was ablaze for a few minutes. Then she too limped back to Ulithi.

Mitscher had come to Okinawa with four task groups. Now there were only enough ships left for three. At 0500 on April 17, he disbanded Task Group 58.2, and augmented the other task groups. The Japanese were not winning, but neither were they losing except in equipment and personnel. An average of twenty to thirty Kamikazes were splashed each day. He sent strikes to Kyushu and raked the fields in desperation, but the Divine Wind kept coming.

Despite constant GQ, life went on in flag country, and Mitscher alternated between his swivel chair, the Flag Plot transom and his sea cabin as the fast carriers steamed on various courses, none of them far from Okinawa. Aside from giving broad instructions to the task-group commanders, he did not have much to do, for escaping the Kamikazes was almost an individual job for ship captains. Everything became routine in these days off Okinawa. Within the larger frame, minor incidents assumed much importance and became deeply imbedded in the minds of the staff.

Mitscher, for instance, was irritated by a pair of Japanese aerial snoopers who seemed to lead charmed lives. They made daily trips to the extremity of the Okinawa island chain, observing the positions of the ships and of the troops ashore.

One morning, after sending two destroyers up the line to vector the *Bunker Hill* planes in for a kill, he launched twelve aircraft. Large patches of fog combined with intermittent rain that morning. After a futile search for the snoopers, the planes ran low on gas and returned to the carrier, where Mitscher had been waiting. The Admiral called Lieutenant Commander Raymond Hill, the squadron leader, up to the flag bridge and asked if any results had been obtained. He already knew that Hill's pilots had missed them.

"No, Admiral, I'm sure they weren't out today," said Hill.

"They came right through you," Mitscher said coldly. He pointed to a radar plot of the Japanese snoopers. Several days later, the snoopers finally were knocked down.

Another routine incident concerned Mitscher's communications planes, used to relay messages. A group of four planes circled at a spot 100 miles from the task force; another group was located at 200 miles. One morning Mitscher sent up a division of four Marine aircraft to the 100-mile position, north of the task force. They orbited and relayed messages from their 12,000-foot sentinel points. About 1100, when it was time for their recall and relief, bad weather set in, and communication with them was lost. So were the pilots.

During the afternoon, search aircraft were launched, but they were still unreported at 1900. At that hour Mitscher came in from the wing and said to Flatley, "Get me a chart and a pair of dividers." He walked off distance, then said, "Those pilots are right here."

Flatley squinted at him. Mitscher pointed to a position between 300 and 400 miles from the task force. "Send a message to the submarines to pick them up," he said. Flatley promptly did so, although he felt the Admiral was miles off in his guess. The next morning American submarines reported that the pilots had been picked up.

Flatley attributed the bull's-eye location to Mitscher's kinship to "seagoing air." Mitscher himself explained it rather simply for Flatley and any of the other students in Flag Plot. The Marine pilots thought they had been flying in a 50-mile wind at the relay position; Mitscher, from close study of his aerology information, estimated it to be a 100-mile wind, and concluded that the Marines must have run out of gas because of a navigation error brought on by their ignorance of the true wind speed.

There were other similar incidents as the task force fulfilled its mission off Okinawa. But by May 1, the pace of Task Force 58 had again slowed to a trot. The strain of two months of continuous tension showed in every face. Some of the men on the *Bunker Hill* had been aboard since her operations at Rabaul in 1943. Washington recognized the need for frequent changes for air groups, but wasn't as considerate of ships' personnel. The men were confined to narrow quarters with the same people day after day, and had been getting only two or three hours of sleep each night; enemy raids and calls to GQ interrupted their normal duties. Their reflexes grew slower and slower. Mitscher was found more often on the soft transom seat in Flag Plot. The calm and quiet of the flag bridge was a forced serenity, achieved by will power.

May 11 was the *Bunker Hill*'s fifty-ninth consecutive day at sea. Task Groups 58.3 and 58.4 were about 100 miles east of Okinawa, furnishing direct air support for the Southern Attack Force ashore and providing a fighter plane cover over Okinawa. The *Bunker Hill* was still in Sherman's 58.3.

At 0200 enemy planes were reported, and a few minutes later everyone went to general quarters. Mitscher rose tiredly from his bunk, and pulled on a light robe and the cap. GQ lasted until 0255, when "Condition One Easy" was set, which left the antiaircraft gunners on partial alert. At dawn, 0441, there was the usual routine GQ of ten minutes. After 0800 there were reports of more bogeys, and at 0900, GQ was set again, and not relaxed for forty minutes. It was often impossible to shave without interruption.

The staff had finally convinced Mitscher he should wear something more than the baseball cap. Since mid-April, at the insistence of Burke, Mitscher had been wearing "battle gear," consisting of a steel helmet and a Mae West life preserver, when he was on the bridge wing. If a Kamikaze appeared likely to fall on the *Bunker Hill*, he would duck into Flag Plot, take off the helmet, and stand behind the steel battle shields, watching the attack through the heavy bulletproof-glass windows.

About 1002, Gus Read, who was flag-duty officer at the time, summoned the Admiral and Commodore Burke into Flag Plot. CIC reported that there were indications that a close-support group returning to the *Bunker Hill* might be a cover for enemy planes. Read asked for further reports, but CIC indicated it could not positively identify the planes as enemy.

As it turned out, an enemy formation actually had tagged along with the *Bunker Hill*'s planes, aided by concealing clouds. At 1004, the radio speaker in Flag Plot tuned to fighter frequency frantically relayed: "Alert! Alert! Two planes diving on the *Bunker Hill!*" Major James Swett, USMC, Mitscher's Medal of Honor winner from Guadalcanal days, had seen the planes diving.

Almost instantly, one Zeke released his five-hundred-pound bomb, which went through the flight deck and out through the side of the ship, and exploded above water. Almost at the same moment the plane plunged into the flight deck in the middle of a group of fighters manned for take-off. Its gas tank exploded and left a searing trail as the plane skidded along the flight deck and over the side.

There was more warning of the approach of the second plane. It roared past the ship at full throttle, made a steep climbing turn to port, and then dove directly for the *Bunker Hill*. The pilot released his bomb, which hit amidships and then exploded on the gallery deck, where there were many staff personnel. Flatley, on his way up from CIC, two decks below, had just passed the flight deck when the second Kamikaze hit, and flame scorched his back.

The plane finally crashed onto the island, less than a hundred feet from where Mitscher stood, and more flame leaped skyward. The Admiral then stepped out on the starboard side of the flag bridge. He had not said a word during the few minutes of attack. He looked about him, then peered down toward the flight deck.

Smoke came into Flag Plot through the door and the ventilators, and Burke soon ordered everyone out. The smoke was so thick Captain Read had to follow the edge of the chart table to reach the door. Burke, the last to leave, emerged choking and coughing, unable to do anything more than gesture and wheeze for a few minutes. As he came out, a third Kamikaze was shot down by antiaircraft fire, and fell, burning, into the water close to another ship.

Mitscher and Burke went up to the ship's bridge to confer with Captain George A. Seitz. Then Read joined them, climbing up a pipe to reach the bridge after he had been blocked from a more usual access by flame. As his hands came over the edge of the bridge deck, someone wearing a steel helmet grasped his wrists to help him. As the man leaned out, his helmet came off, bounced off Read's face, and struck the staff communications officer on the head. So far, these were the only known injuries to the Admiral's staff.

Read saluted the Admiral and asked, "Are you okay, sir?"

Mitscher returned the salute and said, "Yes," quite imperturbably.

Burke sent Read down to the flight deck to collect members of the staff and muster them. Since the ladders were red-hot and gasoline from aircraft tanks was still burning on them, Read and another officer climbed over the gun-directing system to reach the flight deck.

Meanwhile, Mitscher stayed on the ship's bridge to watch the fire-fighting operations. He knew, by now, that he could not continue his command from *Bunker Hill*. By visual signal, he relinquished command of Task Force 58 to Sherman, whose flagship, *Essex*, had not been attacked.

Bunker Hill had slowed to 10 knots, and was developing a slight list. The twenty-millimeter batteries at the edge of the flight deck were all but deserted. There was one exception, well forward on the port side, where the Marine sergeant in charge appeared to have telephone connections with the gunnery department and kept calling out bearings to his gun crew as sporadic attacks on the group of ships continued.

Aft, there were gasoline explosions among the burning planes, and as machine-gun ammunition exploded, tracer bullets set Fourth-of-July patterns. Safety valves popped off and spouted white steam into the billowing clouds of smoke. The air was thick with the unique smell of a burning ship, acrid and nauseous. Mingled with the hiss of planes and the noise of explosions were screams, and sometimes the sound of a man whimpering. Many crew members were dying of burns.

Read found some of the staff members manning hoses to fight hangar-deck fires; others were helping doctors and corpsmen give first aid to the wounded. Two chaplains walked slowly among the twitching bodies, talking in low voices.

When muster was finally held, the missing included Captain Ray Hege, the newly attached staff flight surgeon, Lieutenant Commander Charles Steele, the energetic, completely devoted young flag secretary, Lieutenant Commander Frank Quady, assistant operations officer, and ten enlisted men. Their bodies were found a short time later.

Captain Read went back to the bridge and reported the muster to Burke, who then gave the names of the dead to the Admiral. Mitscher sighed deeply. He had gone through most of the war without a staff casualty.

Meanwhile, the cruiser *Wilkes-Barre* and three destroyers had trained their hoses on the *Bunker Hill,* and were picking up some three hundred men who had been blown off the ship or forced to jump overboard to avoid the flames. About 1130, when the fire was being brought under control, the forward elevator was put into service to bring up casualties and planes, which were spotted forward. As the sun was hot, and there was no other shade, wounded men were placed under wings of aircraft that had not burned.

Three hundred and forty-six of the *Bunker Hill's* crew were killed or died of wounds, forty-three were missing, and two hundred and sixty-four were wounded. Most of the ship's fighter squadron, waiting action in their ready room, were dead from asphyxiation. Thirteen of Mitscher's staff had been killed.

Mitscher was depressed and would not discuss their deaths at all at the time. The situation was very similar to the Torpedo Eight loss. Later, he said he felt personally responsible for Captain Hege's death since he had asked for him by name and had particularly selected him from a group of other eligible officers. Throughout the grind of the Marshalls, the Marianas, and the Philippines, Mitscher had almost always drawn on a vast inner strength to maintain, at least in outward appearance, the façade of vigor and invincibility. Now the facade was beginning to crumble.

The Admiral's sea cabin had been gutted, Burke reported. All of Mitscher's clothes had been burned; most of his scanty file of papers and many personal letters had been destroyed. The flag office, on the gallery deck, had been swept by fire. Mitscher hardly raised his eyebrows when Burke informed him of this.

About twenty staff officers and enlisted men were ordered to gather what possessions they could and report to the hangar deck for transfer to the destroyer *English*, which would take them to a new flagship, the *Enterprise*. The transfer began about 1500. Mitscher, left last, at about 1630.

The men of the *English*, pleased at the presence of a three-star admiral, extended themselves to be good hosts. Hot coffee was provided as the *English* slipped away from the side of the smoldering, listing *Bunker Hill*. For entertainment on the short cruise to the *Enterprise*, the commanding officer of the *English* set up a screen in the wardroom to show excellent color footage of their rescue work after one of the big carriers had been hit. It was packed with dramatic action, full of fire and explosions.

According to Read, Mitscher and his staff, there in the smoky wardroom of the *English*, would have preferred the antics of Mickey Mouse.

CHAPTER

⚓ 44 ⚓

Last Days of Combat

MITSCHER resumed tactical command of the task force at 0800 the next morning—May 12—having installed himself in the *Enterprise*. The flag bridge was above the captain's bridge, instead of below it as on the *Bunker Hill*. Back home, that day, a radio commentator told the world that the Navy was about to announce the death of one of its favorite admirals. Frances did not hear the broadcast but knew something must be wrong when her neighbors in Coronado looked at her with curious sympathy. She telephoned the naval base at San Diego, and was reassured. Marc was all right, she was told.

The *Enterprise* was now a night carrier, and her routine was strange to the staff. Her operations began at sunset and ended shortly before dawn. During daylight the ship was usually at GQ, and the flight deck was clear. This turned out to be fortunate.

Burke and Flatley had been urging Mitscher to hit the Kyushu airfields again in hopes of hampering activity on these Kamikaze breeding grounds. They were tired of the sitting-duck posture off Okinawa. It was Mitscher's belief, however, that they could destroy more enemy aircraft by staying in the area off the island. Furthermore, Mitscher thought that the B-29's should do the Kyushu work, because of the close-support duties of the task force.

But finally, and with reluctance, he bowed to his staff's recommendations and began a high-speed run toward Japan's southernmost home island. Later, Flatley, who has since become a captain and a carrier commanding officer himself, conceded that Mitscher had been right. In fact, excepting only Mitscher's reluctant agreement to attack Kyushu, Flatley himself believed that "Mitscher never made a tactical error in the employment of the Task Force and its aircraft." Mitscher could be charged with overestimating enemy strength on several occasions, and wasting manpower and aircraft because of this, but the result was only a higher score, and the cost was a few added tankerloads of gasoline.

The move against Kyushu was begun on the late afternoon of May 12. The next day was spent off the coast with satisfactory results and no particular opposition. The weather was good, with scattered clouds at 3,000–5,000 feet. A steady, freshening wind blew from the southwest. The staff even managed to relax a bit.

But at 0620 on May 14, Mitscher was notified in his sea cabin that enemy planes were near. He went immediately to Flag Plot. Captain Read, who had the duty watch, had previously called Burke to the bridge. Three enemy planes were shot down over the task force in quick succession, but a fourth kept on, and its course was plotted on the fighter-director board. Read had telephoned other members of the staff to awaken them. Before turning in after the night watch, one of them had said, "Now, damn you, Gus, if you get bogeys on the screen, you wake me up."

The Kamikaze dodged into one cloud, then into a second, while the guns of the *Enterprise* and her escorts groped for him. As the ship was ending an emergency turn, the suicider dropped out of the second cloud, coming in at about 200 feet altitude, and ablaze. Either deliberately or from flipper trouble, he aimed at the carrier. Every trainable gun in Captain Grover B. H. Hall's ship banged away at him.

Flatley, who had rushed out on the wing to take a look, rushed right back in for the first time in anybody's memory. The *Enterprise* flag bridge was in the exposed position on top of the carrier island. Flatley shouted for everyone to hit the deck. There was a tremendous explosion forward, and shock waves drummed through Flag Plot, followed by sounds of metal falling on the deck outside and bouncing off the light armor of the flag deckhouse. As Flatley raised his head and peeked around, he saw Mitscher standing very erect amid the prone bodies, with his arms folded, a bit of a frown on his face.

"Flatley," he said, "tell my task-group commanders that if the Japs keep this up they're going to grow hair on my head yet." His words sliced through the atmosphere and the men in Flag Plot jolted to action.

Smoke began to pour in through the ventilating system, and the starboard door was ordered opened. Commander Frank Dingfelder, the staff communications officer, staggered in, with the remains of his spectacles in one hand, bleeding from a superficial cut below one eye. He was groggy, and Burke led him to the Admiral's sea cabin. Mitscher followed several minutes later to check on Dingfelder's condition and provide him with a drink from the emergency supply in the safe.

Routine was soon restored in Flag Plot but the flight deck of the *Enterprise* was wrecked. Parts of the suicide pilot and his possessions, including his wallet, were recovered. Mitscher and several other officers took calling cards—which the Japanese also carried—as mementos of a suicide pilot's last flight.

Mitscher quickly returned to the flag bridge, where he could see the huge hole forward and the long bulge in the flight deck aft. The *Enterprise* was tough and maintained her speed, and also maintained the Navy's proud boast that no land-based aircraft had ever sunk a major carrier. Working parties, in flash-proof clothing and helmets, cleaned up the debris with a minimum of confusion. Fires which had been started on the hangar deck by the exploding bombs were quickly brought under control. Captain Hall soon had her in order.

Mitscher's own, in-port quarters on the gallery deck—which he had not seen—were a shambles. His unused bunk had collapsed, as had the table in flag mess. At the time, he was carrying most of his personal possessions with him, so little of personal value was lost. Six or seven of the staff were wounded, but none were killed. As there could be no cooking in flag country, Mitscher and his staff in Flag Plot were supplied with K rations. They were also given a portable drinking-water device such as some remembered from Guadalcanal days. Aside from an attack about 0800, in which three bogeys were splashed around the task force, the day passed without further excitement. At dusk, they headed for a fueling rendezvous.

During all of this wild action, both on the *Bunker Hill* and on the *Enterprise*, Mitscher did not once visibly flinch, raise his voice, or become in the least excited, according to his staff members. His nerve control seemed almost inhuman. Some associates say he knew he had a heart condition and therefore would not allow himself the slightest excitement. But those who knew him better believe this view is nonsense, and point out again that Mitscher never really became excited.

The next morning, May 15, Mitscher and his uninjured staff members were transferred to the U.S.S. *Randolph*, where they were welcomed aboard by Rear Admiral Gerald Bogan, one of the momentarily spare task-group commanders attached to the force. By that time, there were but two experienced watch officers on the staff to stand duty in Flag Plot. Bogan lent some of his men to augment Mitscher's staff and for the next two weeks, the task force continued to support the troops ashore, with occasional side missions. The task force was subjected to several more suicide attacks, but none were effective.

In his Action Report, Mitscher wrote:

It is interesting to note that for two and a half months the Task Force operated daily in a 60 mile square area East of Okinawa, less than 350 miles from Kyushu. This was necessitated by the restricted area available and the necessity for being able to cover [the] Amami Gunto airfields, intercept air raids before they could reach Okinawa, and still furnish air support to ground forces. There was no other location from which all these things could be done. It is a degrading reflection on the enemy submarine service that they were unable to make us move or even threaten our ships during that time.

Mitscher, however, did want to move away from Okinawa. On May 18 he informed Admiral Spruance that the continued support of Okinawa by Task Force 58 was of doubtful value and recommended that the force be released. But the Commander, Fifth Fleet, felt otherwise, and kept him near the island.

Finally, on May 27, Admiral Halsey and Vice Admiral McCain took over, and Task Force 58 again became Task Force 38. After several conferences with Halsey and McCain, Admiral Mitscher and what remained of his staff departed for Guam. As the *Randolph* and several escorting destroyers left the formation, Halsey signaled:

WITH DEEP REGRET WE ARE WATCHING A GREAT FIGHTING MAN SHOVE OFF X ALL LUCK TO YOU AND YOUR MAGNIFICENT STAFF FROM ME AND MY WHOLE STAFF AND THE FLEET X HALSEY

They reached Guam, after seventy-nine days at sea. From there, the Admiral, Burke, Read, Flatley, North, Dingfelder, and several other officers and enlisted men, flew back to Pearl Harbor in Halsey's private plane. They held a formation behind the administration building at Pearl Harbor, and awards were presented. It looked very much like a parade of scarecrows, photographs testify. At that, they were lucky, for more than two thousand men in Task Force 58 had not lived through the Okinawa campaign.

PART FOUR

⚓ ⚓
⚓

Peace Again

CHAPTER

⚓ 45 ⚓

Fishing

MITSCHER's fighting days were over. It would be practically impossible accurately to estimate the number of miles he had steamed, the enemy aircraft he had downed, and the full damage he had done since 1942. For instance, on July 23, 1945, the Navy Department announced that Task Force 58 had destroyed or damaged 3,259 enemy planes in seventy-six days of fighting off Okinawa. The task force itself claimed 3,170. And to the achievements of the task force might be added, as a personal Mitscher score, the havoc wrought clear back to Midway, and certainly including those days by the Lunga.

While combat statistics are uncertain at best, one thing was evident—Mitscher and his fast carriers and planes had led the way to Tokyo. The ground troops took the real estate and secured the airfields; then the Army Air Corps moved in for mass destruction with the ponderous B-29's. But Mitscher and his carrier men had led the way.

Said Admiral Towers, in a fitness report: "He has demonstrated to the world at large those outstanding qualifications of leadership and aggressiveness which I have always held in high esteem. I consider him one of the Navy's outstanding flag officers."

Said Admiral Nimitz, even more glowingly: "He is the most experienced and most able officer in the handling of fast carrier task forces who has yet been developed. It is doubtful if any officer has made more important contributions than he toward extinction of the enemy fleet." Attached to that fitness report were thirteen congratulatory dispatches from almost every top-ranking officer in the Pacific and in Washington.

Mitscher flew straight to Washington and on June 5 was again a guest at Forrestal's press conference. He still wore his forest-green uniform, for he had had no chance to replace the clothing burned on the *Bunker Hill*. He made one statement which startled many high-ranking naval officers: "Suicide bombing is the same as dive bombing except the man goes with the bomb." He flatly maintained that the Kamikaze was not too serious a threat, and said that only ten per cent of the suicide planes were getting through. Previously, most Navy Department statements on the subject had expressed great concern about them. Mitscher purposely minimized them because he thought people were becoming unduly alarmed.

Back at Coronado, he began a short rest by going to the Sierras. John Hayward, who had been with Mitscher during the early part of the war, was now at the naval ordnance facility at Inyokern, California, where he had duty in connection with the Manhattan Project. He managed to get several days' leave, and together they went to Bishop, up in the Sierras. There was a lake there, and the trout were hungry.

On midafternoon of the last day, the trout stopped striking and the rowboat drifted lazily along. Both men were silent, but Hayward wanted to talk. He began telling Mitscher about the atomic bomb. He hadn't told anyone else, not even Mrs. Hayward. "General Groves would have hung me," said Hayward, "but I knew the secret was safe with Admiral Mitscher."

Hayward explained Einstein's theory and then began a layman's description of how an atom is split. Mitscher was listening, but his eyes were on the far shore. Suddenly, Hayward realized how ridiculous it all sounded there in the silent, peaceful setting of the lake. He sensed that Mitscher could not comprehend, or would not believe, this story about a bomb of incalculable destruction. Hayward finished, saying, "The war is all over, Uncle Pete."

Mitscher turned his eyes away from the shore and looked directly at Hayward. "Chick, you're my friend . . ." He paused for a long while, then said quickly, "You're completely off the beam. You have to go back to the war!" But in September of that year, after the bombing of Hiroshima and Nagasaki, Hayward received a letter from Mitscher, recalling that afternoon at Bishop. It ends rather wistfully, ". . . this is a young man's business now. There is no place in it for old men."

After his return from the fishing trip, Mitscher held a press conference at his home—a guest house which belonged to friends—and was asked what "other secret weapons the Japs might have ready to spring on us." He answered, "They'll put men in guns and shoot them next." Usually, when the reporters got back to their city rooms and checked their notes, they found they had engaged in some delightful conversation but had brought back little in the way of stories.

He had learned in Washington that he would get an administrative job—as Deputy Chief of Naval Operations for Air. "It is against my wishes and desires," he told the press. He had hoped for at least thirty days' leave but Admiral King would grant only fifteen, so he made plans to go to the capital in mid-July.

One afternoon, while in Coronado, he received a call from the Navy Department. Forrestal had been scheduled to make two Fourth-of-July speeches in Seattle but had had to cancel them. He asked Mitscher to fill in for him. Despite further need for rest, Mitscher agreed to make the talks if the public-information officers at San Diego would write them.

Commander E. Robert Anderson, USNR, worked for days on the speeches and accompanied Mitscher to Seattle. He was eager for the Admiral to approve them, disapprove them, or rewrite them. But Mitscher wouldn't even read the speeches in Coronado or en route to Seattle. When the time came for the major speech in the Olympic Hotel ballroom, Mitscher reached into his pocket, pulled out one of the speeches, examined it to make sure it was the one he was supposed to deliver, and addressed the audience: "I was here two weeks ago on a quiet fishing trip in your beautiful Puget Sound. I didn't get a single fish and ended up eating some fish out of a can. Therefore, you are now going to get a canned speech." Then he read it through in a monotone.

His conclusion was: "Next time if you prefer a fresh speech, see that I get some fresh fish." There was laughter and applause for at least two full minutes.

CHAPTER

⚓ 46 ⚓

Home to Hillsboro

THE farming village of Hillsboro, Wisconsin, had grown since 1887, but not a great deal. It had modernized its name from Hillsborough to Hillsboro, but the people were much the same. In early July of 1945 there were rumors that Vernon County's illustrious son was on his way home, but Mitscher's mother would neither confirm nor deny them. While town officials attempted to get concrete information from her, the Marc Mitschers were heading for Hillsboro in a rattling 1941 Chevrolet sedan. He was never a man of Cadillac tastes.

Mitscher had been avoiding people as if everyone were smitten with a contagious disease. The few weeks in Coronado and the Pacific northwest had been hectic, and the Mitschers wanted to be alone—away from the telephone, hand-wringers, friends, and the United States Navy. The automobile afforded some privacy.

Their luck had been poor. All the way across, he had been recognized. They lodged in motels or sought out unpretentious side-street hotels, and he often removed his hat and insignia, but the reporters, probably abetted by room clerks, usually found him, and news wires pecked off a few more lines on the

Mitscher journey. Once, in a restaurant, two sailors saw him, and said loudly, "Hey, there's Admiral Pete Mitscher." Mitscher rose, motioned to Frances, and they hurriedly left the table, food uneaten.

It was dusk when they entered La Crosse, Wisconsin, to spend the night before going the last fifty miles to Hillsboro. They parked in front of a hotel, and a venerable doorman approached, started to speak to Mitscher, examined the chill on the Admiral's face, and thought better of it. Instead, he whispered to Frances, "They've got a big celebration for you over in Hillsboro."

"We didn't know," she replied, honestly.

Momentarily, she was worried. He had been so edgy since they left Coronado. She decided not to tell him until morning. The hotel opened its dining room for them, and as they ate dinner, she noticed several men lurking outside. She suspected they were newsmen and was relieved when they made no effort to enter. One left a paper at the desk, and Frances retrieved it on the way to their room. Mitscher retired immediately.

The paper was dated July 11, 1945. Hillsboro, she read, had been restless all day. The volunteer fire department had strung a welcome banner over Water Street, the main thoroughfare; the telephone company had arranged to send out a jangle on all lines on Mitscher's arrival. There had been nothing like it in a hundred quiet years, just about Hillsboro's age. As she read on, occasionally glancing over at her husband, his face relaxed in deep sleep but losing none of its tired creases, she knew they would have to face the celebration.

The Koffee Kup had Mitscher clippings plastered over its front window. The Pioneer Garden Restaurant had a window display of pictures of Mitscher's grandparents—Andreus and Constantina—and Civil War muskets, to give it a martial air. The town hardware store was displaying models of Navy ships and aircraft.

Mitscher was awake at dawn, and Frances cautiously broke the news to him. He frowned and grumbled at first; then she sensed that all would be well. They covered the fifty miles to Hillsboro in a rainy hour and rolled the sedan up a side street to stop in front of Aunt Helen Pinch's house. Uncle Doc Pinch had delivered Mitscher. He jumped out of the car and hurried Frances in, dodging photographers who had followed them the last few miles. His mother was just inside the door.

"How did they know I was coming?" he admonished gently.

"I didn't tell them," she said, beaming.

By now, a crowd had gathered on the front lawn and the photographers were clamoring for him to make an appearance. He did, posing between his mother and Frances. The doorbell rang throughout the rest of the morning. People brought in food on huge trays—bacon and molded salads and desserts, hot rolls and preserves. Cakes were stacked on the table.

Mitscher was uncomfortable, but only once did the warm, set smile disappear. The bell had been ringing incessantly, his hand was trembling from the constant handshaking, and there was an endless sing-song of chatter in Aunt Helen's front room. The confusion finally rattled him, and he hastily walked upstairs. He paced the floor for about a half hour, cursing under his breath at nothing in particular. Then he came down, smiling and at ease again. By two, the lawn was filled. Some people had come fifty or a hundred miles. At three, Mitscher smoothed out his slate-gray uniform, an unhandsome wartime creation, and stepped out to the front porch, saluting smartly to the crowd. The narrow street, shaded by massive trees, overflowed with welcomers.

Mayor Moon introduced Dr. MacKechnie, the village physician for almost half a century, a beloved man in Hillsboro. Clad in white trousers and morning coat, with a high, stiff collar which would have choked a lesser man, MacKechnie presented the Admiral with a watch, inscribed from "The Citizens of

Hillsboro," and a state flag. Mitscher responded in a voice so quiet that the reporters caught only fragments of words. Then a parade, led by the high-school band, reinforced by volunteers from surrounding towns, moved through the business district. In the lead car, an open limousine rented in Madison, sat Mitscher, flanked by Frances and his mother. Hillsboro had spared nothing.

The car passed his birthplace, now renovated to two stories, and went by the old brick building where his father had once been a partner in Shear & Mitscher. Once the car stalled from overheating, and spewed steam. The parade ground to a halt, and Mitscher mopped perspiration. The July sun was intense. Aproned mothers, some with babies, stood watching, and the usual herd of small boys, many barefoot, bounced alongside the car as it proceeded slowly back to the Pinch house. There, he thanked the crowd and went inside.

At times, the reception must have seemed unreal; only two months before, Mitscher had been bombed off the *Enterprise*. If a parade had to be held in honor of Admiral Mitscher, Hillsboro's was his kind of show. The ticker-tape affairs of Chicago and New York would not have pleased him half so well.

During the commotion, a phone call came in from Madison, Wisconsin. As Mitscher hung up, he said, "That man has a boy missing from one of my carriers."

"Oh, Marc, you know we can't help him," said Frances, thinking of the torture that often developed in ten or fifteen minutes with a bereaved parent.

"We have to," said the Admiral. "He wanted to come here but I told him we'd stop in Madison tomorrow. He's a retired minister."

As they got out of the car near the dwelling on Commonwealth Avenue, Frances saw an elderly man coming down the walk, and when Mitscher entered the house, the minister's wife, who appeared to be much younger, whispered to Frances,

"Does the Admiral really know our boy?" Frances nodded, although she doubted the Admiral would remember this one pilot out of thousands.

"There's Dick," Mitscher said quickly to the Reverend E. D. Upson, pointing toward a large portrait of a young man with a crew cut and thick mustache. Lieutenant Commander Richard Upson, who had led VT-16 in the *Lexington*, had failed to return from the Truk strike in April, 1944.

The hope in the minister's eyes grew brighter as Mitscher told him the Navy felt sure that many missing pilots were safe on islands in the Pacific. He talked about Dick Upson intimately for almost twenty minutes, and Frances was amazed. As Mitscher left, the retired Methodist clergyman grasped him by the arm. "If Richard doesn't return, he will have done more for humanity than I did in all my years in the pulpit."

As the Mitschers drove away from Madison, finally bound for Washington, Frances noticed there were tears in the Admiral's eyes. Several days later the following appeared on the editorial page of the Madison *Journal:*

Madison was paid a visit the other day by a very distinguished Naval officer, Vice Admiral Marc Mitscher. He stopped here to visit with the Reverend E. D. Upson whose son is missing in action in the Pacific. We don't know how many generals and admirals visit bereaved parents but we do know that Admiral Mitscher has the reputation of looking after his men. His gesture in extending that to these Madison parents is one worthy of recognition. We feel safer when humble men like Admiral Mitscher are running the war.

CHAPTER

⚓ 47 ⚓

The Lessons Learned

ADMIRAL MITSCHER reported as Deputy Chief of Naval Operations for Air, unimpressed by job and title, settling in a comfortable, homey office in the long white maze on Constitution Avenue. Paintings of early naval-air triumphs were spread over the walls, and on his desk were models of modern aircraft. His feet were often propped up there, too. He did as little as possible, unless higher command sent for him, and his door was usually open to visitors, whether on business or to discuss a trout fly.

Said Rear Admiral Robert Pirie, "Plainly, Pete was mad." And bored. Previously, Flatley had voiced fears at Mitscher's return to Washington. "They'll rip him to shreds," said Flatley, referring to the political aspects of the job. But it was apparent that Mitscher did not intend to place himself in a position where he could be ripped to shreds.

Speaking engagements were scheduled for him immediately, and, regarding these as a duty, he made five speeches during August. He also made a statement through a Navy Department press release on August 11, which aroused some controversy.

Japan is beaten, and carrier supremacy defeated her. Carrier supremacy destroyed her army and navy air forces. Carrier supremacy destroyed her fleet. Carrier supremacy gave us bases adjacent to her home islands. And carrier supremacy finally left her exposed to the most devastating sky attack—the atomic fission bomb—that man has suffered.

When I say that carrier supremacy defeated Japan, I do not mean airpower by itself won the Battle of the Pacific. We exercised our carrier supremacy as part of a balanced, integrated air-surface-ground team, in which all hands may be proud of the roles assigned them, and of the way in which their duties were discharged. This could not have been done by a separate air force, exclusively based ashore, or by one not under direct Navy control.

This statement, coming two days after Nagasaki was subjected to an atomic bomb, and with victory a certainty, was one of the first public presentations by a high-ranking officer of a thesis that was to get much attention. Mitscher repeated the statement on carrier supremacy several times in other speeches during that month and the two following. His opinion was not well received by the Tokyo raider, General Doolittle, for one. Later, on November 12, before a Senate Military Affairs Committee hearing on the arms merger, Doolittle said, "Our B-29 boys are resting uneasily in their graves as a result of these comments." But Mitscher stood fast, saying what he honestly thought; maintaining that the Navy carriers had led the way to the Japanese downfall, and it was exceedingly difficult for anyone to refute him. Mitscher was not baiting the Army Air Force, although subsequent Pentagon statements indicated the Army thought he was.

Late in August, on the occasion of naval aviation's thirty-second anniversary, Mitscher got into difficulty with Admiral King. The cause of King's sharp annoyance was a press release which seemed to begin innocuously:

Vice Admiral Marc A. Mitscher, USN, Deputy Chief of Naval Operations (Air) declared today in marking the 32nd anniversary

of Naval Aviation tomorrow (August 30) that the carrier supremacy established in the war just ended will be devoted fully to en-
suring peace.

The release followed the regular pattern of those issued as
routine on birthdays of governmental agencies. But Admiral
King apparently objected to formalizing the phrase "Naval
Aviation" in such a manner. To him all parts of the Navy were
as one. Perhaps he was disturbed by the capitalization, and the
inference that naval aviation was indeed a select branch of the
Navy. At any rate, in a few days King sent Mitscher a memorandum which said, in effect, "Please explain your use of 'Naval
Aviation,' in your remarks."

Later, Mitscher showed Captain Read a copy of his answer.
It said, according to Read, "What am I supposed to do, say
meow?" Mitscher told Read that Admiral King had looked
dark and forbidding when he received it, then said, "Well, let's
forget it."

Mitscher was not in the mood, nor in physical condition, to
play a cat-and-mouse game on Constitution Avenue. The King
incident is but one example of the rather senseless irritants he
had to cope with. Less than six weeks after his arrival, finding
himself involved in the sort of squabble he detested, he began
to lay the groundwork for regaining a sea command.

Of the various members of his war staffs, only two remained
with him in Washington. Captain Read was still with the Admiral, and Commander Everett Eynon had rejoined him as personal aide. Read was scheduled to return to his banking business
in early fall. Commodore Burke had gone on to other duty,
since there was no billet in DCNO-Air which he could occupy,
although the Admiral had plans to claim him as a chief of staff
if the sea command could be arranged.

Two sudden deaths in this period must have caused Mitscher
to think about himself. Vice Admiral John Sidney McCain died
of a heart attack shortly after returning from the surrender

ceremony, and Vice Admiral Willis A. Lee died of a heart attack aboard his flagship on August 25 in Atlantic waters. McCain, Lee, and Mitscher—three big names in naval tactics. Now McCain and Lee were gone. Their hearts had lasted until the pens scratched the surrender documents.

It was now September, always hot and steamy in Washington. The memorandum Mitscher prepared at the request of Secretary of the Navy Forrestal is dated September 24. Although Mitscher could not foresee the Communist strategy of attacking peoples through political infiltration, and then open aggression, most of his comments are as true, and as applicable today as they were in 1945. Pertinent excerpts follow:

. . . It is extremely likely that the next war will be started in the same way that the Japanese started this war. It is probable that the first definite indication of hostile intent will be the actual attack, and it is equally probable that the nation that makes this attack will have profited by the mistakes of the Japanese in their Pearl Harbor raid; that is, the attack will be followed through. It will be quick, vicious, and, the enemy will hope, decisive. It is unlikely that there will be time to prepare for defense after the attack is initiated. The nation will fight with what it has at the moment. The existence of the United States may depend upon what the United States can accomplish in a matter of days. No wise nation will attack slowly or on the outer rims of periphery of our defense. Our enemy will probably attempt to neutralize our efforts very quickly and destroy our means for continuing the war just as quickly as he possibly can. We have the means now to counter such an attack. Other nations will have the means to conduct such an attack in a matter of a few years. The research facilities of all large nations who are concerned with protecting themselves from an aggressor, or have intent of becoming an aggressor, will be devoted to producing their own versions of atomic bombs, guided missiles, and a navy from which to launch them, as well as long range fighters and bombers.
. . . Since the defense of the United States will depend upon its ability to wage an immediate offensive destructive war, a powerful Navy must be maintained ready to go (not in any back chan-

nel). The Navy must be capable of launching this offensive in either ocean and must have a sufficient force in each ocean capable of immediate attack against any enemy.

. . . The only two nations powerful enough in the near future to wage war against the United States are Russia and Great Britain. Russia now has a small navy and a large air force. Great Britain has a medium sized navy and air force. It is unlikely that Great Britain will attempt an aggressive war in the near future. Therefore the major portion of our Fleet should be kept in the Pacific.

In his recommendations for the composition of the postwar Navy, Mitscher outlined the minimum deployment of naval forces in both the Pacific and Atlantic which would be necessary to thwart an enemy attack successfully. Then he outlined what he considered the ideal composition for fast-carrier task groups:

. . . Four carriers, six to eight support vessels and not less than 18 destroyers, preferably 24. More than four carriers in a task group cannot be advantageously used due to amount of air room required. Less than four carriers requires an uneconomical use of support ships and screening vessels.

Mitscher described in detail the elements needed to back up the fast-carrier spearhead: A large amphibious force for invasion purposes, a hundred submarines, and a solid nucleus of mine layers and mine sweepers.

. . . It will be noted in this discussion I have not mentioned the battleship, but prefer to use the term "support ship." It has been my experience that the battleship possesses three definite limitations that preclude its use as a permanent support ship for fast carrier task forces.

First, it cannot use the main battery of 14" or 16" turret guns and its anti-aircraft guns at one and the same time, so that it forces the carrier task forces not to be dependent on this type vessel if a main engagement is imminent.

Second, under the present concept of warfare, for tactical reasons a battleline must be reorganized before a main engagement with an enemy battleline. This requires all battleships to leave

task force formation, plus a certain number of cruisers and destroyers to support the battleline, thus detracting from the gun support of carriers, and at the same time requiring the carriers to
furnish air support for the battleline.

Third, the large battleship gun is outranged and outmoded. The
range of the aircraft carrier is about 250 to 300 miles with full load.[1]
The range of the battleship gun is 25 miles at the most. Due to range
of enemy patrol planes and submarines, the chance of an engagement with enemy main fleet of battleships is so remote that it is
questionable that it should be used.

. . . The frequently stated argument that we should keep the
BB type in active condition as long as any other power maintains
that type is fallacious, in my opinion.

. . . In future considerations for a Post-War Navy, the below
types have assumed, in my opinion, importance in the order that
they are listed:

Aircraft carriers	Troop support forces
Patrol aircraft	Amphibious forces
Submarines	Minesweepers
Destroyers	Battleships
Cruisers	Battle cruisers

Then Mitscher wrote:

In my opinion the most important lessons to be derived from the
past war in the Pacific area are noted below. I feel strongly that
future consideration for a Post-War Navy should be based around
these lessons, with a view toward benefiting from their teachings
rather than accentuating the individual performances of types of
vessels, under the conditions existing in the Pacific during the first
year of the war. . . .

1. It is indicated that there will never be another war fought,
on land or sea, without the assistance of air. This, therefore, indicates that the airplane assumes the most important consideration.

2. The many disappointments of the present type of gun design
and control, and aircraft bomb and torpedo development to meet
the problems to be solved in the Pacific war, in bombardment as
well as in attacks on enemy surface ships and enemy aircraft. This
leads probably to the conclusion that in the past our ideas have been

[1] Modern, large carrier aircraft have almost tripled that range.

so concentrated on gunpower that we have failed to foresee the possibility of the development of more effective weapons for our campaign, such as the one just concluded in the Pacific.

3. The tremendous importance of ground attack troops and the complete necessity for invasion and occupation of areas to establish bases.

4. The relative importance that the smaller vessel, such as the destroyer, has assumed in comparison with the larger vessel, as a defense against aircraft attacks.

5. The importance that the submarine has assumed in connection with the offensive and defensive operations.

6. The importance of re-servicing combatant ships at sea in operating areas, rather than the development of far-away bases for this purpose.

7. The complete dependence of any nation on trained manpower to carry on future wars. This in itself constitutes the frightening part of the problem for this nation when we consider that there is a possibility of a large part of a world combine against this country. This in itself indicates the necessity for the utmost foresight in the development of methods and weapons to conserve manpower for future generations.

8. It would now appear to be the time to thoroughly appraise our investments in terms of obtaining the most offensive power for our money, to the extent of minimizing the developments that do not possess this quality.

Mitscher's recommendations combined what is now termed the Eisenhower "new look" in the military establishment, and older, tried and trusted weapons. Mitscher did not believe in a one-concept weapon or a one-concept defense. He was profoundly impressed by the atomic bomb, and was convinced of the capability of science to produce greater weapons. On October 17, testifying before the House Appropriations Committee, Mitscher said that the atomic bomb might eliminate naval surface forces within ten years.

CHAPTER

⚓ 48 ⚓

The "Super Carrier"

AT EVERY opportunity in conferences or informal chats with other naval officers in key positions, Mitscher continued pushing the large-carrier idea. His earlier pressures, beginning with the Philippines campaign, had already achieved a start. On April 27, 1945, while Mitscher was off Okinawa, an informal board had been appointed to restudy carrier requirements. The study was known as "C-1."

By the time he returned to Washington, the board was approximately halfway through its work. There was also a need for new big planes to operate from the projected carrier. After consultations with the Chief of the Bureau of Aeronautics, Mitscher forwarded a Bureau of Aeronautics Conference letter, dated December 11, 1945, to the Chief of Naval Operations, Admiral Nimitz, recommending that a co-ordinated design study for heavier aircraft and a carrier capable of operating these aircraft be made. It appeared that chances of building a flush-deck carrier were good.

Mitscher spent the rest of the uneasy fall of 1945 making speeches, sitting on various boards, and performing his duties as DCNO-Air. Once, when testifying before the Navy's General Board, he stopped, alarm showing in his eyes, and took a deep breath.

In November, he returned to Oklahoma City for a war-bond drive and was honored with a homecoming parade. He rode down the main street with Vice Admiral Clark. It was bigger and flossier, but not more enthusiastic than the Hillsboro celebration. That day, also, Mitscher held a press conference. Unification pressures were building constantly. At the time, every top military officer was being asked for his views. Mitscher took a go-slow position:

In mountain climbing it is a rule to move no faster than you can breathe through your nose and take no step forward until you are sure one foot is firmly in place. This proposal is climbing a mountain. I favor going the whole way to make unification work efficiently. But it seems to me that it will take as long to work out difficulties under tightened conditions after you pass legislation as it will to work out the difficulties first, then pass legislation in the light of what we've found. It's a revolutionary step whichever way you take it.

He was asked by a reporter, "Isn't it true that the United States ended the war with the only carrier Air Force in the world?"

"I have frequently stated" he replied, "that by going to the development of its land force, and neglecting its naval air arm, one great nation [Great Britain] saved its home islands but lost its empire."

On December 4, 1945, Secretary Forrestal, who was also opposed to a quick merger, issued a statement to the press on another subject:

About four months ago, I said: "Aviation in the Navy is an integral part of the Navy and is becoming increasingly dominant." The influence of airpower on the Navy will be an evolution, not a revolution. The actual fact is that the Navy is becoming an air Navy. It is becoming that by a natural evolution of its activities and a natural reflection of the increasing preponderance of Naval aviation in our activities. The leading commands of the Navy will in time be occupied by men who deal with air in one form or another.

The Secretary of the Navy had publicly placed naval aviation in the lead role. The statement was greeted with quiet cheers by the Pensacola canvas-backs and their younger counterparts. Announcing a series of command changes, Forrestal said further:

A further evolution also of aviation within the Navy is to take place with assignment of officers to command fleets. For the first time, Naval aviators are to become fleet commanders. Admiral John H. Towers, now Commander, Fifth Fleet, is eventually to relieve Admiral Raymond A. Spruance, as Commander in Chief of the Pacific Fleet. Vice Admiral Marc A. Mitscher will in due course leave his position as Deputy Chief of Naval Operations for Air and become Commander of the Eighth Fleet.

Because these men pioneered aviation in the Navy, the Navy looks to them, as well as to all their fellow officers of all origins, to be equally and fully alert to the effect of new weapons on the further evolution of sea power.

When he read Forrestal's announcement, Mitscher might have recalled his testimony before the Morrow Board on October 6, 1925. Now aviators were finally going to receive Fleet commands. Time and a war had taken care of that.

Although Mitscher was delighted at the prospect of getting a sea job again, Frances thought he had done enough, that it was time for him to rest. She told him so, many times, but he stubbornly insisted that he was in good physical condition and that a sea job was not nearly so trying as the Washington arena. Actually, the Eighth Fleet didn't exist. It would be created especially for Mitscher, to serve as a nucleus around which carrier aviation could be revitalized and become the core of the new fleet. He expected to leave Washington in early March.

One of the first good signs of the new year occurred in early January, when the C-1 study board submitted its findings on the big carrier. Its conclusions were favorable, and it was decided that the project should be made a design study for the 1948 Shipbuilding and Conversion Program.[1] As the concept and specifications of the carrier became clearly defined, it was decided to push legislation to include the first of the carriers, labeled by the press a "super carrier," in the 1949 building program.

The last of many memorandums, but the first in which Mitscher formally proposed a flush-deck carrier, was dated May 26, 1946 and addressed to the Chief of Naval Operations:

SUBJECT: *Aircraft Carrier Design—Comments and Recommendations Concerning*

1. Basic aircraft carrier design has progressed steadily from the days of the converted collier *Langley* to the present in which the CVB class represents the latest in carrier thought. . . . [But] our new CVB class represents but relatively slight improvement over the *Essex* class with the armored deck as the outstanding difference.

2. . . . it is believed that these existing carriers [CVB] approach the ultimate in basic design under existing limitations. Foremost among these limitations is the island structure. This structure places a definite restriction on the size of aircraft which may be operated. The foreseeable future may well find that this limitation is unacceptable. Therefore it is considered that our thoughts as to carrier design should include design and construction of a flush deck type.

Mitscher then outlined the obstacles that would have to be overcome: decreased radio performance because of low antennae, decreased radar performance because of low antennae, elimination of elevated position from which carrier launching and landing operations are controlled. "If retention of this high position proves necessary an elevator arrangement [placing the entire structure on an elevator] may be feasible."

[1] Informal Advisory Board of DCNO, memorandum dated January 23, 1946.

On the other hand, he said, advantages of the flush-deck carrier would be: include the capacity for operating larger aircraft, and the elimination of the danger, in armored-deck carriers especially, of loss of all radar and radio outlets as a result of the explosion of bombs on the flight deck. Also, it would force "new radar-radio type development through creation of requirement therefor." Finally, he wrote:

In light of the above, it is recommended:
(a) That design study of a flush deck type aircraft carrier be started immediately.
(b) That upon completion of this study, immediate modifications of an inactivated *Essex* type carrier to a flush deck type be undertaken.
(c) That development of correlated radio and radar apparatus, including AEW (airborne early warning), be pressed.[2]

The Bureau of Ships objected at the time to elimination of the island structure, because they had not developed a satisfactory method of disposing of stack gases. Nevertheless, plans for design of a flush-deck carrier were soon underway.

Mitscher could not have realized that the dream carrier he fathered would someday be a contributory cause of the resignation of a Secretary of the Navy, and set off a controversy that is still reverberating. The "super carrier" was part and parcel of the Navy-Air Force controversy over strategic bombing in 1949. There have been no politically stormier ships than the ill-fated U.S.S. *United States* and its present, canted-deck, slightly smaller successor, the U.S.S. *Forrestal*.

Construction of the big carrier was approved by Congress on June 24, 1948; President Harry Truman approved the name *United States* for the vessel in March, 1949. It was to be designated CVA-58. The "58," inevitably reminiscent of Mitscher's task force, was a coincidence, for carriers are numbered in the

[2] AEW planes had been introduced by the Navy and used by the Fast Carrier Task Force late in the war.

order in which the keels are laid. The *United States* would have been 65,000 tons of fast carrier, certainly capable of carrying aircraft loaded with atomic weapons. Some engineers envisioned a small island on an elevator apparatus, as Mitscher had anticipated, which would be lowered during flight operations; others considered the use of television "eyes" to view flight-deck operations and aid in docking, since the stationary bridge would be below flight-deck level. She would have been able to operate aircraft of up to 100,000 pounds.

Opposition to the construction of the *United States* had been mounting steadily. Air Force proponents attacked the ship as being too costly and vulnerable, at the same time introducing arguments against the entire concept of carriers. Meanwhile, funds to build it were approved by the House of Representatives on April 13, 1949.

Two days later, Secretary of Defense Louis Johnson, who had succeeded James Forrestal, sent a letter to General Eisenhower, then temporary presiding officer of the Joint Chiefs of Staff, asking for the Joint Chiefs' current views on the proposed carrier. Johnson stated that he had "no preconceived notions with respect to this carrier."

On April 18, the keel of the *United States* was laid at Newport News. This accomplishment did not decrease the opposition, and behind-the-scenes maneuvering continued briskly. On April 20, General Eisenhower sent a memorandum to the Joint Chiefs of Staff suggesting that the subject be placed on the agenda, and studied in his absence. On April 23, a Saturday, the views of the Joint Chiefs of Staff were submitted to the Secretary of Defense. That same morning, Louis Johnson summarily ordered work on the construction of the carrier stopped.

Secretary of the Navy John L. Sullivan was in Corpus Christi, Texas, when he received a phone call informing him of Johnson's action. On his return to Washington, he resigned his post, sending letters both to President Truman and Secretary Johnson. To Johnson, he wrote on April 26, 1949:

On Saturday, April 23, without discussion with the Chief of Naval Operations, without consultation with the Secretary of the Navy, you directed the discontinuance of the U.S.S. *United States*, the construction of which had twice been approved by the President.

This carrier had been the subject of intensive study in the Navy Department since it was first proposed early in 1945 by the late Admiral Marc A. Mitscher whose combat experience convinced him of its necessity.

Professional naval men, charged with the task of planning a Navy adequate to the defense of America believe that the construction of the *United States* is so indispensable to the continuing development of American seapower that they have twice sacrificed other substantial construction because of the carrier's highest naval priority.

I am, of course, very deeply disturbed by your action which so far as I know represents the first attempt ever made in this country to prevent development of a powerful weapon. The conviction that this will result in renewed effort to abolish the Marine Corps and to transfer Naval and Marine aviation elsewhere adds to my anxiety.

So Sullivan resigned, and the keel, the tons of blueprints, and other preliminary work, were scrapped. Halting the construction cost the government more than $2,000,000, and intensified the already strained atmosphere within the National Military Establishment, which had come into being in September, 1947. A few months later, the controversy between the Army and Navy over the strategic-bombing concept and the value of the all-out heavy bomber program, flared up. To some elderly naval aviators it seemed the calendar had been rolled back about thirty years to the equally sulphuric days of Colonel Mitchell.

Although the big carrier itself was but a dusty pile of blueprints, the idea remained alive in the the minds of top Navy admirals, a good number of whom were aviators. Many of them had served with or under Mitscher, and they were still convinced that such a carrier must be built if the United States Navy was to keep pace with new weapon development.

Then came the conflict in Korea, and in an atmosphere more receptive to new weapons of any kind, efforts to restore the big-carrier program were doubled and redoubled. Finally, on July 12, 1951, the Navy Department announced a contract for a new large aircraft carrier (CVB-59), to be built at Newport News.

On July 30, 1951, came a joint resolution from Capitol Hill:

> Be it resolved, that when and if the United States completes construction of the aircraft carrier known as the *United States*, the construction of which was discontinued on April 23, 1949, or the aircraft carrier authorized in Public Law 3, Eighty-Second Congress, first session, it shall be named the *Forrestal*.

The *Forrestal* has some innovations that Mitscher did not envision. It is not flush-decked. A British design, the canted deck, allows flight operations without island interference. It has powerful steam catapults, and is able to handle large jet bombers.

The *Forrestal* is the largest warship in existence; at 59,900 tons, with an over-all length of 1,039 feet, it is only slightly shorter than the Empire State Building is high. Already contracts for two more sister carriers have been let, and the Navy plans to use atomic propulsion as soon as engineering difficulties have been surmounted. The U.S.S. *Forrestal* is the fruition of Mitscher's early determination to bring into the Navy a vessel which would reflect the needs of the day.

CHAPTER

⚓ 49 ⚓

Eighth Fleet

IN MID-JANUARY, Captain Truman Hedding returned to Washington from Tokyo, where he had been a member of the United States Joint Strategic Bombing Survey. He brought with him a pair of swords so heavy he could not lift them both at once. Sheathed in silk-covered wooden scabbards, magnificently decorated, the swords represented the remainder of Japanese naval might.

One, formerly the property of Admiral Toyoda, was presented to Nimitz; the other, which had been owned by Mitscher's opposite, Ozawa, was given to the Admiral, who packed it carefully away for later display in the trophy room he hoped to build.

January was devoted to closing out his duty as DCNO-Air. He was detached on January 31, and on March 1 he broke out his flag as Commander, Eighth Fleet, over the carrier U.S.S. *Lake Champlain*, at Norfolk. Also on March 1, Mitscher was promoted to full four-star admiral. Of the Pensacola flyers who could properly be classified as pioneers, only one other, John Towers, had attained four stars. At fifty-nine, Mitscher was one of less than seventy-five officers in the entire history of the

Navy who had reached the rank of full admiral before retirement.

As soon as his sea command had been confirmed, Mitscher made arrangements for Burke to rejoin him. The relationship between Mitscher and Burke, so cool at first, was now warm, almost that of father and son. With Burke as chief of staff, Mitscher knew he would not have to be greatly concerned with administration of the command. Shore headquarters for the Eighth Fleet were in the administration building at the Norfolk Naval Base.

Preliminary planning for extensive maneuvers in the Atlantic was well underway by the time the Admiral arrived. There was to be a high-level audience at the maneuvers. Admiral Nimitz, who had relieved Fleet Admiral King as Chief of Naval Operations in December, had persuaded Secretary Forrestal to invite President Truman to go along for several days.

Some months earlier, Admiral DeWitt Ramsey had requested Mitscher to make available any records or papers he had for inclusion in a naval command study, and in mid-March, Mitscher replied:

My thoughts of command relations are stored away in the back of my mind. At some time later I shall be glad to spend some time and reduce my ideas to writing.

The only two times I was really in trouble with the task force occurred in the first and second battles of the Philippine Seas, in which battles my forces were dispersed to such an extent that we could not concentrate and it proved a considerable handicap in my future movements. I was impressed with the absolute necessity of *quick* concentration, particularly when operating against so many shore bases plus carrier groups in both cases. It immediately puts one on the defensive and I personally prefer the offensive when I have the superior force, particularly a fast carrier force.

In operating against land based aircraft I find it less nerve wracking not to select targets that require the carrier task force to attack targets almost completely surrounded by enemy bases as we were when we went into Formosa. A determined enemy could have murdered us, because they could come in from any direction, of course.

Better cooperation with the Army Air Forces from Southwest Pacific could have relieved things to a certain extent, at least from the South, but we did not have the coordination and consequently had to take it on the chin. We were able to do so because we kept concentrated and the groups could help each other when the going was roughest.

Some day the lessons of this war should be handed down to posterity but I am afraid that many points will be missed.

This brief memorandum was apparently the last in which Mitscher discussed lessons learned from the war. A few naval aviators have been prone to term Mitscher a Mahan of naval aviation, forgetting that the great sea-power thinker achieved his fame, and made his lasting contributions to global military strategy, with the pen and not the sword. Mitscher was a field commander and a fighter—not a military philosopher.

April 19 had been set as the date for opening the Eighth Fleet maneuvers, and Burke and Commander Ernest Snowden, who had been ordered to the staff as operations officer, were busy with plans, taking extra care since the President would be there.

Mitscher was glad to be away from Washington, where the unification argument was becoming more tangled daily. He kept informed about it, but tried to remain aloof from the fight —which was impossible to do. In January at Milwaukee, he had made a plea for continued study prior to merger, and now, on April 8, he was scheduled to make a speech in New York. In the original version of the prepared text, he outlined his *personal* views on the merger plan, which the President had urged Congress to pass. Several days before the New York speech, however, instructions were received that any antiunification speeches by high-ranking military officers would be considered anti-Truman and might cause embarrassment. A considerably tamer speech was delivered in New York, from which all references to unification had been deleted.

Throughout his Navy career, Mitscher had forthrightly spoken his beliefs and had been intellectually honest. Never before had there been occasion to evade an important issue. Even the Billy Mitchell disagreement had been out in the open, although Mitchell himself was mainly responsible for this. The Admiral was distressed, confused, and angry over the New York incident and was still smarting on April 11 when President Truman held a press conference and denounced Navy admirals for what he termed "lobbying." Mr. Truman said that the Navy was not justified in fighting unification after he had clearly stated the administration policy. It was the third major rebuke President Truman had given the Navy within recent months.

After the account of the press conference appeared in the Norfolk morning papers of April 12, Mitscher dictated a letter to Admiral Nimitz:

If the enclosed article from the Norfolk papers represents fact, I hope that you will consider this my application for retirement from the Naval service.

I want you and the whole country to understand that I consider a merger of the armed forces in the near future will seriously jeopardize the defense of the country.

I also want it to be clearly understood for the first time in so far as I know, the honesty and integrity of the administration of Naval Officers have been questioned. I see no stable future for our Country's defense.

Mitscher was now convinced that the unification controversy had become hopelessly involved in politics. Surcharged with jealousy and rivalry, buffeted by outside lobbying, the conflict could have no really sound resolution. The apparent suppression of the right of experienced naval officers to voice their views alarmed him; the public reprimand by the President was more than he could accept. Admiral Nimitz, however, would not agree to his resignation.

Mitscher was in a better frame of mind a week later, when the fleet left port. "You can't learn much from fighting behind a desk, you've got to go out and do it," he told newsmen just before the ships got underway.

The carrier *Franklin D. Roosevelt* was Mitscher's flagship for the exercise, and on April 22, President Truman, with a party including Secretary Forrestal, Admiral Leahy, Admiral Nimitz, and the presidential aide, General Vaughan, boarded her at sea about a hundred miles southeast of the Virginia capes for a two-day cruise. It was the first time a president of the United States had been in an aircraft carrier at sea. Flight operations were conducted under a cloudless sky for more than two hours, culminating with a brilliant dive-bombing exhibition.

The *Roosevelt* was scheduled to demonstrate her shooting ability for the President's benefit, and Mr. Truman was on the flag bridge, near Admiral Mitscher, when a target drone was launched. After the drone had passed back and forth several times, something went wrong with the remote-control system and it headed for the ship. On the carrier's flight deck were about a dozen planes, armed, their gas tanks full, ready to go. They were highly explosive. If the drone hit them there would be a nasty fire.

Mitscher and the members of his staff, on the flag bridge, knew instantly that the drone was out of control. Finally, it skimmed breathtakingly close to the ship and dove into the sea, splashing harmlessly into the water by the carrier's stern. If it had come down a few feet forward, it would have crashed into the planes. President Truman applauded vigorously, thinking that the close pass was intentional.

After the presidential party debarked, Mitscher took the fleet south to train in the Caribbean for five weeks, and went aloft himself at Culebra to observe bombing runs. Along for the cruise was Robert L. Biggers, a Detroit industrialist who had been a World War I naval aviator and was an old acquaintance of Mitscher's. He asked, "What was the toughest duty you ever had, Pete?"

Mitscher thought for a while and said, "Guadalcanal." Although he had since then been blasted off two ships, at Okinawa, Mitscher could not forget the miserable days in the camp by the Lunga.

On May 28, he brought the fleet into New York harbor, and immediately began his official duties as a visiting dignitary. These included calling on Mayor O'Dwyer at City Hall, dropping a horseshoe of flowers around Assault's neck for winning the Belmont Stakes, and participating in Memorial Day services.

He spoke at The Lambs club: "Some people have been pushing the Navy and Marines around. I have a suspicion the Navy will get tough."

Frances had joined him, and they went to the theater and the movies and made plans to accompany the Gus Reads to Canada on a short leave. On June 6 the fleet returned to Norfolk, without Mitscher. He'd gone fishing. This trip was memorable to Mitscher because Frances caught her first fish, and because of an Indian guide, a gruff, contentious expert in hooking salmon. One afternoon their luck was poor and Frances grew uncomfortably cold.

"All right," said Mitscher, "we'll go in now."

"No, by God," said guide George Martin, "you'll fish three more drops."

Mitscher obediently fished the three more drops. Arriving back in the lodge, Mitscher had a twinkle in his eye. "You know," he said, "I am not used to being given orders what to do, especially in a boat."

C H A P T E R

⚓ 50 ⚓

The Last Effort

HEARINGS on S. 2044, the unification bill, had been in progress several months when Mitscher was invited to submit his views to the Senate Naval Affairs Committee, presided over by Senator David I. Walsh. Forrestal, Nimitz, Halsey, King, and Spruance had already expressed disapproval of the bill as it was then drawn up. On July 11, 1946, Admiral Mitscher added his statement for the record:

My comments on this bill are my own personal opinions. In my capacity as a naval officer, I will naturally do my utmost to carry out orders of the President or of the Navy Department without regard to my personal views. However, having been asked by this committee to give my views, I feel it is my duty as a citizen to speak my own opinions regarding the important matter of future security of our country.

I think that the present is not the time for legislation of this nature; that widespread propaganda has been used to make the catch phrase of "merger" and "unity" appear as an automatic panacea of all the ills that beset the armed forces during the war. Let us not forget that the machine we are considering scrapping won the pennant in World War II by a very healthy margin.

Mitscher had not changed his mind since November, 1945, when he had cautioned against rushing headlong into unification. He could not understand why there was not time to study thoroughly the World War II campaigns, "land, sea, and air," and then, in the light of what was learned, draft corrective legislation. He appreciated the Army Air Forces' desire for autonomy—and had publicly so stated—but felt there was no emergency which demanded precipitate action.

Mitscher recommended that the analysis of World War II campaigns include consideration of the correctness of the decision to conduct the particular campaign; study of the planning and conduct of the campaign, and its over-all effect on the strategy of the war; and examination of the co-ordination of the various branches (Army, Navy, and Army Air Force) before and during the campaign in regard to logistics, employment of forces, and command:

The facts brought out by such an analysis should indicate whether or not the past war would have been fought more efficiently by merged armed forces. Such an analysis in conjunction with a study of the policy of the United States and the policy of foreign countries should also indicate whether a merged armed forces would be efficient in wars in the predictable future.

After pointing out the basic differences between the philosophies of war of the Army and of the Navy, and maintaining they were "still fundamental, natural and purposeful," he said:

A third philosophy of war has been in the process of development in the last thirty years if recent publicized statements are correct. Army air personnel are its principal proponents. This theory is based on the premise that air power alone—with no assistance from any other agency—can subdue an enemy nation by bombing cities and installations and terrorizing the populace. This theory depends on aircraft being capable of repulsing any attack by any means on the United States, whether that attack is delivered by air, submarines, surface ships or amphibious forces, or invading armies. It assumes that aircraft can do sufficient damage to an enemy to make sure that enemy sues for peace even though that enemy knows he will not be invaded.

With this theory I disagree. Wars cannot be won without air power—strong air power—but I know of nothing in this past war which indicates that air power itself can bring an enemy to its knees. It is my firm belief that all armed forces are necessary to win a war.

Mitscher was fearful that the bill, which he said was "vague, and incapable of being strengthened by amendment," would eventually enable the Air Force to annex naval aviation, or by limiting or stripping fleet functions, would render it impotent.

Now Army air apparently aspires to control all the services including the Ground Forces and the Navy. I believe that the disability which they have demonstrated at times, in war, does not justify confidence now. The viewpoints expressed by Army Air officers in the press confirm this judgement. I have seen, and I am sure you have seen, public statements made by high ranking officers in the Army Air Forces, to the effect that there is no need, in the future, for any Navy—that all that is needed is an Army Air Force—B 29's, and these are the people who aspire to control all of our armed services—and who will have control if the presently planned merger is made law.

It is my belief that if the merger is hastily effected without careful analysis and without adequate checks to prevent Army Air from strangling the other arms, the control of all armed services will gradually be appropriated by Army Air. This will certainly imperil the national security, for Army Air will inevitably relegate all other services to low priority, and when the need arises, those services will be impotent and demoralized.

Mitscher's lengthy attack on the bill was no more and no less violent than those made by the Navy officers preceding and following him. Their combined efforts, along with those of a number of ground-force officers, succeeded in killing the bill, and the measure was postponed. A year later, unification legislation, more moderate and better defined, was passed—but without benefit of any exhaustive study of World War II campaigns. An analysis of all of Mitscher's statements about unification and the establishment of a national military organization indicates that he felt it was inevitable. His concern was at the prospect that it might be done too hastily and that an overbalance in air power might result.

Admiral Jonas Ingram, Commander in Chief, Atlantic, and Atlantic Fleet, was ill most of the summer of 1946, and Mitscher assumed additional duty as acting CINCLANT several times in July and August. During this period he was preparing to make a European trip to visit naval installations overseas and attend a number of conferences with Allied military leaders on the rollback of American naval power in Europe and North Africa. On August 19, Mitscher, the late Admiral Forrest P. Sherman, then a vice admiral, and Burke left Anacostia Naval Air Station for a whirlwind tour which was to include London, Berlin, Naples, Paris, Rome, and North African bases.

There were the usual formal dinners and cocktail parties at every stop. Mitscher made a practice of leaving the parties no later than 10 P.M., and it was Burke's duty to seek him out at that time. Until they were out of earshot of other members of the party, Mitscher would berate Burke for taking him away. When they got back to the hotel, however, they might sit up and talk until one o'clock. On September 2, Mitscher arrived in Rome for a three-day inspection tour of the naval forces still in Italy. The next day, he was received by Pope Pius XII at Castel Gondolfo, the papal summer residence. There was a continuous grind of tightly scheduled arrivals and departures, conferences, and official functions.

For a number of months, Mitscher had been warned that he had symptoms of chronic appendicitis, but he scoffed at the warnings. On September 5, while flying over the Mediterranean, he was suddenly stricken, and the aircraft was ordered to Malta, where he was operated on on September 6. On the same day, he was notified by dispatch that even more work was ahead. Admiral Ingram was to be retired because of illness, and Mitscher would assume command of the Atlantic on September 20. His title of acting CINCLANT would remain in effect until that time.

Less than forty-eight hours after his operation, Mitscher held a bedside conference with the British on forthcoming joint fleet maneuvers in the Mediterranean. This was the man many had thought could not last through the war. Doctors at Malta recommended that he not fly back to the United States, and Admiral Sherman arranged to have the light cruiser *Little Rock,* then on a good-will tour, diverted to bring Mitscher home. Not too much of importance had been accomplished. It was impossible to come to sensible military decisions when major political decisions were still to be made.

After his return, Mitscher refused to ease up appreciably. Despite the operation, he looked better than when he had departed. However, Frances noticed that he seemed to tire more easily. When he went duck hunting in Elizabeth City, North Carolina, he came back exhausted. Commodore Burke flew up to Washington during this period, and came back with a set of leave orders, which he placed on Mitscher's desk. The Admiral looked at them, grunted, and tore them up.

In October, he was appointed to the Order of the Bath, Grade of Companion, by Great Britain. In the years since he had received the Navy Cross for the NC flight in 1919, many medals and awards had been conferred upon Mitscher. He had received the Navy Cross twice more for World War II actions; he held the Legion of Merit, with Combat "V"; he had won the Distinguished Service Medal twice; and he was entitled to Presidential Unit Citations for the *Yorktown,* the *Lexington,* and the *Bunker Hill.* He held the Order of Tower and Sword, Grade of Official, from Portugal, and he was posthumously awarded the Croix de Guerre with Palm, and the title of Grand Officer of the Order of the Crown with Palm, by the Belgian government.

In late October, he was off on another round of official duties. He went to sea on the U.S.S. *Pocono* for a six-day inspection tour of Atlantic naval establishments, which included stops at the Naval War College, the Atlantic destroyer command at Newport, Rhode Island, and the Casco Bay, Maine, naval station. Maine, he knew, had fine bird grounds. One day, with the governor and several admirals, he went after pheasant near North Whitefield. He got his bag in an hour or so, marveling at the abundance of the birds, and he vowed to return to Maine at the first opportunity and shoot again.

Mitscher never knew, said Rear Admiral Frank Beatty, that the pheasant, crammed full of wheat, had been placed in the field the night before by game wardens to make certain he would be successful. It was just as well that he didn't know. Very probably, he would have been angry.

December was a routine month, but already there were plans for heavy maneuvers later in the winter. Burke tried to assume as much of the burden as possible. At the same time, the Navy Department was making an effort to transfer Burke to other duty. Mitscher resisted each time the subject came up, and Burke himself wanted to stay with the Admiral a while longer.

It was quite evident to most of the staff members that Mitscher could not drive himself much further. Mitscher himself had long believed that the statutory retirement age should be sixty years instead of sixty-five. According to existing regulations, however, unless he voluntarily retired he would spend five more years in active service. Sunday, January 26, was his sixtieth birthday. He and Frances were at the Princess Anne Golf Club, and during the afternoon the Admiral complained of feeling ill. He had a cold. Frances called a doctor, and the next day he was admitted to the naval-base hospital. At first it was announced that he was suffering from bronchitis, but soon his illness was properly diagnosed as a heart attack.

On February 1, the White House wired:

THIS IS JUST A LINE TO TELL YOU I AM SORRY TO HEAR YOU ARE IN THE HOSPITAL. KEEP YOUR CHIN UP AND GET WELL SOON. HARRY S. TRUMAN

The Fifth Naval District medical officer, Rear Admiral J. C. Adams, an old friend, returned from a Washington trip to confer with doctors attending Mitscher and discovered he was still trying to keep in touch with Atlantic Fleet administration. Operations plans were being formulated for a southern cruise, and many questions were undecided.

Adams immediately went to Mitscher. He sat by his bed, grasping the tanned, freckled hand, and told him that he had had a coronary attack. Mitscher had not known his exact ailment. Adams explained the treatment, and warned that all energy must be devoted toward recovery. Then he proceeded to the mission for which he had entered the room. It was one of the most difficult assignments the veteran flight surgeon had ever had.

"Pete," he remembers saying, "we've always been honest with each other, so what I'm going to tell you is in all honesty. You've got to realize, once and for all, that you have made your last contribution to the Navy. You will not be returned to active duty."

Mitscher eyed Adams steadily. Not once did he blink, nor did his face change expression. Adams found himself looking into an inscrutable mask.

"There won't be any more visitors from the staff. No more Navy talk!"

Mitscher grasped Adams's hand a little tighter, his only

show of emotion at the ending of his naval career. He said huskily, "Thanks, Cy. I knew you'd come in here and tell me the truth. I'm tired as hell and ready to take time out."

Then he rolled over, as if to go to sleep, and Adams, who felt he had hit Mitscher harder than the Japanese had, left quickly. The flame had been lowered. Mitscher did not have enough energy left to fight death. Still comparatively young in years, he was an old and weary man.

The next day Frances visited her husband. Bothered by a cold and afraid he might catch it, she had seen him only once since he had entered the hospital. "Are you worried about anything, Marc?" she asked, standing about ten feet away from his bed.

"No, I'm not worried," he answered, but he told her about Dr. Adams's visit, and said that he was through with the Navy. He seemed cheerful enough under the circumstances. As she was leaving, he called out, "Thank Luis for the medicine." Luis de Florez had sent down several bottles of 1916 bourbon. Frances went down the corridor fifteen or twenty feet and then hesitated. She felt compelled to return to his room, and went back and looked in. The Admiral had closed his eyes. She recalled later that he looked very fragile. She stood for a moment. Then she silently closed the door and walked away. At 0120 the next morning, February 3, Admiral Mitscher died of coronary thrombosis. Whatever the medical term, he died of a tired heart.

At muster that morning, in ships of the Atlantic Fleet, tied up at piers at the naval base, and farther up the drab, muddy Elizabeth River at the Navy yard, and at Key West, Charleston, Philadelphia, New York, Boston—all along the Atlantic coast—Admiral Mitscher's death was announced, and the flag was two-blocked and lowered to half mast.

There were many ways to say that the Admiral was gone, but Arleigh Burke, in personally informing many of the Admiral's friends, wrote or said simply, "The Admiral has slipped his chain." In Navy parlance the term means to let go by unshackling the anchor cable, so that the ship is free to stand out to sea.

Epilogue

⚓ ⚓

Two days later, on February 5, in biting cold, Admiral Mitscher was buried in snow-spotted Arlington National Cemetery. His grave is on the eastern slope, below Lee Mansion. After the seventeen-gun salute was fired, a young naval officer told a reporter from the Washington *Evening Star:* "If we have another war we will be a lot less able to win it without him."

President Truman wired: "The Armed Forces have lost a brave and gallant leader."

Admiral Nimitz wrote Frances Mitscher: "You may well be proud of the services he gave so unselfishly for his country, and the great contribution which he made in bringing peace to the world." To the Associated Press, Nimitz said: "I always had the feeling of confidence and security when Admiral Mitscher was out with Task Force 58. He needed no detailed instructions."

Said the Charlotte *Observer:* "Experts in sea warfare have said that the United States Navy developed an entirely new set of tactics in the Pacific, and Mitscher was the field captain who executed the strategy and led the team to victory. It was a task to break great hearts."

Said the Baltimore *Sun:* "When the United States entered into the war with Japan, the aircraft was, theoretically, a mere side wing of the fleet. In actual practice, it soon became the main capital ship of the modern task force. Certainly no one had a more important part in implementing the revolutionary change than Admiral Marc A. Mitscher."

Said the Washington *Post:* "If you wished to give an appellation to Admiral Marc A. Mitscher, it might have been Raider of the Pacific. He was the man who demonstrated that the Navy air arm was the most powerful striking force in the sea warfare against Japan."

Said *The New York Times:* "He did not die in action. It is one measure of a sea fighter's success not to die in action. But he died of wounds as surely as any hard hit soldier ever did."

But perhaps the most fitting epitaph did not appear on an editorial page, nor was it spoken by a president or admiral. A young man whom Mitscher had bounced on his knee, and who later fought with Mitscher in the Pacific, wrote a letter to his mother. His name was Henry Mustin, Jr.:

"A bad day. Because of Pete, of course. I found myself pretty moist around the eyes at the news of his passing. This in spite of knowing it could not help but happen before so very long. Men do not live that way and spend a great old age telling grandchildren about it.

"How peaceful the passing was in contrast with the fierce, stormy nature of the little man! It was almost a joke of nature that he should have been spared a flaming death in battle to go thus quietly, in bed, in his sleep.

"He will be greatly missed, in a way, and yet I believe it was fortunate in another sense he is gone. He was all fighter, a breed in failing popularity today—though bravery is never out of fashion. He was not happy in peace, having found his ultimate manly purpose in the holocaust of war. Of all the pictures taken of him, I have seen only one which caught him with a smiling countenance. In it, he stands on a carrier's bridge, looking out over the sea to where his air groups are forming for a strike against the enemy.

"How he hated the enemy! Only such a hatred, fierce, bitter, uncompromising, can fit a man to blast and batter others into eternity. Wars are scarcely desirable, but when once waged, such men are needed that they may be waged unremittingly until victory.

"I remember very well the 'lift' that came with him to the carrier fleet. One attack with him was all it took to let us know we were sure to win. Until he took command, there still seemed doubt; afterward, none. Surely, there is some Valhalla for him."

Bibliography

⚓ ⚓

PRIMARY SOURCES

INDIVIDUALS

Rear Admiral John C. Adams, MC, Rear Admiral Frank Akers

Rear Admiral Frank H. Beatty, Vice Admiral Patrick N. L. Bellinger, Robert L. Biggers, Mrs. Laura E. Bracht, Joseph Bryan III, Rear Admiral Arleigh A. Burke

Commodore Penn L. Carroll, Admiral John H. Cassady, Admiral Joseph J. Clark

Rear Admiral Luis de Florez

Brigadier General John P. Edgerly, USAF, Joseph R. Eggert, Jr., Lieutenant Colonel Charles Endweiss, USMC, J. R. Eyerman, Commander Everett Eynon

Admiral Aubrey W. Fitch, Captain James H. Flatley

Commander Roy Gee, Rear Admiral Claude S. Gillette, Rear Admiral Hugh H. Goodwin, Rear Admiral Marshall R. Greer, Dr. Frederick L. Gwynn

Rear Admiral Grover B. H. Hall, Fleet Admiral William F. Halsey, Mrs. Eva F. Hamblin, Rear Admiral Edward B. Harp, Jr., Lieutenant General Field Harris, USMC, Captain John T. Hayward, Rear Admiral Truman J. Hedding, Rear Admiral George R. Henderson, Mrs. Zoe Mitscher Hoevel, Rear Admiral Lester T. Hundt, Dr. Jerome C. Hunsaker

Mrs. Ada Jarboe, Vice Admiral Alfred W. Johnson

Rear Admiral Ernest W. Litch, Lieutenant Colonel Herbert H. Long, USMC

Vice Admiral Harold M. Martin, Max Miller, Mrs. Marc A. Mitscher, Captain William A. Moffett, Jr., Vice Admiral Alfred E. Montgomery, Rear Admiral Charles J. Moore, Colonel Luther S. Moore, USMC, Captain Thomas Moran, Henry Mustin, Jr., Commander John Myers

Thomas A. Nicholson, Fleet Admiral Chester W. Nimitz

Vice Admiral Ralph A. Ofstie

Vice Admiral Frederick W. Pennoyer, Jr., Rear Admiral John Perry, Rear Admiral Robert B. Pirie, Vice Admiral John D. Price, Vice Admiral Alfred M. Pride

Admiral Arthur W. Radford, Admiral DeWitt C. Ramsey, Rear Admiral Albert C. Read, Duncan H. Read, Rear Admiral William A. Read, Admiral John W. Reeves, Jr., Captain Holden C. Richardson, Rear Admiral Stanhope C. Ring

Admiral Frederick C. Sherman, Mrs. Mary A. Smith, Captain Ernest W. Snowden, Rear Admiral Apollo Soucek, Admiral Raymond A. Spruance, Admiral William H. Standley, Admiral Felix B. Stump

Admiral John H. Towers

Captain Herbert W. Underwood

Captain Newton H. White, Jr., Captain Theodore H. Winters

Admiral Harry E. Yarnell

MEMORANDUMS AND CORRESPONDENCE

Letters from Admiral Mitscher to Mrs. Marc A. Mitscher, 1917, 1921, 1944, and 1945. Correspondence to Mrs. Marc A. Mitscher following Admiral Mitscher's death.

Memorandums and correspondence during 1920–1921, Fleet Air Base, San Diego, California, now in the possession of Kenneth S. Reightler, Tilghman, Maryland.

Memorandum to the Secretary of the Navy, dated September 24, 1945, Secretary of the Navy files.

Official letters in the files of the Bureau of Aeronautics, Chief of Naval Operations, including memorandum to Admiral DeWitt C. Ramsey, dated March 20, 1946, in reference to naval command studies.

Letter from Admiral Mitscher to the Chief of Naval Operations, dated May 24, 1946, on the subject of large carriers.

History of 6A Carrier Project, prepared by the Judge Advocate General, dated May 11, 1949, lent by Admiral Arthur W. Radford.

OFFICIAL SOURCES

NAVAL RECORDS CENTER, ARLINGTON, VIRGINIA

Commanding Officer, U.S.S. *Hornet*, Action Report, serial 0015, 28 April 1942; War Diary, 22 April 1942; Operations Plan 1–42, serial 007, 27 February 1942; all concerning the Doolittle-*Hornet* raid on Tokyo.

Commanding Officer, U.S.S. *Hornet*, Action Report, serial 0018, 13 June 1942; also serial 01849, 28 June 1942; Operations Order 1–42, 22 March 1942, concerning the Battle of Midway.

Commander, Patrol Wing Two, War Diary, July, August, and November, 1942.

Commander, Carrier Division Three, Action Reports of Task Force 58, serials 00151, 00153, 00154, 6, 8, and 12 March 1944; also a War Diary covering 10 December 1943 to 29 February 1944, signed by Truman J. Hedding.

Operations Plan 1–44, serial 00113, 10 January 1944; Post FLINT-LOCK Operations, serial 00122, 5 February 1944; Operations Plan 2–44, serial 00123, 10 February 1944, and Operations Plan 3–44, no serial, 19 February 1944.

Fast Carrier Task Forces—Action Reports, Task Force 58, 29 March 1944, no serial; also serials 00195, 00196, 00290, and 00306, 12 April, 1 June, and 3 June 1944; Operations Plans 4–44, serial 00173, 22 March 1944; 5–44, serial 00192, 9 April 1944; 7–44, serial 00255, 24 May 1944; serial 00287, 8 June 1944 (supplemental orders covering plans GUS, JOHNNY, and JEEPERS); 8–44, serial 00316, 21 June 1944; 9–44, serial 00353, 31 July 1944; also a War Diary signed by Arleigh A. Burke.

First Carrier Task Force—Action Reports, serials 00388, 0045, 00222, and 00505, 11 September and 3 November 1944 and 13 March and 18 June 1945; Operations Orders 10–44, serial 00421, 20 August 1944; serial 00020, 1 October 1944; serial 0001, 1 January 1945; Task Force instruction, serial 003, 20 January 1945; Operations Order 2–45, serial 00029, 1 March 1945; Task Force instruction, serial 0222, 1 April 1945, and Communications Plan 3–45, serial 00216, 24 May 1945.

Of minor interest are operations plans and orders for Commander, Eighth Fleet, and Commander in Chief, Atlantic Fleet.

OTHER TRANSCRIPTS AND RECORDS

Scholastic transcripts and conduct records, U.S. Naval Academy, and Naval Academy Section, Bureau of Naval Personnel, Arlington, Virginia.

Accident reports, Naval Aviation Safety Center, Norfolk, Virginia.

Official orders, fitness reports, and correspondence files, Bureau of Naval Personnel, Arlington, Virginia.

NAVAL AVIATION HISTORY UNIT, OFFICE OF THE DEPUTY CHIEF OF NAVAL OPERATIONS, WASHINGTON

Aircraft Yearbooks, 1919–1940, Doubleday, Page & Co., Aeronautical Chamber of Commerce, and D. Van Nostrand Co.

The Navy's Air War, edited by A. R. Buchanan, New York, Harper and Brothers, 1946.

Plane Talk, ship's newspapers, U.S.S. *Saratoga*, 1934 and 1935.

U.S. Naval Bureau of Aeronautics Newsletters, a collection of newsletters including bulletins published prior to 1921, and chronologically assembled through 1943.

Miscellaneous papers and reports in which Admiral Mitscher is mentioned.

OFFICIAL PUBLICATIONS

Introduction to Naval Aviation, Bureau of Naval Aeronautics, Washington, Government Printing Office, 1946.

Japanese Naval and Merchant Shipping Losses during World War II, Joint Army-Navy Assessment Committee, Washington, Government Printing Office, 1947.

The Japanese Story of the Battle of Midway, Washington, Government Printing Office, 1947.

Naval Aviation, 1943, Annapolis, United States Naval Institute, 1943.

Navy Department Communiqués, 1–624, Office of Public Relations, Navy Department, Washington, Government Printing Office, 1946.

Pacific Islands, Volume I, Hydrographic Office Publication No. 165, Washington, Government Printing Office, 1938.

U.S. *Naval Aviation in the Pacific, a Critical Review,* Washington, Office of the Chief of Naval Operations, 1947.

U.S. *Strategic Bombing Survey,* Summary Report, Washington, Government Printing Office, 1946.

HEARINGS

Aviation Hearings, General Board, 2 Volumes, Washington, Navy Department, 1925.

House of Representatives, Hearings on Operations of U. S. Air Services, 1924–1925, Volumes I–VI, Washington, Government Printing Office, 1925.

House of Representatives, Sixty-eighth Congress, Inquiry into Operations of the United States Air Services (Lampert Committee), 4 Volumes, Washington, Government Printing Office, 1925.

Rodman Board Report, Washington, Government Printing Office, 1923.

COMBAT ACCOUNTS

Battle of Midway, combat narratives, Washington, Office of Naval Intelligence, 1943. A report by Commander Frank Akers, following the Battle of Midway, on file in the Naval Aviation History Unit. An account of the Battle of Midway by Commander William J. Widhelm. Critical Analysis of Battle of Midway, Newport, Naval War College, 1947.

Monthly summaries, Operations in the Pacific Ocean Areas, January, 1944–May, 1945 (mimeographed), Commander in Chief, Pacific Fleet, and Commander in Chief, Pacific Ocean Areas.

Three narratives by Commodore Arleigh A. Burke covering his experiences as Chief of Staff to Admiral Mitscher.

Two narratives by Rear Admiral William A. Read covering his experiences on the staff of Commander Aircraft, Solomons, and on the staff of Commander, Task Force 58, with a detailed account of operations off Okinawa.

GENERAL SOURCES

BOOKS

Alden, Carroll Storrs, and Allan Westcott, *The United States Navy*, second edition, revised, Philadelphia, Lippincott, 1945.

Aviation History Unit OP-519B, DCNO (Air), *The Navy's Air War*, edited by A. R. Buchanan, New York, Harper and Brothers, 1946.

Bryan, Joseph, III, *Aircraft Carrier*, New York, Ballantine, 1954.

Bryan, Joseph, III, and Philip Reed, *Mission Beyond Darkness*, New York, Duell, Sloan and Pearce, 1945.

Cant, Gilbert, *Great Pacific Victory*, New York, John Day, 1946.

Craven, Wesley F., and James L. Cate, *The Army Air Forces in World War II*, Volume IV, Chicago, University of Chicago Press, 1948.

DeChant, Ralph, *Devil Birds*, New York, Harper and Brothers, 1947.

Driscoll, Joseph, *Pacific Victory, 1945*, Philadelphia, Lippincott, 1944.

Fahey, James C., *Ships and Aircraft of the United States Fleet*, victory edition, New York, Ships and Aircraft, 1945.

Field, James A., *The Japanese at Leyte Gulf*, Princeton, Princeton University Press, 1947.

The Forrestal Diaries, edited by Walter Millis with the collaboration of E. S. Duffield, New York, Viking Press, 1951.

Griffin, Alexander R., *A Ship to Remember* (the U.S.S. *Hornet*), New York, Howell Soskin, 1943.

Halsey, William F., and Joseph Bryan III, *Admiral Halsey's Story*, New York, Whittlesey House, 1947.

Haugland, Vern, *The A.A.F. Against Japan*, New York, Harper and Brothers, 1947.

History of Vernon County, Madison, Wisconsin State Historical Society, 1934.

Jensen, Oliver O., *Carrier War*, New York, Simon & Schuster, 1945.

Jordan, Ralph B., *Born to Fight*, a biography of Admiral Halsey, New York, John McKay, 1946.

Karig, Walter, and others, *Battle Report*, Volumes III, IV, and V, New York, Rinehart, 1947–1949.

King, Ernest J., and Walter Muir Whitehill, *Fleet Admiral King*, New York, W. W. Norton & Company, Inc., 1952.

Levine, Isaac Don, *Mitchell, Pioneer of Air Power*, New York, Duell, Sloan and Pearce, 1943.

The Lucky Bag, Naval Academy yearbooks, 1904–1910.

Marshall, George C., Henry H. Arnold, and Ernest J. King, *The War Reports*, Philadelphia, Lippincott, 1947.

Mears, Frederick, *Carrier Combat*, New York, Doubleday, Doran, 1944.

Miller, Harold Blaine, *Navy Wings*, New York, Dodd, Mead, 1943.

Mitchell, William, *Winged Defense*, New York and London, Putnam, 1925.

Morison, Samuel E., *History of U. S. Naval Operations in World War II*, Volumes III, IV, V, VI, VIII, Boston, Atlantic–Little, Brown & Company, 1947–1953.

Pratt, Fletcher, *The Navy's War*, New York, Harper and Brothers, 1944.

Reynolds, Quentin, *The Amazing Mr. Doolittle*, New York, Appleton-Century-Crofts, 1953.

Sherman, Frederick C., *Combat Command*, New York, Dutton, 1950.

Sherrod, Robert, *History of Marine Corps Aviation*, Washington, Combat Forces Press, 1952.

Turnbull, Archibald D., and Clifford L. Lord, *History of U. S. Naval Aviation*, New Haven, Yale University Press, 1949.

Winston, Robert A., *Fighting Squadron*, New York, Holiday House, 1946.

Woodward, C. Vann, *The Battle for Leyte Gulf*, New York, Macmillan, 1947.

NEWSPAPERS AND PERIODICALS

"Airmen's Admiral," *Time*, February 10, 1947.

Busch, Noel, "Task Force 58," *Life*, July 17, 1944.

Kearney, Paul W., and Blake Clark, "Pete Mitscher, Boss of Task Force 58," *Reader's Digest*, July, 1945.

Scott, J. D., "Ship That Haunted Mitscher," *Saturday Evening Post*, October 20, 1945.

Waite, Elmont, "He Opened the Airway to Tokyo," *Saturday Evening Post*, December 2, 1944.

Portraits and sketches in *Time*, *Newsweek*, and others during the period 1944–1945.

Material from the following newspapers:

Hillsboro, Wisconsin, *Sentry-Enterprise*, July 26, 1945.
La Crosse, Wisconsin, *Tribune*, July 12 and 13, 1945.
Milwaukee *Journal*, July 12, 13, and 14, 1945.
The Daily Oklahoman, Oklahoma City, July 25, 1943.
Wisconsin State *Journal*, July 13 and 14, 1945.

CLIPPINGS AND FILES

Department of Defense, Office of Public Information—files (for information on the unification hearings and on the U.S.S. *United States* and the U.S.S. *Forrestal*.

Navy Department, library of the Office of Public Information—clippings, speeches, press releases.

Navy Department, Officers' Biography Section, Office of Public Information—news clipping file.

The New York Times, library—news clippings.

PHOTOGRAPHS AND FILMS

Approximately a thousand photographs in which Admiral Mitscher appears, on file in the Naval Photo Center, Washington.

Considerable footage on carrier operations in World War II, on file in the Naval Photo Center, Washington.

The Fighting Lady, Twentieth Century–Fox film.

The History of Naval Aviation, U. S. Navy Department film.

Index

The **Naval Institute Press** is the book-publishing arm of the U.S. Naval Institute, a private, nonprofit professional society for members of the sea services and civilians who share an interest in naval and maritime affairs. Established in 1873 at the U.S. Naval Academy in Annapolis, Maryland, where its offices remain today, the Naval Institute has more than 100,000 members worldwide.

Members of the Naval Institute receive the influential monthly magazine *Proceedings* and discounts on fine nautical prints, ship and aircraft photos, and subscriptions to the quarterly *Naval History* magazine. They also have access to the transcripts of the Institute's Oral History Program and get discounted admission to any of the Institute-sponsored seminars regularly offered around the country.

The Naval Institute's book-publishing program, begun in 1898 with basic guides to naval practices, has broadened its scope in recent years to include books of more general interest. Now the Naval Institute Press publishes more than forty new titles each year, ranging from how-to books on boating and navigation to battle histories, biographies, ship and aircraft guides, and novels. Institute members receive discounts on the Press's more than 375 books.

Full-time students are eligible for special half-price membership rates. Life memberships are also available.

For a free catalog describing the Naval Institute Press books currently available, and for further information about U.S. Naval Institute membership, please write to:

Membership & Communications Department
U.S. Naval Institute
118 Maryland Avenue
Annapolis, Maryland 21402-5035

Or call, toll-free, (800) 233-USNI. In Maryland, call (301) 224-3378.